Max Lambert spent most of his working life with the New Zealand Press Association Wellington, and reported for the news agency from Sydney (1969–71), from Washington (1975–80) and from the Antarctic in the summer of 1974–75. He still works occasionally for NZPA. He co-authored *The Wahine Disaster* in 1968 and wrote *November Gold*, an account of New Zealand horses in the Melbourne Cup, in 1985 before *Night after Night* in 2005. He and his wife live in Wellington.

MAX LAMBERT

DAY AFTER DAY

New Zealanders in Fighter Command

HarperCollinsPublishers

HarperCollins*Publishers*

First published in 2011
by HarperCollins*Publishers* (New Zealand) Limited
PO Box 1, Shortland Street, Auckland 1140

Copyright © Max Lambert 2011

Max Lambert asserts the moral right to be identified as the author of this work.
All rights reserved. No part of this publication may be reproduced, stored in a retrieval
system or transmitted in any form or by any means, electronic, mechanical, photocopying,
recording or otherwise, without the prior written permission of the publishers.

HarperCollins*Publishers*
31 View Road, Glenfield, Auckland 0627, New Zealand
25 Ryde Road, Pymble, Sydney, NSW 2073, Australia
A 53, Sector 57, Noida, UP, India
77–85 Fulham Palace Road, London W6 8JB, United Kingdom
2 Bloor Street East, 20th floor, Toronto, Ontario M4W 1A8, Canada
10 East 53rd Street, New York, NY 10022, USA

National Library of New Zealand Cataloguing-in-Publication Data

Lambert, Max, 1936-
Day after day : New Zealanders in Fighter Command / Max Lambert.
Includes bibliographical references and index.
ISBN 978-1-86950-844-9
1. Great Britain. Royal Air Force. Fighter Command. 2. Great Britain.
Tactical Air Force, 2nd. 3. World War, 1939-1945—New Zealand.
4. World War, 1939-1945—Aerial operations, British. 5. Fighter pilots—
New Zealand. I. Title.
940.544941—dc 22

ISBN: 978 1 86950 844 9

Cover design by Mark Thacker
Cover photo: A Spitfire VB of 243 Squadron in England. New Zealander Evan Mackie
later commanded the squadron in the Middle East. Courtesy Air Force Museum
Typesetting by Springfield West

Printed by Griffin Press, Australia

70gsm Classic used by HarperCollins*Publishers* is a natural, recyclable product made
from wood grown in sustainable forests. The manufacturing processes conform
to the environmental regulations in the country of origin, Finland.

Contact Max Lambert at:
maxlambert@paradise.net.nz
Phone 04 973 9436

For Kathleen and Sally

Contents

Acknowledgments		9
Note for readers		15
Chapter 1	Disaster in the north	17
Chapter 2	Air war in France — the fighters	31
Chapter 3	Slaughter of the Battles and Blenheims	62
Chapter 4	Jimmy Paterson — an extraordinary young man	79
Chapter 5	Life in the pre-war RAF — Wilf Clouston and Derek Ward	91
Chapter 6	Dunkirk — a victory inside defeat	98
Chapter 7	The Battle of Britain	119
	Brian Carbury — a wasted talent	153
	Bill Hodgson — my little heart went pitter-pat	165
	The deaths of Cecil Hight and Terence Lovell-Gregg	175
	Jack Fleming — guinea pig	183
	Mindy Blake — pilot and inventor	186
	'We gotcha, we gotcha'	191
	92 Squadron — a wild bunch	198
	Geoff Wellum — 'many snappers; keep a good lookout'	216
	Frank Gill and Bernie Brown	218
	Roll of Honour: New Zealand pilot deaths in the Battle of Britain	225
Chapter 8	Horry Copland goes to war	229

Chapter 9	ASR — aircrew saviours	243
Chapter 10	485 and 486 Squadrons begin to fly	254
Chapter 11	Dieppe	269
Chapter 12	Evaders	287
Chapter 13	The years between	298
Chapter 14	Divers	323
Chapter 15	Invasion and victory	333
Bibliography		359
Index		363

Acknowledgments

First and foremost I am greatly indebted, as I was with *Night After Night: New Zealanders in Bomber Command*, to Errol Martyn of Christchurch, who gave me an incredible amount of help with this book. He had the answers to all my many questions, with his unrivalled knowledge of New Zealand aviation history. The three volumes of his masterful *For Your Tomorrow — A Record of New Zealanders Who Have Died While Serving with the RNZAF and Allied Air Services Since 1915* made the writing of this so much easier. Without these volumes I would have had a difficult, sometimes impossible, task to pin down dates and other facts. My heartfelt thanks.

I'm also hugely grateful to Wellington friend Colin Smith, whose computer wizardry made so many of the photographs here possible. His knowledge and skill accomplished what I could not do and for that I shall always be grateful.

I also greatly appreciate the help I received from a number of aviation historians and writers. At the head of the list is Martyn Ford-Jones, who lives in Somerset, England. He is the historian of 15 Squadron, a bomber unit which flew from the start of the war to the finish. It operated Battles then Blenheims in the early stages of the war before transferring in November 1940 to 3 Group, one of whose members was 75 (NZ) Squadron. Many New Zealanders served with 15 Squadron, no fewer than fifty-five losing their lives. Ford-Jones, who has written a number of books about 15 Squadron, gave me unstinting help and much valuable material about the sad story of 15 Squadron Blenheims in the Battle of France. He also sent me several photographs appearing in these pages. He helped me no end.

Likewise Colin Ford (268 Squadron historian) and Steve Brew (41

DAY AFTER DAY

Squadron historian), both in Australia, generously provided material enabling me to write respectively about New Zealanders Owen Chapman and William Hawkins, pilots of two of the four Mustangs that made the first Allied fighter penetration of German air space in 1942, and of Mac Mackenzie and Hawkeye Wells in the Battle of Britain.

I'm also grateful to: Peter Cornwell for permission to quote from his magisterial *The Battle of France — Then and Now* and for the photograph of Edgar Morton's crashed aircraft; likewise Brian Cull's generous approval to quote from both his *Twelve Days in May*, co-written with Bruce Lander and Heinrich Weiss, and *Diver! Diver! Diver!,* also co-written with Bruce Lander. Without the latter book it would have been much more difficult to write my chapter on the anti-V1 campaign in 1944; Stephen Bungay for permission to quote from his *The Most Dangerous Enemy — A History of the Battle of Britain*, a marvellous read; Norman Franks for kind permission to quote from his *Air Battle for Dunkirk* and *The Greatest Air Battle — Dieppe*; Derek Palmer for permission to quote from *Fighter Squadron* (the story of 19 Squadron); Nigel Walpole who allowed me to quote from *Dragon Rampant* (the story of 234 Squadron) and to use photographs from the book. I also owe a special thanks to David Ross, aviation historian and author, who lives in Northumberland, England. He has written several books including *'The Greatest Squadron of Them All' — The Definitive History of 603 (City of Edinburgh) Squadron, RAuxAF*, the squadron with which Brian Carbury flew, and is currently writing the biography of Carbury. He generously permitted me to quote from his book and checked over my chapter on the New Zealander, thus saving me from a couple of blushes.

I need to thank Larry Hill, author of *An Aviation Bibliography for New*

Zealand, published in 2009, for kindly loaning me books and memoirs from his remarkable collection and for his help in other ways.

Someone who merits a special word is Shona Scott of Southland, daughter of Horry Copland, whose story is told in these pages. She didn't hesitate to let me have a copy of her father's memoir *From the Farm to the Spitfire*, from which I've quoted extensively, answered questions and provided the photographs reproduced here.

Likewise Aucklander Richard Lumsden, whose father flew Hurricanes and Typhoons and wrote an engaging memoir called *The Byron Lumsden Story*.

Also Jim Dillon of Wellington, who tells the story of his uncle Jimmy Paterson in his *Grand Blitzing Day 1940*, a tribute compiled from Paterson's letters and diary. Before I made contact with Dillon I had found, in the manuscripts section of the Auckland War Memorial Museum, a copy of the amazing letter Paterson wrote to his parents after escaping from France. Dillon also supplied photographs from his cache.

Janice Alford in Lower Hutt helpfully allowed me to read the letters of her uncle Tony Dini and to quote from them.

Particular thanks also to John Jameson in Auckland, son of Jamie Jameson, who willingly passed on a huge pile of his father's letters and found photographs and other material. He was a great help. Thanks are also due to Claire Bunt of Onehunga, who originally led me to the Jameson family through a chance meeting in a Mt Eden bookshop.

Richard Clouston in Waipukurau was extremely helpful with letters written by his father Wilf Clouston and photographs of his dad, who survived the Battle of Britain but was then unfortunate enough to fall into the hands of the Japanese. Many thanks.

My thanks also to Sue Pattison of Upper Hutt, daughter-in-law of

Battle of Britain pilot John Pattison — a meeting with her led me to a copy of a long interview Ministry for Culture and Heritage historian and writer Alison Parr had with John Pattison not too long before his death in September 2009. I'm grateful for Parr's permission to quote from that interview.

Angela Hutchings of Kamo, Derek Ward's niece, was extremely helpful with letters and details about Ward's service and background. So also were members of Cecil Hight's family in Te Puke and Tauranga. Robyn and Rex Smith's wonderful property in Te Puke was indeed an interview bonus.

I'm also grateful to the many other people who talked to me about husbands, brothers and more distant relationships with men who flew the fighters — and of course I am indebted to the fast-dwindling band of pilots who participated in World War II. It was a pleasure to meet and interview Bernie Brown and John Gard'ner, the last two New Zealanders who flew day fighters in the Battle of Britain, both of whom live in Tauranga. I thank them for giving me their time and providing photographs.

I also want to thank John Scullin of the Hawke's Bay Aviation Heritage Association for his amazing helpfulness, and for introducing me to John Caulton and Max Collett at a pleasant Sunday function at the Napier Aero Club in February 2010. As a result I was able to talk to both men and use their stories in this book. Collett used a camera extensively in the war while serving with 485 Squadron and several of his photographs are reproduced here.

Thanks too to Ric Stevens of *The Press*, Christchurch, an old friend, who went to so much trouble to get me a useable copy of the photograph the newspaper had published seventy years ago of the 'Hodgson draft'. Also Joan Keate and Katrina Willoughby in the

ACKNOWLEDGMENTS

Defence Force Library in Wellington who were unfailingly helpful, and Kent Atkinson of the New Zealand Press Association, Wellington, who can always find what I can't on the internet.

I'm also grateful for help of various kinds from Vince Ashworth, Jim Hartley, Dick Fernyhough, Arthur Arculus, Nick Lambrechtsen, John Bickerton, Graham Kitchen, Tevor Glassenbury and Tony Eyre in New Zealand, Mickael Simon (France), Murray C Meikle (Singapore) and Alan Jasper and Peter Nutt (England). A special thanks to Scott Harrison, librarian at the *Daily Echo*, in Bournemouth, England, who photocopied wartime pages of the newspaper that helped so much in the writing of Cecil Hight's story. I need to thank the helpful staff at the Air Force Museum in Christchurch, in particular Matthew O'Sullivan, Keeper of Photographs. And, of course, my sharp-witted reader and editor, Lorain Day, who tweaked my copy no end. Thank you to everyone.

Finally, to my wife Eileen whose knowledge of grammar and sentence construction far surpasses mine and whose ability to pick up errors and omissions is hugely helpful, my thanks, admiration and love.

Max Lambert
Wellington
November 2010

Note for readers

This book is about New Zealanders who flew single-engined day fighters in World War II in Fighter Command and the Second Tactical Air Force (2TAF). They fought in Norway and France in May-June 1940 and then from bases in Britain and, after the invasion of Europe in 1944, from French, Belgian, Dutch and finally German airfields. The one major exception is the early chapter on the New Zealanders involved in the Battle of France as pilots of Blenheims and Battles on the suicidal bombing operations in vain attempts to halt the Germans — an integral and major role in this doomed campaign. Their bravery and deaths, largely untold until now, should never be forgotten.

The stories throughout *Day After Day — New Zealanders in Fighter Command* are representative. For every man mentioned here — the survivors, those taken prisoner, the dead — there are countless others. It is simply impossible to mention them all. Each story mirrors what happened to many more.

The majority of the best-known New Zealand fighter pilots, men like Colin Gray, Alan Deere, Johnny Checketts, Des Scott and Johnnie Houlton, wrote their own books in the postwar period — this being the case I have not gone into great detail about them here. Instead I have concentrated on telling the stories of some of the flyers almost unknown to most New Zealanders. They all played their part in winning the war.

Readers will perhaps note that I have not often attached ranks to pilot names. That is deliberate. Ranks repeated endlessly simply clutter up the text. All ranks at war's end and aircrew decorations can be found in the index.

And now a brief word about the fighter war in the European theatre.

Unlike the bomber campaign, which grew steadily and remorselessly in intensity and direction as the war progressed, true fighter-on-fighter combat reached its peak in 1940, in the Battle of France and the Battle of Britain. After that, with the exception of the large-scale fighter engagement over Dieppe in August 1942, fighters were engaged in sweeps over occupied northwest Europe, anti-shipping strikes and in bomber escort, where fighter combat was an incidental to such roles, and not normally on a large scale. From 1943 until mid-1944 the RAF concentrated on the build-up to the invasion with the fighter combat role increasingly subordinated to that of the fighter-bomber. Even Spitfires began carrying bombs. After D-Day the fighter-bomber reigned supreme, with its prime role the support of Allied ground forces.

Chapter 1

DISASTER IN THE NORTH

Even in June, early summer, the Arctic water was unimaginably cold. Without a lifejacket, New Zealander Jamie Jameson swam a quarter of a mile to a raft from the sinking aircraft carrier HMS *Glorious*. Men were already dying around him. Waterlogged and frozen, Jameson still managed humour as he reached the packed Carley float. Spotting his squadron commander, he called out, 'Permission to come aboard, sir?' Squadron Leader Kenneth 'Bing' Cross hauled him on.

By about 6 p.m. on that disastrous 8 June 1940, off the northwest coast of Norway, the Carley was loaded with twenty-nine men. They didn't see *Glorious* go down — the huge pall of smoke from the flames shrouded her sinking. Eleven-inch shells from the powerful German battle cruisers *Scharnhorst* and *Gneisenau* had quickly shredded the carrier. The warships made no attempt to rescue the hundreds of men from *Glorious* and her two escorting destroyers, now struggling in the water. Appallingly, British naval authorities were unaware of the disaster until a day later, when German radio hailed the sinking. More than 1500 perished, with fewer than fifty men surviving from the three British ships.

Jameson and Cross were among the handful who lived. The sea was flat most of the time, but they were above the Arctic Circle and although the sun shone brightly and never properly set, the night air was killingly cold. Four hours after *Glorious* sank, hypothermia claimed its first victim on the raft and by morning only ten of the original twenty-nine were left. Two hours short of three days after they abandoned ship, a Norwegian trawler rescued just seven men. One died as the little ship steamed towards the Faroe Islands, another succumbed ashore in hospital.

Jameson was born on 10 November 1912 in Lower Hutt. He was often called Pat and sometimes signed his letters 'Mike', but to most of his friends, and especially in wartime, he was Jamie. He learned to fly at the Wellington Aero Club, soloing in early 1934 after just two hours fifty minutes' dual. 'I loved flying and seemed to have a natural aptitude,' he wrote years later. But flying was costly, an hour's solo all but ate up the paltry week's wages he earned as a clerk. 'I remember thinking how wonderful it would be if I could get into the RAF and be paid to fly.'

In early 1936 his parents paid his passage to England and Jameson was accepted for a Short Service Commission (SSC). He passed out top of the class at his initial training course on Tiger Moths at Hatfield, Hertfordshire, the de Havilland flying school where many New Zealanders trained pre-war. A distinguished pass followed at No. 8 Flying Training School, at Montrose, on Scotland's east coast north of Dundee, where he flew Hawker Harts, Audaxes and Gloster Gauntlets. In December 1936 he was posted to 46 Squadron, then at Kenley, London, before a 1937 move to Digby, Lincolnshire. He served with 46 Squadron for more than three years and was one of three squadron pilots forming a Gauntlet aerobatic display team.

In February 1939 the squadron began re-equipping with Hurricanes and Jameson was promoted to flight lieutenant, commanding a flight. He noted that everyone was sorry to see the Gauntlets go: 'With their low stalling speed and open cockpits they were a delight to fly. However, it was a great relief to get the much more businesslike Hurricane, which had about three times the speed and about five times the firepower and vast improvements in blind-flying instrumentation.'

In the lead-up to war, 46 Squadron shared Digby with 73 Squadron, but within a week of the outbreak of hostilities 73 Squadron was whisked off to France, one of the two Hurricane squadrons in the Advanced Air Striking Force (AASF). Its pilots were to win fame in France, none more so than Jameson's New Zealand friend Cobber Kain.

In April 1940, 46 Squadron, now commanded by Cross, was still at Digby, bored with convoy patrols and a lack of action. That month they learned 46 Squadron was also likely to go to France, with an aerodrome already chosen. In a BBC broadcast to New Zealand in March 1943, Jameson recalled that in mid-April he and Cross

> flew over to France to see what our aerodrome was like. We expected to leave England in about a week's time. Cobber had already shot down his first Hun and one or two more and when we visited 73 at Reims the whole squadron was on top of the world. We broke a bottle or two of champagne.

As 46 Squadron readied for the move to France, the squadron was suddenly issued with Arctic clothing and told to fly their fighters north to join *Glorious* on the Clyde, bound for Norway.

DAY AFTER DAY

On 9 April 1940 Germany had invaded Norway. German troops, landing by sea and air and backed by the bombers of Fliegerkorps X, quickly captured Oslo and key western coastal ports — Kristiansand, Trondheim, Bergen, Narvik. The last was ice-free in winter and Hitler wanted to secure Norway's coastal waters for shipment of vital supplies of Swedish iron ore. The Royal Navy retaliated, particularly at Narvik, where Captain Bernard Warburton-Lee, killed in action, won the first Victoria Cross of the war and a strong German destroyer flotilla was destroyed.

Supported by the Norwegians, the British, French and Polish units forced the Germans out of Narvik on 28 May but by then the Nazi blitzkrieg in France and the Low Countries had drastically altered the strategic situation. The decision had already been made to withdraw the Allied forces, and between 4 and 8 June they pulled out of Norway.

46 Squadron flew their fighters to Abbotsinch, now Glasgow Airport, miles from where *Glorious* was moored, at Greenock. After landing, the planes were taxied down winding country lanes and across open fields, to a jetty on a canal leading to the Clyde. There they were loaded on to barges, one to a barge, for the trip down river to the waiting ship, where slings hoisted them aboard on 10 May.

Getting the fighters ashore in Norway proved tediously slow. The carrier reached Narvik where an airfield was being built for the Hurricanes at Skaanland, seventy miles north of the port, but heavy rain and melting snow made the strip unusable. *Glorious* couldn't wait for the field to become operational and returned to Scapa Flow in the Orkneys to refuel, with the planes still on board.

In a letter from the carrier, Jameson wrote to Hilda Webster, his fiancée in New Zealand:

> My darling, I have been cruising about in this carrier for the last two
> weeks. Unfortunately I cannot tell you where I am or where I am going,
> but no doubt when I get there, which I think will be tomorrow, I shall be
> able to let you know … we were shot off from Digby at short notice and
> I must say we were glad to leave, for the inactivity was getting us down.

One other New Zealand pilot was aboard. Reg Miles, 24, a former RAF officer transferred to the Fleet Air Arm (FAA) in 1938, was serving with 802 Squadron, a Sea Gladiator unit stationed on the carrier. He was the only son of Brigadier Reggie Miles, 2NZEF's artillery commander, who was in England by chance, in charge of New Zealand troops diverted from the Middle East to the south coast, in anticipation of a German invasion.

Three other New Zealand pilots served in the Norwegian campaign, all on the RAF's Gladiator-equipped 263 Squadron, based at Bardufoss — James Wilkie, 20 (Mangaweka), Lou Jacobsen, 25 (Wellington) and Harold Vickery, 26 (Invercargill). Wilkie died in combat near Narvik and the other two lost their lives when *Glorious* was sunk.

The Gladiator, developed from the Gauntlet, was the RAF's last biplane. A nippy little fighter, its top wing was forward of the enclosed cockpit and it had four machine guns. It was no match for the new generation of monoplane fighters but was effective against bombers, as Jacobsen was to show.

Eighteen 263 Squadron Gladiators, the first RAF unit in Norway, had flown off *Glorious* on 24 April — in a snowstorm with only four maps among the pilots — to bleak Lake Lesjaskog, 100 miles from Trondheim, where the squadron was to support an army attack. A ground crew with local labour and horse-drawn transport improvised a landing strip, brushing away snow on the ice-covered lake. Overnight the engines froze and the planes were sitting ducks when the ever-observant Germans bombed next morning. Thirteen Gladiators were destroyed, with the remainder flying to a temporary strip near Andalsnes, near the coast, where another was destroyed and one crashed.

Re-equipped, the squadron went north again on the carrier HMS *Furious*, flying in bad weather to Bardufoss, where they went into combat. On 30 May, flying alone, Jacobsen attacked a German truck convoy, destroying two and inflicting many casualties.

On the afternoon of 2 June Jacobsen made his name and won the Distinguished Flying Cross (DFC); he was said by some sources to have claimed no fewer than four German aircraft in running scraps stretching from Narvik to the nearby Swedish border. The encounter began disastrously when Jacobsen and Wilkie tackled a pair of twin-engined Messerschmitt 110s (Me 110s), one flown by the legendary Helmut Lent, the German pilot who was to become an outstanding night fighter. Jacobsen zoomed down on Lent from the beam and fired a burst.

Wilkie followed up with a rear attack but was hit by return fire and shot down. His Gladiator crashed east of Rombaken Fjord, the wreckage and his body not found until some years after the war. His remains now lie in a grave in Narvik. Australian-born Wilkie came to New Zealand as a youngster and was working as a farm hand at Mangaweka when he was accepted for an SSC in the RAF, sailing for England in 1939, in February.

Jacobsen chased Lent into cloud, then emerged to claim a Dornier, which force-landed inside Sweden. Now just over the Swedish border, Jacobsen spotted a bunch of Heinkel 111s (He 111s) and Junkers 88s

(Ju 88s) and, disregarding the odds, plunged into the attack. In a swirling engagement the lone little Gladiator is said to have bagged three Heinkels in a few minutes. Out of ammunition, his windscreen smothered in oil from damage he'd sustained, he broke away and flew home to Bardufoss, his immediate DFC recognition of a brilliant afternoon.

Little is known of Vickery's operations in Norway but he is not thought to have scored any victories. On 30 May, in his last letter, just a few short paragraphs to his mother, then in England, he said: 'I am still hale and hearty. I am fairly busy, as you may imagine, and since the sun never sets this business goes on forever. I sent a suitcase to Caterham Station before I left. I hope you got it … Your affectionate son, Harold.'

Good at short takeoffs and landings, 263 Squadron's Gladiators had no trouble operating from carriers but a carrier takeoff had never been tried by a plane like the Hurricane. Anxiety levels ran high when it finally came time to fly ashore from *Glorious*, a converted World War I cruiser with a short 700-foot flight deck. Jameson watched Cross make the first takeoff on 26 May:

> I couldn't help wondering how he felt when he was running his engine up on the brakes, and then accelerating along the tiny deck. Would he get flying speed in time? Leaving the front end of the flight deck, his Hurricane sank momentarily but then I breathed again as I saw her climb away.

Jameson and the other Hurricane pilots followed safely.

The Skaanland runway, said to be ready, was not, and the steel-mesh matting, on squelching, sodden ground, couldn't take a Hurricane's

Day after Day

weight. Cross's fighter, first in, tipped on its nose as its wheels sank into the mud. The second went over too, though the third staggered down okay. Cross jumped back into his cockpit and called up Jameson on the R/T, telling him to take the fifteen other aircraft to Bardufoss, about 25 miles away. The aircraft all landed there and stayed until the squadron left Norway.

Ashore, the squadron began operations immediately, their main role the air defence of the Narvik area and attacks on German troops and installations. Because of the almost perpetual daylight the squadron flew long hard hours. According to Jameson, the squadron claimed almost 30 enemy aircraft for the loss of just two pilots of their own.

Two days after landing Jameson was told German transport aircraft were unloading troops in one of the fjords south of Narvik. His section scoured several without finding anything before investigating Rombaken Fjord, which ran inland from Narvik. Inside the fjord they spotted two German flying boats hidden in a small cove and protected on three sides by high cliffs. Flying in and over Norway's deep fjords, with their high sheer-sided rock walls, was a new deal and the RAF pilots quickly learned to manoeuvre sharply and carefully.

> To strafe the flying boats we had to dive steeply down the side of one cliff, firing as we went, and then do a steep turn along the fjord [to avoid hitting] the cliff on the other side. We each carried out four attacks and left both flying boats blazing merrily and sinking.

Later the same day Jameson and another pilot encountered two He 111s and a Ju 88 over Narvik. Jameson got the Junkers, his No. 2 one of the Heinkels. 'I surprised the bomber by climbing up under his tail. There was a bright flash and my windscreen was obscured by oil. Breaking away I could see black smoke coming from his starboard engine.' Jameson bored in again. 'No return fire so I assumed I had knocked out the rear gunner during the previous attack. I fired another burst and the starboard engine began to burn, the fire gradually spreading to the fuselage.'

The enemy aircraft went down, crashing on the face of a fjord.

On 6 June, two days before the Hurricanes were evacuated, Jameson had what he later called 'one of the most interesting flying experiences of my life'. He and another Hurricane escorted five amphibian Walruses of FAA Squadron 701 on a bombing trip south of Narvik.

The Walrus was an ungainly, lumbering biplane with a pusher engine mounted above the fuselage between the wings. Despite limitations, it played an invaluable role during the war. The aircraft were used from catapults on the navy's big ships until 1943–44 and employed for ship to shore communication flights, spotting for ships' guns and coastal patrols. One even sank a submarine with bombs. For all that, the 'Shagbats' are best remembered for their air-sea rescue (ASR) role with their brave, skilled pilots saving hundreds of aircrew downed in the English Channel, the North Sea and the Mediterranean.

One thing the Walrus was not designed for was dive-bombing but on 6 June that's exactly what Jameson saw. 'Because they were very slow I rendezvoused with them at 500 feet about halfway to the target. Nothing I could imagine looked less like an effective bomber force.'

The target: a warehouse just back from a jetty poking out into water at the inward end of a fjord. Behind it an almost vertical wall rose 1000 feet to a plateau running back to the mountains.

One by one the Walruses flew low across the plateau and when each got to the cliff the nose was stuffed down and a dive-bombing attack

DAY AFTER DAY

was carried out … I certainly would not have believed it if I hadn't seen it. Not only did they dive bomb, they did it successfully.

The warehouse, full of explosives or ammunition, dissolved in an enormous explosion.

The next day 46 Squadron was told Narvik was to be evacuated and the pilots taken home. They had two choices for their fighter planes — either burn them, as originally ordered, or fly them on to *Glorious*. The pilots were unanimous — try for the carrier and get them back to England, where they were sorely needed. Such a landing had never been attempted but Cross flew to the carrier in a Walrus and Captain Guy D'Oyly-Hughes promised maximum speed. The planes had no tail hooks to catch an arrestor wire, and Jameson figured that somehow they had to lose some of the Hurricanes' nose heaviness, caused by the new metal three-blade props. In the grand New Zealand number-eight-fencing-wire tradition he found that a 14-pound bag of sand strapped in the very end of the fuselage permitted the use of full brake.

The aircraft carrier HMS *Ark Royal*, then in company with *Glorious* and her destroyers, had a longer, more attractive flight deck but her lifts were too narrow for the wingspan of the Hurricanes. Those on *Glorious* were wide enough.

Jameson led two other fighters out to sea for the first attempt. When they arrived over the carrier, 150 miles west of Narvik, she was at cracking speed but her flight deck looked awfully small. Awaiting the signal to land a sergeant-pilot suddenly peeled off, dived and landed perfectly. When Jameson tackled him about it later the man said he had engine trouble, but Jameson suspected he really wanted to be the first to land a Hurricane on a carrier.

Jameson:

The flight deck had a round-down at the stern, which was moving up and down like a cantering elephant's backside. We had to touch down as near the top of the heaving rump as possible to minimize the chance of over-shooting and crashing on to the fo'c's'le. The flight deck didn't go right up to the bow of the ship. I came in on the approach at just above stalling speed, feeling my way, because the sand bag affected the flying characteristics of the aeroplane.

Suddenly, as I was getting near the touchdown point, the Hurricane dropped rapidly and it seemed she was trying to land on the quarterdeck, the one below the flight deck. I slammed on full throttle and that beautiful, lovely Rolls-Royce Merlin engine never faltered. It dragged us up onto the flight deck and the Hurricane stopped about a quarter of the way along. All three of us got down okay.

A few hours later Cross's Hurricane and the six others still flyable after the campaign landed without incident. That made ten. The carrier also took on board 263 Squadron. Jameson later remembered having a brief chat with Jacobsen and Vickery on *Glorious* but feeling 'knackered' after round-the-clock ops went to his cabin for a long sleep. He wakened to hammering on his door and the news that German warships were in sight. He never saw Miles, Jacobsen or Vickery again.

The loss of *Glorious* on 8 June 1940 is a great blot on the Royal Navy's history, one of its worst embarrassments. While the official inquiry report is still hidden from public scrutiny under the 100-years secrecy rule, later investigations pin the blame for the disaster on the folly of the ship's captain in sailing with only two accompanying anti-submarine destroyers, and not putting up patrols. The battle cruisers appeared on the horizon without warning; the Admiralty had no idea they were anywhere near. By the time *Glorious* ordered planes and torpedoes for takeoff it was too late. The Germans opened fire at 4.31 p.m. with an early salvo from *Scharnhorst's* guns slamming into the carrier's flight deck and exploding in the hangar where the Swordfish and Hurricanes were stored. The bridge erupted in flames from a direct hit, killing D'Oyly-Hughes and senior officers. More shells, more damage, more fires. The 'abandon ship' order was given about 5.20 p.m. and ten minutes later the big carrier was gone, her distress calls either not picked up or jammed.

The escorting destroyers *Ardent* and *Acasta* laid smoke in a vain attempt to shield the carrier and both attacked the German ships in the best navy tradition, firing to the last. Totally outgunned they didn't stand a chance, and were both blasted out of the water. In a final gasp, one of four torpedoes fired by *Ardent* struck *Scharnhorst* abreast of her rear turret, doing significant damage. Jameson sheltered on the quarter deck as *Scharnhorst* and *Gneisenau* battered the carrier.

Shells from the little [4.7 inch] guns on *Glorious* dropped into the sea about halfway to the targets! I could see the great flames spout from the German guns when they fired; but it seemed an eternity before the shells came crashing in. They sounded like a large firecracker being let off in a big tin can multiplied a thousand times. They were coming in thick and fast and *Glorious* began to list to starboard. [He heard the order, 'Prepare to abandon ship,' and watched the sailors with admiration.] I shall always remember the calm way in which the men of the Royal Navy set about their tasks. The discipline was superb and there was never the slightest sign of panic. They could have been getting ready for a picnic or boat race.

Jameson tried to go below to get his greatcoat, but watertight doors prevented access to his cabin; his lifejacket was on the tail of his Hurricane in the burning hangar. When he decided it was time to go, the ship was a ball of fire and listing so much one side of the quarter deck was under water. When he jumped into the sea *Glorious* was still moving at about 10 knots.

The Carley float, a copper tube surrounded with kapok or cork and covered with waterproofed canvas, had a wooden trellis grate on the bottom. Twenty-nine shivering men, without food or water, sat on the tube with their feet in the sea. Jameson recalled how it was bitterly cold and nineteen men died from exposure that first night. The next day three more died, leaving only seven, who never gave up hope. Eventually Jameson's blunt pocketknife severed the ropes holding the grating and somehow the men managed to wrestle it on to the top of the raft, get their feet out of the water and lie on it. Some even slept, before they were rescued.

> We saw the trawler coming up. To see that it was flying the Norwegian flag gave me the sweetest moment of my life. I went down [below] and slept on the catwalk round the engine. They put some old clothes on the walk and I think it was the most comfortable bed I ever had. It was a bit noisy and smelly, but it was warm and the smell of the oil was as good as eau-de-cologne to me.

Jameson, Cross and other survivors plucked from the sea by a second trawler were carried home from the Faroes by a destroyer and taken to Scotland's Gleneagles Hotel, then a wartime hospital. There Jameson spent six weeks while his painful feet mended. 'They were swollen and white with the immersion in the water, and I remember that when I touched the skin my finger made a little hole as though it had gone into a soft pudding.'

Staff tried massage with all sorts of oils. Nothing worked until a woman who owned some stables nearby brought along a bottle of something called 'Mermaid Oil'.

It said, 'For use in stables, kennels and piggeries.' But I didn't care; the oil certainly did my feet good! … My DFC came through while we were in hospital and we had a grand party that night.

Chapter 2

AIR WAR IN FRANCE — THE FIGHTERS

Seventy years on the 1940 aerial Battle of France is now an almost forgotten conflict, overshadowed by later events, particularly the Battle of Britain. It included the long, so-called phoney war between September 1939 and the German onslaught that began on 10 May 1940 and the three weeks to Dunkirk, followed by the period leading up to the French capitulation and armistice in late June. France was as much a defeat for the British and French air forces as it was on the ground, where German armoured columns, aided by waves of Stukas, overwhelmed the armies of Belgium, Holland and France, and the divisions of the British Expeditionary Force (BEF).

The RAF, though grateful for the eighteen months or so it was given to equip its squadrons with modern Hurricanes and Spitfires and develop its radar and radio communications after the Munich crisis, was in no shape to fight the air war as it developed over France. Its squadrons of Fairey Aviation's Battles (light bombers) were hopelessly slow, under-powered and under-gunned, as dozens of young aircrew were to find. The Bristol Blenheims, in their role as ground-attack aircraft, were every bit as deadly for their crews. Hurricane squadrons in France were too few despite reinforcements, and Fighter Command leader Hugh Dowding successfully, and rightly, resisted attempts to send Spitfires, while the French air force fought gallantly but unavailingly.

When war was declared the RAF ordered two distinct forces to France — the Air Component of the BEF based at airfields in the Pas de Calais and headed by Air Vice-Marshal Charles Blount, and the Advanced Air Striking Force (AASF), which had been No. 1 Group of Bomber Command, under Air Vice-Marshal Pip Playfair. The Air Component's basic job was to protect the BEF. When it settled down it had Hurricane squadrons 85 and 87, Gladiator squadrons 607 and 615 to be re-equipped with Hurricanes, various Army Co-operation squadrons with Lysanders and Blenheims, plus its squadrons of Blenheims and Battles.

Headquartered at Reims in northeast France, the AASF was in theory based where its Battles and Blenheims could bomb targets in the nearby Ruhr Valley, Germany's industrial heartland. The Allies withheld bombing while the phoney war was on and when the real thing began the squadrons were too busy to do anything but attack the German invaders. The Battles and Blenheims were useless for this sort of role, but there was nothing else available and their crews suffered the consequences, with catastrophic losses.

In October 1939 two Hurricane squadrons, initially attached to the Air Component and both commanded by Irishmen, switched from the Pas de Calais to the AASF. No. 1 Squadron was commanded by the imposing Bull Halahan, and No. 73 Squadron was under Red Knox. The latter squadron was to gain the most fame and oceans of newsprint, mainly because of New Zealand pilot Eddie 'Cobber' Kain. The AASF's Battle and Blenheim squadrons were dotted at airfields in the beautiful Champagne area, some for long periods at the same field while others shuffled about. Some returned to England at various stages to re-equip.

When it flew to Le Havre from Tangmere on 8 September 1939, 1 Squadron had one New Zealander, Bill Stratton ('Stratters') in its ranks and 73 Squadron arrived in France the following day with two. Confusingly both were called Kain, although Cobber and Dereck were not related. Stratton, still a lowly pilot officer in A Flight when he took off for France, had joined the RAF on an SSC in July 1937 and was posted to No. 1 Squadron in May 1939. He was at the start of what turned out to be a steady upward air force climb, culminating in his appointment in 1969 as RNZAF Chief of Air Staff, ranked Air Vice-Marshal.

On 73, Cobber Kain hogged the limelight — first RAF 'ace' of the war, first fighter pilot to win the DFC, and with a rising tally of downed enemy aircraft. Fleet Street adored him. Stuffy RAF brass were displeased by the adulation but the public lapped it up. Cobber's exploits filled the pages from November 1939 to early May 1940, when there was little to write about.

Dereck Kain — Bill to everyone who knew him — was a different character, not nearly so flamboyant, a solid performer who got on with the job quietly. He was to have a distinguished war, commanding squadrons in North Africa and Palestine and fighting over Malta before returning to New Zealand as a wing commander. He'd had a terrible time in 1934 trying to get into the RAF because he didn't have matriculation (university entrance), but he persisted and in October 1935 won his prized SSC.

On 29 September 1939 Bill Kain was the first RAF fighter pilot shot down over France, a victim of friendly fire when French artillery

DAY AFTER DAY

clawed him down over Calais. Several Battles had been lost in clashes with German fighters over the Nazi frontier but fighters had not yet been engaged. Years later he told the story.

> My section were in readiness up at this place called Estreblanch on the border between France and Belgium … sitting in the tent playing a record, *Little Sir Echo*. The record had been played so much that eventually it began to stick, repeating the words 'Hello, hello, hello' over and over again. The phone rang and I lifted the receiver and put it alongside the gramophone. Unfortunately, it happened to be the CO Knox, ringing up to say he had a job and I could jolly well do it. 'I hope it breaks your neck,' he joked. He said I had to fly up to Calais. [Kain was to circle Calais at 5000 feet to show the French anti-aircraft gunners what a Hurricane silhouette looked like from the ground.] … I arrived south of Calais and flew around the outskirts. Suddenly the aircraft began jolting. I looked around and saw smoke so did a very sharp turn and went slap bang into an anti-aircraft burst. It blew part of the propeller off and nearly took the engine out. The motor wouldn't run so I quickly looked around to see where I could land.

All Kain could find was a beach with the tide out. As he glided down he could hear French machine guns firing at him. He waggled his wings; the gunners took no notice. Kain lined up for a beach landing, pumped the wheels down by hand and then, to his anguish, saw a deep gash across the beach, carved by a stream. The Hurricane charged across the sand and into the stream before nosing into the far bank, knocking Kain out, cutting his chin and smashing two teeth.

Kain revived to find French cavalry galloping towards him. They arrived as he climbed groggily out of the cockpit. No one spoke

English and Kain was made to walk up the beach, hands up, a bayonet prodding him in the backside. The French then dumped him in a police cell. At last an interpreter, realising he was an RAF pilot, told him he'd been shot down because he had the incorrect roundels on the fuselage. The interpreter phoned Estreblanch, and Knox arrived on the scene. 'He got stuck into the Froggies well and truly,' Kain remembered years later. 'He called them a few names but they just laughed. Eventually they turned on a terrific party and we stayed the night.'

Champagne Department sparkled in the autumn of 1939 and once fears of immediate war evaporated and the phoney war set in, squadron life was immensely enjoyable — as it was everywhere in the RAF. The flying schedule was not too demanding and the pilots found themselves at airfields near villages thick with cafés, bars and all else France had to offer. The very best champagne flowed like water and squadrons made sure they invited leading vintners for mess dinners, who duly delivered crates of champagne. Paris was not far away.

Paul Richey, who flew in the same section as Stratton in 1 Squadron, wrote about it in his 1941 *Fighter Pilot*, a classic superbly evocative of that early period of the war. His squadron was based at Le Havre for a couple of weeks after its arrival.

> Our evenings usually kicked off at about six at the *Guillaume Tell*, where we sat over Pernods or vermouths watching the life on the boulevards, and ended in the *Normandie* or elsewhere. We all felt that our first taste of service in France would probably be our last of civilisation and peace for a long time and we wanted to make the best of it.

While 1 Squadron settled in at Vassincourt, a scant fifty miles east of Reims, 73 Squadron were based at Rouvres near Verdun, in 1916 the site of awful slaughter. 'No. 1' looked enviously at 73 Squadron's position, which was closer to the German frontier and the path of German reconnaissance aircraft over northern France. Nevertheless, 1 Squadron scored the first victory, when, on 30 October, Peter 'Boy' Mould shot down a Dornier 17 from 18,000 feet. In the words of Richey, 'The Hun caught fire immediately, went into a vertical spiral, and made a whopping hole in the French countryside … There were no survivors.'

A week later 73 Squadron had its initial 'kill'. Cobber Kain was credited with the victory, also a Dornier, this one from 27,000 feet. The first success by a Commonwealth pilot reverberated around the world, especially in New Zealand. The *Southland Times* trumpeted, 'New Zealand Airman Wins Fame — German Plane Shot Down — Wellington Pilot's Victory — Vivid Description of Thrilling Fight.' The paper's report quoted a BBC eyewitness account:

> The fight took place four to five miles above the earth. As the German came out of the clouds it looked as big as a swallow. Suddenly a British fighter … dived into the attack. Even at that tremendous height we could hear the rattling of his machine guns … The German plane went into a spiral dive, but when about 23,000 feet above the earth, the pilot lost control, apparently having been hit. The aeroplane hit the ground at a speed of about 600 mph. I have never seen a smash like it. The New Zealander told me afterward he had spotted the German by sheer chance and had followed him down … he said it was just a bit of luck.

New Zealand war correspondent Alan Mitchell, who talked with Kain in Reims, wrote in his 1945 book *New Zealanders in the Air War* that Kain was attracted by puffs of anti-aircraft fire, spotted the Dornier and climbed to intercept. He attacked twice, his machine guns scoring hits. He fired constantly from a distance of 250 yards until he closed to within 50 yards before breaking off the second attack, after which the Dornier began to go down.

Kain watched the German crash in the middle of the crossroads of a village called Lubey, a few miles from Rouvres. It dug a hole 10 feet deep, scattered wreckage far and wide and left just a few fragments of the crew's bodies. After Kain landed he drove to the village and souvenired a machine gun — now in the Air Force Museum at Wigram. That night the squadron staged a big party. By the time Kain was killed seven months later he was a celebrity, myths abounding. Some obituaries said he had forty kills to his credit, but in fact he had fourteen confirmed victories, with perhaps one or two more, which was still an astonishing number in such a short time.

Cobber had apparently vied with Bill Kain and another pilot to get at the Dornier and Peter Cornwell's *The Battle of France — Then and Now* has a long section by 73 Squadron's then adjutant Edward Hall, who writes of the Kains: 'Bill duly turned up [at the crash scene]; no one would have guessed the disappointment which lay beneath the honestly expressed tribute of appreciation to the better man when the two Kains met.'

Cobber Kain, born 27 June 1918, grew up in Wellington, but his parents sent him to Christ's College, Christchurch. When he finished there at the end of 1935 he returned to the capital where he worked for his businessman father, though the RAF was his objective. He wanted to be a pilot, a fighter pilot, but had slacked at school and lacked the necessary qualifications for an SSC. Now anxious to do well, he studied at Victoria University College in Wellington to fill in the gaps, while his supportive parents paid for him to learn to fly.

In November 1936 he sailed for England. Fresh off the ship, Kain failed his first medical but passed his second easily and was accepted by the RAF. He whizzed through training on Blackburns, Hawker Harts and Furies and it was soon clear he was above average. Kain scored highly on gunnery and that, along with his passion for aerobatics, clearly destined him for fighters. A year after leaving New Zealand he was posted to 73 Squadron, then at Digby, Lincolnshire.

Formed in July 1917 flying Camels, 73 Squadron was later disbanded but re-formed during the 1930s expansion of the RAF. When Kain arrived it was equipped with Gladiators pending a switch to Hurricanes. The squadron shared Digby with 46 Squadron's pilots, one of them Jamie Jameson. The New Zealanders swam, played golf, drank together and generally had a good time in their off-duty hours. 'A most likeable chap,' said Jameson of Kain in Michael Burns' 1992 biography *Cobber Kain.*

> Cobber was a brilliant and completely fearless pilot. It could be that his lack of fear cost him his life. He may well have been alive today if he had had a little fear built into his make-up to give him warning of approaching danger and to temper his judgments.

Paul Richey, who also knew Kain well, called him a split-arse pilot, one who takes foolish, unnecessary risks.

Fleet Street and BBC correspondents flocked to Rouvres to cover Kain's victory and reporters descended again when he shot down his second Dornier later in the month. The RAF forbade the use of individual pilots' names in print so British reporters referred to Kain as a 21-year-old New Zealander or just 'Cobber', although this was also frowned on by the RAF. But there were no restrictions in the United States and the identity of Kain soon became widely known, with New Zealand papers lapping up Kain stories.

The severe winter of 1939–40 put a damper on flying and it was not until 2 March 1940, a fine sunny day, that Kain scored his third German aircraft, this time an Me 109, his first. He and his wingman chased a group of Heinkels and were bounced by covering Me 109s; dogfights developed and the New Zealander became trapped between two Germans. Kain took the one in front of him with a long burst but was then hit from behind, cannon fire thudding into his engine. Mitchell quoted Kain:

> The motor caught fire, and smoke poured backwards. I thought I was done … I was prepared to jump, but I found the straps of my parachute harness had slipped so I had to stay there. The fire went out for a while but then it started again, and the fumes were so bad I turned on my oxygen to breathe. I managed to glide far enough to land on an airfield (Metz) behind the Maginot Line. By this time the fire had stopped and I climbed out and fell flat on my face. When I woke up I was in hospital. I was feeling fine and there was a French pilot in the bed next to me who had force-landed just before me. So we had a party. Then I got up, hopped into a British machine and flew back to my squadron.

It's always been widely speculated that Kain was shot down by the budding German ace Werner Molders, something Cornwell in *The Battle of France — Then and Now* admits is a possibility.

It was an unhappy day for 1 Squadron at Vassincourt, as they also lost their first pilot of the war — New Zealander John Mitchell. Like Kain,

Mitchell was just 21 and from Wellington, and had the misfortune to go into the records twice, as the first New Zealander killed over France and the first to die flying a Hurricane. Mitchell joined 1 Squadron in France in November 1939, two weeks after his 21st birthday and because of the onset of winter had flown only 11 ops before his death. He and fellow sergeant Francis Soper attacked a Dornier over Metz, and while their machine guns claimed the bomber, return fire smashed into Mitchell. Richey says Mitchell called, 'I'm hit in the engine and must go down.' Soper abandoned the scrap and went down to pick out a field for Mitchell, who couldn't see for smoke. As the pair neared the ground Soper lost sight of the New Zealander. While Errol Martyn's *For Your Tomorrow* notes different eyewitness accounts, Richey says 'Mitch' spun in. He added, 'Mitchell was a New Zealander, a big cheerful boy.' The young man was buried in Chambieres French National Cemetery at Metz.

Mitchell, born the day before the Armistice in World War I, studied at Wellington College and Victoria University College and was working as a city council clerk when he was selected for an SSC. He sailed for England in late September 1938 in a draft of eighteen, only eight of whom survived the war. In July 1941 Mitchell's parents farewelled a second son, Stuart, on his way to England for attachment to the RAF as a trained pilot. What agonies they must have gone through. In England Mitchell, like his brother, learned to fly Hurricanes and then was posted to the Middle East, joining 112 Squadron flying Kittyhawks. He died in Libya on 31 May 1942 while bombing and strafing enemy forces. During the army's later advance, Mitchell was found buried alongside his wrecked fighter near Derna, but postwar his grave could not be found, obliterated by sandstorms. Dead at 21 like his brother, he is commemorated on the Alamein Memorial.

AIR WAR IN FRANCE — THE FIGHTERS

Two days before Mitchell's death in France, Horace Trenchard (28), another Wellingtonian, became the first New Zealander killed on a Spitfire, dying in a flying accident at Duxford, Cambridgeshire. He'd been posted to 19 Squadron in October 1939 and on 29 February 1940 was practising night circuits and landings when he crashed. At 28, Trenchard was old for a tyro fighter pilot.

In France, Cobber Kain and his squadron learned in mid-March 1940 that he had won the DFC for 'exceptional gallantry' and he and his fellow pilots partied in the mess before heading off for a dinner and show in Verdun. The decoration was gazetted in London on 29 March, three days after Kain had become the first RAF fighter ace of World War II, shooting down two more Me 109s in a single engagement to take his tally to five, the number qualifying an airman for ace status. The day he got the pair of Messerschmitts, the Germans also got him again. Kain and the two other men in his section tangled with nine Me 109s. Kain hammered his victims down, one, two in quick succession, but as the sky cleared after the whirling melee, his Hurricane was picked off by German fighters who'd been lurking above. Kain told Mitchell:

> There was nothing behind me and then — *bang!* The cockpit covering was blown off. I didn't have time enough to know what had happened, or where it came from. Flames and hot oil came up from the engine, and I thought the top of my head had been blown away. I passed out.

Kain revived as the Hurricane plunged steeply but flames scorched his face as he leaned forward to switch off the petrol. He pulled the fighter out of its dive, undid his straps, rolled the plane over and fell out. His parachute opened over what Kain knew to be the border with France and he landed near a German village. He skedaddled towards France and was lucky, picked up by French troops with shrapnel fragments in one leg and a red and swollen face.

Any remaining shred of Kain's anonymity vanished when his DFC was announced — with news and feature stories, radio broadcasts, photographs and interviews with his family in New Zealand. He had become an international hero. On leave in England he was congratulated by High Commissioner Bill Jordan and Mitchell met him again.

> He was much thinner than when I had seen him in France … for the squadron was flying up to six hours daily, and on the day he was shot down Kain had been interrupted at the grapefruit stage of breakfast … there were no mock heroics about Kain, and he admitted quite frankly that he'd been scared stiff of using his parachute, and had only done so when there was no other option.

Kain took the train to Peterborough where his girlfriend, actress Joyce Phillips, was appearing. Hot on his trail, reporters followed and Movietone News filmed them. They announced their engagement and Phillips was soon flashing a ring with three big diamonds. She told a reporter, 'Of course, I am terribly proud of him. Naturally, I worry … but he has as good a chance as the next man, except that men of his type go looking for trouble.'

Journalist Eric Baume, also a New Zealander, reported from London that Kain

> finds himself willy-nilly on society pages and in gossip columns. If he wants a quiet lunch at Simpson's … autograph hunters rush after him.

If he stands on a street corner for a moment, his six feet two of New Zealand brawn is at once noticed and he gets no peace. If he goes to a theatre he is mobbed and asked to step up on the stage.

Britain needed heroes in the spring of 1940 and Kain filled the bill.

While 73 Squadron ranged well into Germany in those spring days, searching out the enemy, 'No. 1' was more circumspect, and cursed its lousy luck at not having seen any German fighters. But it still remained the squadron's policy to be cautious and bide its time, Richey wrote, adding:

> We seldom crossed the German frontier and when we did we went over as high as possible and did a sweep round and back again to draw the enemy fighters out. If we saw a Hun we'd cross the lines and attack if he was within reasonable distance, and we'd always chase across if there was a chance of catching one. But the Bull gave strict orders that there was to be no fooling around, no 'daredevil ace' stuff. To eliminate temptation he excluded the brigade of press correspondents in France from contact with the squadron [unlike 73 Squadron]. This was a training period, and very useful experience; our turn would come with the German push, said the Bull, and when it did we would be more than ready as a cohesive and disciplined team.

Halahan was right. Once the Germans invaded, the highly trained and cohesive 1 Squadron, despite overwhelming odds, claimed more than 100 enemy aircraft for the loss of only three pilots killed and one taken prisoner.

After the German attack, 73 Squadron helped to cover Allied

airfields and bases, falling back as its airfields were bombed or became untenable. On 18 June, the squadron returned to England, where it concentrated on night fighting during the Battle of Britain. Operations ceased on 20 October to allow it to prepare for transfer to the Middle East.

At daybreak on 10 May RAF pilots had no shortage of targets. The skies over Holland, Belgium and northern France were black with German aircraft — bombers, troop-carrying transports, Stukas on ground attacks and swarms of fighters. Reconnaissance aircraft had already marked dozens of Allied airfields and other key sites in the Low Countries and from dawn the droning bombers began unloading.

That morning Cobber Kain shot down a Dornier 215 reconnaissance bomber and saw it crash east of Metz. Day after day for the rest of the month and into June, Kain and his fellow pilots flew unceasing patrols in their own base areas, attacking German bombers and their escorts flying to the battle zones, and where possible trying to protect the vulnerable Battles and Blenheims. The 73 Squadron pilots also endured attacks on their airfields and were soon exhausted by constant action and long hours in their cockpits. Now they were only occasionally able to get into Reims for a bath and a decent meal.

Kain's tally mounted. Another Dornier on 11 May, a Henschel 126 (a battlefield reconnaissance aircraft) the next day, an Me 109 two days later. RAF fighter pilots were flying at the limits of their endurance, grim with exhaustion as the German army spread panic and rolled up the opposing French as it speared through the Ardennes into northeastern France, wheeled and headed for the sea. Charles Gardner, a BBC correspondent who'd become friendly with Kain, is quoted in *Cobber Kain* saying the New Zealander walked into his hotel room in Reims 'looking as though he had just come out of a coal pit'.

> I turned the bath on while he peeled off his clothes — for the first time in six days. He was dazed for want of sleep, and said hardly a word … after about ten minutes I looked into the bathroom … and Cobber Kain's chin was resting on his massive chest, his eyes were closed, and the water was making little bubbles as he snored a fraction of an inch from the surface.

Kain's successes continued. On 19 May he claimed an Me 110 and a Ju 88 and perhaps shot down a third. He had three more victories the following week. Two days before his own death he destroyed another Me 109; he had honed his tactic of getting in very close before firing his machine guns. It paid off.

Details in Burns' book account for fifteen victories but the squadron's operations record book says fourteen. Kain himself mentioned various other slightly higher totals. Christopher Shores and Clive Williams in *Aces High* say sixteen. Some breathless reporters boosted his record to forty, but whatever the precise tally, Kain was a skilled and brave fighter pilot.

Had fate not intervened towards the end, he might have survived. Kain and other tour-expired pilots were rostered to return to England on 23 May but at the last minute the New Zealander was held back and returned to battle. Eventually new pilots arrived and on 6 June Kain learned he was to go home for rest and posting as an instructor. He was weary and anxious to leave; his fiancée was busy organising their wedding. That night he dined at Maxim's in Paris with Richey who remembered later that Kain seemed nervous and preoccupied. 'Like the rest of us he'd had enough for a bit.'

The following morning he climbed into his fighter to 'beat up' — fly noisy, almost ground-level passes — the airfield at Echemines, a few miles northwest of Troyes, where 73 Squadron was stationed. One last flight before departure. He couldn't resist a farewell aerobatic fling, and had he not been so worn down, Kain might have landed safely, his loops, dives and rolls accomplished without incident. But as the Hurricane flick-rolled across the airfield it stalled, spun into the ground, broke up and burned. Kain, thrown clear, died instantly. He didn't have a chance. The Court of Inquiry found the accident occurred 'as a result of doing aerobatics at too low an altitude' and it was said his *joie de vivre* had overcome his judgment.

Flying Officer Edgar James Kain, 21, DFC, mid, RAF, was buried locally but after the war was reinterred in Choloy War Cemetery near Nancy. Fourteen other New Zealand airmen lie there, all Bomber Command aircrew killed between 1942 and 1944. Kain's mother and his sister Judy were on their way to England by sea for his marriage when he was killed and on 4 September 1940 they received his DFC from the King at Buckingham Palace.

New Zealanders were sprinkled through most squadrons attached to British Air Forces France, and more joined as reinforcements flown to France after the German offensive began, usually as part squadrons. While this was one way of meeting French requests for more fighters without denuding Britain of full squadrons, the move was not entirely satisfactory. Putting flights from different squadrons together with pilots who did not know each other or the way they flew was asking for trouble.

The first New Zealand fighter pilot to lose his life from a French base after 10 May was 87 Squadron's Gordon Saunders, 23 (Wellington). He joined 87 Squadron at Lille/Seclin, one of several aerodromes around Lille. Saunders had a mixed opening day of the blitzkrieg. He claimed one victim in a clash with He 111s but according to Peter Cornwell was hit by enemy crossfire, badly damaging his radiator. Saunders got the plane down safely. Four days later Saunders was shot down and fatally burned, while intercepting an incoming bombing raid. He died in Lille Hospital. It was a terrible day for 87 Squadron, which suffered badly with three pilots dead and a fourth with an amputated leg.

Saunders and Roland 'Bee' Beamont, an English tyro on 87 Squadron but a pilot who was to write his name in wartime history, were good mates. Beamont wrote of Saunders' death and others in his 1989 autobiography *My Part of the Sky:*

Then Saunders … perhaps my closest friend in France. The day before [he was killed] I had asked him how many Huns he had got. His reply was, 'Oh, only one but as long as old Saunders is walking along the streets enjoying the sunshine after this war, he doesn't mind.' Messerschmitts got him … he was alive when they got him out but died in hospital later that day of the usual complaint those days — burns.

New Zealanders Ken Tait, Derek Ward and Harry 'Buzz' Allen also flew with 87 Squadron in France. Tait, like Gordon Saunders, was an old boy of Wellington College, and was on the squadron when it first went to France. Ward and Allen were with 151 Squadron at Martlesham Heath when they ferried Hurricanes to 87 Squadron at Lille/Marcq on the morning of 16 May, as replacement planes. The

New Zealanders and four others arrived to find the squadron as short of pilots as it was of planes, and without specific orders to return to England they stayed, welcomed and adopted by 87 Squadron.

Tait and the other two survived France and went on to fly in the Battle of Britain, Tait and Ward remaining with 87 Squadron. But Allen, back with 151 Squadron, was killed on 12 July, the third day of the Battle of Britain, and the other two died later in the war. Allen joined HMS *Conway*, the merchant navy school ship, in England in 1931, and subsequently served on the Blue Funnel Line but decided flying was more attractive, and in 1937 was selected for an SSC. He was slightly wounded in the left arm by return fire from a Henschel 126, a German observation aircraft he attacked on 19 May with Ward and two Australian pilots. Despite evasive low-level flying the 126 stood little chance against four Hurricanes and eventually exploded, losing its tail.

Tait was among twelve prospective pilots who left New Zealand in September 1937 to take up SSCs in the RAF. By the time he was killed in 1941, shot down while attacking an enemy bomber over the North Sea, he'd been credited with five enemy aircraft. *The Battle of France — Then and Now* notes the loss of an Me 109 that struck the ground during combat with Hurricanes near Arras on 20 May, 'possibly one of those claimed by P/O Tait of No. 87 Squadron'. This was the day 87 Squadron hurriedly moved back to Merville as the German advance threatened Lille's airfields. *Aces High* credits Tait with three victories in France, one shared, and three destroyed in the Battle of Britain.

Southlander Bob Yule, who was to become one of New Zealand's notable fighter pilots and commanders of the war, had his first taste of action with 145 Squadron in France. Yule, born in Invercargill in

January 1920, was educated at Southland and Timaru Boys' High Schools and nominated for a cadetship at RAF Cranwell when he was not quite eighteen. Such a nomination, signed by the Governor-General, was regarded as a singular honour — just one cadetship was available to New Zealand each year from 1932 until the outbreak of war when the scheme ended. Yule was accepted and in March 1938 sailed for England. He graduated from a course shortened by the approach of war and was granted a permanent commission in October 1939, was then posted to newly formed 145 Squadron and flew Blenheims until March 1940, when the squadron was re-equipped with Hurricanes. The unit saw its first action In France. Yule flew his fighter to Merville early in the afternoon of 16 May and saw action before returning to England for the night. He and his flight lieutenant, Roy Dutton, shared an attack on an He 111 near Brussels, Dutton machine-gunning one engine into flames and Yule finishing off the bomber.

In the chaotic lead-up to Dunkirk as the Germans approached, French airfields were littered with damaged and abandoned aircraft, some flyable, some not — French, British, Dutch and Belgian. Ken Wynn in *A Clasp for 'The Few'* quotes an unnamed newspaper saying Tait flew an abandoned Dutch aircraft back to England — in an old uniform and with no shirt. Brian Cull's *Twelve Days in May* quotes one 85 Squadron pilot who scoured rows of aircraft that had been strafed by Me 109s: 'I eventually found one Hurricane which, apart from a few bullet holes, seemed OK. We started her up and I was soon heading out over the Channel towards England. Landed Gatwick and on to Northolt.'

Cull notes that Air Vice-Marshal Blount flew home to England in a Tiger Moth from Merville on 21 May, with nothing left of his command. Blount hunted the airfield for a flyable aircraft — about twenty RAF wrecks were strewn around — Gladiators, Lysanders, Tiger Moths, Hurricanes, a Blenheim and a Dominie. He eventually found a Moth that seemed, miraculously, to have nothing wrong with it. The engine burst into life. Cull adds that Blount studied the controls for a few minutes, asked for directions to England, then took off. He reached home safely but died in a crash at Hendon a few months later.

Ward shot down a Henschel on 18 May, shared in the destruction of another with Allen and the others the following day as well as damaging an Me 109 and a Do 17 the day after. The squadron was told to retreat to Merville and from there was ordered back to England. It was at Merville that Ward lost Whisky, his little black Scottie who flew countless times on non-operational flights. Ward took the dog to France and Cull says ground personnel at Lille were surprised to see the small animal pop its head over the side of the cockpit when Ward landed, and quotes Ward as saying, 'He was a real doggie airman. Nothing gave him greater pleasure than to sit on my knee in the Hurricane. With his ears cocked up, he'd stare before him as we often did 300 mph. He'd been on the squadron since he was six weeks old.'

Ward had a battered and damaged Hurricane to fly home and thought the flight might be too risky, so the dog would be better off in one of the transports carrying air and ground crew. Beamont in his autobiography blames himself for the missing dog. The transport turned out to be a KLM airliner, its crew in spotless uniforms, but Beamont says he was only given ten minutes to be aboard. 'That left no time to collect any gear, or even my flying helmet from dispersal where also was Derek Ward's dog ... which I had promised to take home with me.' It was not surprising there was little thought for a spare dog as people scrambled for the transport. As Beamont later recalled:

> Jeffries, whom we thought killed on Saturday, was there with an armful of splinters, a sergeant pilot with terrible burns on his face and hands was hobbling about cheerfully as if nothing was wrong, Woody Woods-Scawen whom we had seen bale out a few days ago, was there telling fearful stories as usual; Squadron Leader Oliver of 85 had just arrived looking grey and haggard — he had been shot down a number of times himself and had finally received a heavy dose of glycol fumes. [Glycol was an essential element of the engine-coolant system of in-line engines. If it was lost due to combat damage the engine quickly overheated and seized.]

Ward's Hurricane lacked a gunsight and had no functioning instruments except compass, oil and petrol gauges. He got the fighter off the ground but, according to *Twelve Days in May* quoting Ward's combat report:

> The seven guns were loaded but there was no incendiary tracer. I intended to land [on the way home] at Abbeville to collect some kit which I had left there. Approaching Abbeville I saw that the town was in flames and two [Dorniers] were dive-bombing. I climbed and attacked one of the planes and got in two bursts at 300 yards, pointing my guns in the general direction of the e/a [enemy aircraft]. The e/a dived into cloud and I followed and gave the e/a some more bursts in the cloud. I came out and circled for ten minutes and saw

another Dornier between clouds and attacked again. My engine began to overheat badly and some 109s attacked me from behind. I dived into cloud and eventually landed at Abbeville. [Ward switched off the engine to find petrol spraying from a punctured starboard tank, the aerodrome being evacuated and unserviceable machines, Lysanders mainly, burning. French ground crews, about to leave, wanted to destroy Ward's Hurricane rather than risk starting it again with Ward in the cockpit and petrol spraying.] ... I stuck a bayonet into the starboard tank to empty it and managed to persuade two airmen to fill my port tank. I had to leave without being rearmed. I took off and two miles east of the aerodrome I encountered six Dorniers 17s and six 109s. I attacked the leader of the 109s, which were coming head-on towards me, and gave the leader a burst. He swerved left and I dived past him towards the ground. Fortunately the 109s continued to escort the bombers and did not give chase. I then flew the aircraft to North Weald and landed it.

The unsuperstitious Ward's regular Hurricane bore a coat of arms of his own design — a quartered shield bearing a broken hand-mirror, a hand holding a match lighting three cigarettes, a man walking under a ladder and the number 13. Under the shield, the words 'So what the Hell'. Ward sent a photograph of it home.

Other New Zealanders fighting in France included superb pilot Johnny Gibson, and Cam Malfroy on 501 Squadron. Both emerged from the war with distinguished records, Gibson with a DSO and DFC and Malfroy with a DFC and DFC (US). Gibson won SSC selection in 1938 and sailed with seventeen others for England in April that year. Only four of the eighteen survived the war.

Born in England, Gibson arrived in New Zealand with his family at the age of four. He was educated at Auckland Grammar and then New Plymouth Boys' High School, where significantly he was the school's champion rifle shot. Just six days before he left New Zealand the young man changed his name by deed poll from Axel John Albert von Wichmann to Axel John Albert Gibson and entered the RAF as such. A sensible move given the climate of the times.

After earning his wings Gibson was posted to Farnborough and the RAF's School of Photography to become an Army Co-operation pilot. But France changed all that and Gibson was thrown in at the deep end, posted to the battlefield as a reinforcement for 501 Squadron, which had flown to Betheniville on 10 May to bolster the AASF. Gibson had never flown a Hurricane when he joined 501 Squadron but that didn't seem to matter. He was a natural. By the time the squadron returned to England on 18 June it had flown from seven different airfields. Its final base had been two days at St Helier on Jersey in the Channel Islands, where it covered the evacuation of troops from Cherbourg.

Gibson shot down one He 111 and shared in the destruction of another on 27 May but then was hit by return fire and crash-landed in a field at Rouen. He was unhurt, and in succeeding days downed another 111, claimed two more which were unconfirmed and damaged three others, knocking down his first Me 109 on 10 June. In the free-for-all with the Messerschmitts over Le Havre, Gibson's Hurricane was badly damaged and he baled out over Le Mans.

Cam Malfroy was a top-flight international tennis player in the 1930s, just short of the very best. He won the New Zealand national championship in 1933, represented New Zealand in the Davis Cup and played Wimbledon no fewer than nine times between 1930 and 1947. He made the fourth round in 1931, and again in 1936, when England's Fred Perry beat him on his way to the title. In the last Wimbledon before the war Malfroy lost in the third round to American Bobby Riggs. Malfroy served with the Cambridge University Air Squadron in 1931–32 while studying at Cambridge, and in 1935 was posted to 501 Squadron in France. During the Battle of Britain, he instructed at an Operational Training Unit (OTU), rejoining 501 Squadron in February 1941 before being posted as CO of a Canadian fighter squadron. He served with Allied headquarters in 1944 and ended the war a wing commander, as CO of RAF Warmwell. The New Zealand Fighter Pilots' Museum lists Malfroy as an 'ace' with five victories but *Aces High* gives him only one, an He 111 near Betheniville on 11 May, and calls five 'unlikely', saying only one claim had been found for him.

Gibson and Malfroy flew on 501 Squadron with a young sergeant pilot born in Yorkshire in February 1917, who, like most RAF pilots, was unblooded when he went to France. But he had a special talent — leaving France with a Mention in Dispatches, a Croix de Guerre, and five enemy planes to his credit in the space of fourteen days. James Henry (Ginger) Lacey was to become one of the RAF's top scorers in the Battle of Britain.

New Zealander Tony Dini matched Lacey's tally in France on Hurricanes with 607 (County of Durham) Squadron but, cruelly, never got a chance to show what he could do in the Battle of Britain. A few days after returning from France he died in an aircraft accident.

Antonio Dini was born on 7 January 1918, in Christchurch. His grandparents had emigrated from Corsica, taking their family to

Queensland so their sons would escape conscription. In Australia Dini's father ran away from home and joined a circus, which toured New Zealand. He spotted a young woman in the front row of a performance. Somehow he found out who she was and presented himself, all spick and span, at her home one night, where he charmed her parents and won her heart. The couple settled in Christchurch, raising a family of seven.

Dini did well at school and when he was chosen for an RAF SSC was working as a mechanic in the Post and Telegraph's automatic exchange. In December 1937 he was in a party of twelve that sailed for England. Only three of the twelve would come home. Among the draft were Bill Frankish, killed in France attacking the Maastricht bridges, Ken Wendel, killed in the Battle of Britain, and notable Sunderland pilot Alex Frame, who rescued 200 Allied servicemen from Greece in 1941 in a series of daring flights. He ended the war a wing commander and CO of a Sunderland squadron in West Africa.

Half of Dini's draft went to Hatfield to begin pilot training. Four days after arrival one of them was dead. Brian Grieves, 22 (Auckland), died with his civilian instructor, 30-year-old New Zealander Theodore Paviour Smith, when their Tiger Moth collided with a Gloster Gauntlet at 800 feet, whose pilot was also killed. It was a sharp lesson to the trainees that flying was a dangerous business. Dini wrote home: 'I suppose you heard about one of our chaps being killed, but don't let it worry you. It was unfortunate it should happen so soon but will probably never occur again.'

Dini, who was told he had a very good touch, went solo after nine and a half hours and received a good report. After winning his wings Dini was posted in October 1938, on loan to an FAA squadron flying Walrus aircraft. In his letters home, Dini constantly told his parents not to worry. A few days after war was declared, he wrote:

> I don't regret a thing I've done and if I'm unlucky enough to get my packet, I want you to know I wouldn't have had it any other way ... This is the job I want to do; I'm never happier than when flying ... Mum, I'll be okay. I know in my own heart I'll be back to see you all some day.

On 1 May 1940 Dini joined 607 Squadron and flew to join them at Vitry-en-Artois, just northeast of Arras. The unit had been in France since mid-November 1939. It stayed at Vitry until 18 May when it moved to Norrent-Fontes, two days before being withdrawn to England. The squadron, as did all RAF units, suffered heavily after the blitzkrieg began. Its CO was killed on 15 May and his successor was shot down and captured four days later. The sky over France offered a target-rich environment and Dini, a talented fighter pilot, made the most of his opportunities.

Dini might even have been the first New Zealander into action in France when the Germans struck on 10 May; a driver interrupted Dini's breakfast in 607 Squadron's mess in a village near Vitry, dashing into the room shouting that the Germans were bombing the airfield. At 4.15 a.m. Dini was airborne with two other pilots, chasing Heinkels. His combat report, quoted in *Twelve Days in May,* says: 'First attack at 300 yards, down to 200 yards — ten seconds. Silenced rear gunner and black smoke from port engine. Second attack, smoke from starboard engine.' He claimed the German as 'damaged' on his first of at least four sorties that day.

Just after 3.30 p.m. he shared a 'kill' claim. 'Carried out attack with Red 3 [on an He 111] and both e/a's engines gave out great quantities of oil and smoke, covering my windscreen and I had to return to base.

When last seen e/a was diving for the ground.' Two hours later he had a victory on his own. 'Attacked last aircraft of formation, first from rear then from quarter. E/a broke away, dived and crashed (in flames) … returned alone.' Finally, as the sky was darkening, Dini damaged another He 111, a straggler. 'Attacked starboard aircraft and fired one-second bursts from 300–150 yards. Engines smoked but oil on windscreen prevented seeing what happened to e/a in bad light.'

Cull wrote that 607 Squadron claimed an impressive eighteen 'confirmed' that day, six probables and a dozen damaged — all He 111s. None of the bombers had fighter escorts and paid the price. It wouldn't happen again. Dini was in the thick of the air battle from then on, shooting down a 109, a Do 17 and a brace of Heinkels on succeeding days.

On 14 May Ken Newton of 151 Squadron was among a group of pilots who flew into Vitry to strengthen 607 Squadron and make up for losses. Newton, 24, was an English-born New Zealander who sailed to England in 1937 to join the RAF. Another New Zealander was among the newcomers — Jim Humphreys, who had been born in Greymouth in 1918 and educated at Christ's College, Christchurch. In 1938 he had been working in the Audit office in Wellington when he was selected for an SSC, and sailed for England. Training completed, he was posted to 245 Squadron. The squadron had converted to Hurricanes in March 1940, and the new pilots had hardly had time for a cuppa in France before they were ordered into action. *Twelve Days in May* says Humphreys lodged claims for a damaged Hs 123 and an Me 109, while Newton claimed two enemy aircraft possibly destroyed or damaged and adds, of the squadron claims, 'Few, if any, of these victories were, or were considered, conclusive.'

During the afternoon of 17 May strong formations of Me 109s and

110s raided Vitry, base for several squadrons and flights. All Hurricanes were ordered off but the Germans caught some aircraft before they were in the air. Dini's Hurricane was hit and forced back to the field. New Zealander Geoff Simpson, lost in the final days of the Battle of Britain, was involved in the fighting above and around Vitry that afternoon. He'd arrived at the field just two days earlier in B flight, 229 Squadron. According to his combat report he saw half a dozen Me 110s at 20,000 feet and joined in the attack.

> I closed to about 30 yards, giving a good long burst. E/a did a stall turn to the left and appeared as if it would dive into the ground. I broke away to the right. E/a recovered itself and flew eastwards at about 20 feet. I attacked again from the starboard beam, using up the last of my ammunition in a full deflection shot. E/a hit the ground … and broke up.

Dini wrote his last letter home on 16 May, apologising for not writing for 'so long' and saying, 'Well, I am quite O.K. There has been nothing wrong at all. I am now in France, have been for some time, and the last few days have had plenty of action. Shot down four certainties and six probables … Feel a little tired sometimes, but a good sleep puts me on top line again.' He finished: 'I'm getting along fine, so don't worry 'bout me. Your ace pilot son. Kid XXXX.'

Fifteen days later he was dead. Home from France on 20 May, Dini was posted to 605 (County of Warwick) Squadron. On 31 May he took off in a Hurricane from Hawkinge on the southeast coast bound for Scotland. *For Your Tomorrow* says his engine failed shortly after, the fighter rolling over at low altitude and diving into a road six miles north of Folkestone. Dini lies in Folkestone New Cemetery, Hawkinge.

Heartbroken, Dini's mother carefully transcribed all her son's letters by hand and put them in a folder. She wrote at the end of the last one: 'I received this letter a month after Toni was killed. He was killed in Kent, England, May 31st, 1940.'

Another New Zealander in 229 Squadron who flew in France was Timaru-born Vic Verity, who was working on his father's farm when he was selected for an SSC. He'd had a couple of months on Hurricanes when he was posted to France with two others to reinforce 615 Squadron. On 20 May, flying from Norrent-Fontes, he and his section fought twenty enemy aircraft, half and half Ju 88s and Me 110s. He attacked two of the 88s then broke away into clouds, emerging to be hit in the wings by 110s but able to scuttle back into the clouds before resuming fire at one of the 88s, exhausting his ammunition and seeing smoke pouring from the enemy's port engine. The Me 110s came at him again, planting cannon shells in the armour plating behind his back and in the fuselage. 'I dived to the ground evading e/a, I found my engine temperature was now registering 145 [degrees] and fumes were coming from my engine, so switched off to prevent being overcome. Made forced landing on aerodrome but overshot, causing undercarriage to collapse. Aircraft was badly damaged.'

The Hurricane was unfit for flying when the squadron departed that night and because of the shortage of planes, Verity was left to his own devices to get home to England — by road to Cherbourg, then a ship across the Channel.

Twenty-three New Zealanders, fourteen of them on Battles and Blenheims, died over France, Belgium and Holland between the start of the blitzkrieg on 10 May and France's capitulation in late June. Four

Hurricane pilots were lost, including Ken Kirkcaldie, 28 (Wellington), killed on an offensive patrol over northern France from an English base. A grandson of a co-founder of Wellington department store Kirkcaldie and Stains, he was a barrister and solicitor working in London as an advisor to United Dominions Trust in late 1938 when he joined the London University Air Squadron. John Coleman, 27 (Christchurch), died when his photo reconnaissance Spitfire, stripped down, unarmed and equipped with long-range tanks, was shot down by a 109 over Belgium on the return leg of a trip to Bremen and Hamburg. Three New Zealand pilots of little Lysanders were among the casualties — Alan Ollerenshaw, 19 (Auckland), crashed in Belgium, Ian Dromgoole, 24 (Lyttelton), was shot down west of Amiens on a ferry flight to Abbeville and Ern Howarth, 20 (Dunedin), was killed when his machine crashed in flames near Calais on a supply drop from England. Dromgoole's grave could not be found postwar and he is remembered at Runnymede, as is his brother Syd, 28, a 75 Squadron navigator, killed two years later on a bomber attacking Le Havre. The Air Forces Memorial at Runnymede, overlooking the Thames, commemorates the names of over 20,000 airmen with no known graves, who were lost during operations from bases in the United Kingdom and North and Western Europe.

The other two deaths were those of bomber crew flying operations from England. Flight Lieutenant John Collins, 23 (Christchurch), was the pilot of a 75 Squadron Wellington hit by flak at low level as it attacked a bridge at Dinant, Belgium, the night of 21–22 May, an almost impossible task. The Wimpy crashed in Belgium but Collins' body was not recovered and he is also commemorated at Runnymede. Three of the crew, none of them New Zealanders, survived to be captured. The Wellington was 75 Squadron's first loss of the war. The other bomber crewman killed was Leading Aircraftman (LAC) Ray Nuttall, 28 (Dunedin). His 10 Squadron Whitley was shot down near Abbeville the night of 11–12 June.

A handful of RAF fighter units stayed in France until late June, after the Germans regrouped and stormed south on 5 June to destroy the remainder of the French Army behind the Somme River line. They flew protection over west coast ports where evacuation of Allied troops, many of them landed after Dunkirk, went on until 25 June, the day the armistice between France and Germany took effect. Between 16 and 25 June the navy lifted 144,000 British, 18,000 French, 24,500 Polish and small numbers of Czechoslovakian and Belgian troops from Cherbourg, St Malo, Brest, La Pallice and St Nazaire. The only major British unit lost in this final act of the Battle of France was the 51st Highland Division, trapped and captured at St Valery.

Chapter 3

SLAUGHTER OF THE BATTLES AND BLENHEIMS

In near silence on the night of Sunday, 12 May 1940, the stunned pilots of 15 Squadron picked at their food in the officers' mess at Alconbury airfield in Huntingdonshire, not believing what had happened that morning. The empty chairs reminded them this nightmare was real.

At 7.50 a.m. twelve of the squadron's long-nosed Blenheims had taken off to bomb the Maastricht bridges across the Albert Canal in the Netherlands. Two days after their lightning attack on Belgium and the Netherlands, German units were streaming over bridges foolishly left intact by the defenders. A storm of small-arms fire and a curtain of shells from rapid-firing 20 mm cannons met the Blenheims as they began shallow dives from 5000 feet to release their bombs at low level and break away at almost ground level.

In quick order six of the twelve aircraft were smashed down by intense, accurate German flak. Three hours and forty minutes later the surviving aircraft, all badly shot up, landed, two of the pilots wounded. It was a repeat of the Charge of the Light Brigade. Of the eighteen crew in the six lost Blenheims, fourteen were dead, the rest POWs. Among the victims were Tom Bassett, 22, and Bill Frankish, 25, the first New Zealanders to die in the Battle of France. Bassett's aircraft crashed and burned just north of Maastricht, Frankish's at Genk, just inside Belgium.

Both men had been selected for SSCs in the RAF. Bassett learned to fly at Wigram and sailed for England in April 1938; Frankish had gone the previous December to do his flying training in England.

Bassett was born in the second last year of the Great War at Te Kopuru, a pioneer settlement on a bluff above the Northern Wairoa River, seven miles south of Dargaville. He'd gone to high school in Dargaville before joining the local branch of the Bank of Australasia there, and had passed his professional accountancy examinations. He rode a fast, very noisy motorcycle to work every morning from Te Kopuru to Dargaville on a pot-holed metal road which was dusty in summer, a bog in winter.

Frankish, born in Wanganui, was christened Claude Randolph — Claude after an uncle and Randolph after an early relative who arrived in New Zealand on the *Randolph*, one of Canterbury's first four ships. But he was Bill from the moment he was born in 1914 when the doctor who delivered him held him up and exclaimed, 'He looks like Bill Massey' — the Prime Minister. Frankish had a privileged upbringing — his father owned a farm supplies store and he was educated at Wanganui Collegiate. Frankish was working on a farm when he applied for an SSC. As his younger sister Marjorie recalls, 'He was bitten by the flying bug after he flew down to Nelson or Blenheim for a holiday. He decided he wanted to fly.'

Frankish had been married a week when he died that awful morning, married to a New Zealander who went all the way to England to walk down the aisle. Marjorie Townend was Marjorie Frankish's best friend at nursing school in New Plymouth and Frankish met her there at his sister's 21st birthday party. Romance blossomed. The young woman waved farewell to him when he sailed from Auckland and accepted his proposal in a letter from England. Strings were pulled and Townend was given a passage to England. They were married in Luton on Saturday, 5 May 1940, just a few days after her arrival. Their honeymoon was cut short when Frankish was recalled from leave when the Germans burst into the Low Countries.

Another New Zealander flew with 15 Squadron's Blenheims on that disastrous morning. Leonard Trent, who won the Victoria Cross over Amsterdam three years later leading 487 (NZ) Squadron's similarly disastrous raid on a power station, somehow survived Maastricht and, miraculously, the next two or three weeks. He won a richly deserved DFC after the fighting in France and over Dunkirk.

Trent wrote a letter that's quoted in his biography *Venturer Courageous* by James Sanders:

Bert Oakley [an Australian] and Tom Bassett are missing. My two best friends in the squadron. Of course … no one saw them shot down, they may have landed anywhere with engine trouble. No one saw much at all except the target, then ack-ack fire, then the tree tops … we haven't heard from Bert or Tom yet but it is still early … I won't give up hope for a month.

His hopes were misplaced. Oakley and Bassett were dead. When Trent arrived in New Zealand postwar he invited the Bassett family to lunch on the ship to tell them about the events of that day and what he knew about Tom's death, a gesture still remembered with gratitude.

The massacre of 15 Squadron continued. Six days after Maastricht it mustered six Blenheims, all it could manage, for an attack on a German armoured column in France. Three were shot down by flak and fighters, eight of the nine men aboard killed. Another aircraft was damaged beyond repair. Trent also survived this raid. He continued to fly over France and then Dunkirk on recces and bombing trips, often without fighter escort, and continued to lead a charmed life while others fell. Sanders quotes Trent: 'We wandered about the sky without fighter escort, looking for targets. Why we were not shot down, God only knows.' Exhausted after fourteen hours-long operations, he was sent on leave and then posted to an OTU to train others. Of 15 Squadron's original eighteen officers, only five were alive a month later, one of them in hospital and another busy evading capture in France. Two of the five were killed later.

However, 15 Squadron was not the only one to suffer that black Sunday. Blenheim and Battle squadrons of Bomber Command, based in both England and France, lost about 35 aircraft all up, shot down by flak or the swarms of Me 109s and other German aircraft patrolling the bridges and battlefields.

Based at Amifontaine, near Reims in northeast France, 12 Squadron put up five Battles in an attempt to destroy two bridges over the canal in Belgium. None returned. Three Battles attacked the steel crossing at Veldwezelt. One, its wings aflame, flicked into the ground. The second, also on fire, its pilot badly burned, crash-landed on one bank of the canal, its crew taken prisoner. Shredded by flak and trailing smoke, the third crashed on the bridge itself, bombs exploding. Pilot Don 'Judy' Garland and sergeant navigator Tom Gray were awarded posthumous Victoria Crosses the following month, the first of the war. Shamefully, the aircraft's gunner, LAC Lawrie Reynolds, who shared death with the others, did not share in their decoration, nor even received a mention. The *Battle of France — Then and Now* quotes one report describing 12 Squadron crews' action as 'devoted heroism … in undertaking a virtually suicidal task'.

The heroics of Garland, Gray and Reynolds were in vain. Pontoons swiftly anchored alongside the structure by German engineers bypassed the damaged bridge and traffic resumed within an hour. According to *Air War Over France* by Robert Jackson, a German officer lectured captured aircrew: 'You British are mad. We capture the bridge early Friday morning. You give us all Friday and Saturday to get our flak guns all around the bridge, then on Sunday, when all is ready, you come along and try to blow the thing up.'

The Bomber Command aircraft and crews are covered here because they played such a prominent part in the Battle of France — unsuccessfully it must be said — and sustained such terrible losses. Little has been written about the New Zealand pilots who flew them, and their role deserves to be remembered.

Two other New Zealanders died on 12 May — Osborne Keedwell, 26 (Levin), and Edgar Morton, 25 (Auckland). Keedwell, a member of 107 Squadron, based at Watton, Norfolk, had been shuffled around Blenheim squadrons before arriving at 107 Squadron in 1939.

Unlike many New Zealanders making their combat debuts in France, Keedwell had flown eight operations before perishing over Maastricht. He'd taken part in an attack on German naval units in the North Sea and crash-landed at base after being damaged over Norway on 17 April. Attacking at Maastricht he fell in Belgium, shot down by fighters after flak broke up his squadron.

Morton, flying a 103 Squadron Battle from its French base at

Betheniville, took off at 4.30 in the afternoon to bomb a bridge at Bouillon, Belgium, near the French border, in an effort to stem the headlong German dash out of the Ardennes. Shot down, the Battle smashed into a field on the outskirts of a village just north of Bouillon, killing Morton and his gunner.

Battles and Blenheims were used more or less as fighter-bombers in the May-June conflict, a role for which they were totally unsuited. The single-engined Battle, a dreadful aircraft already obsolescent before the war started, was slow and ill equipped for any realistic role, basically defenceless against enemy fighters. It had a lone machine gun in the starboard wing and a Vickers gas-operated 'K' machine gun in the rear cockpit. The gunner stood up to fire, cockpit cover thrown back. The Battle carried 1000 pounds of bombs, normally 4 by 250, and was well-named 'the flying coffin'.

The twin-engined Blenheim bomber was no better in ground-attack. The long-nosed version, a development of the first mark, was also vulnerable to fighters although it had more fire power. It also carried 1000 pounds of bombs.

In September 1939, 15 Squadron, then flying Battles, was posted to France but returned to England in January 1940 and stayed, re-equipping with the Blenheims on which Bassett and Frankish would die. There is no record of what they thought about the 'new' planes but the prescient Bassett had written home in 1939, saying, 'The Battle is absolutely the rottenest machine imaginable for bombing … they are just death traps … couldn't possibly hope to get out of it alive if we had a war.'

The Battles and Blenheims were forced to play the role they did because the RAF simply had no other aircraft capable of ground attack and support — certainly nothing like the Luftwaffe's dive-bombing

DAY AFTER DAY

Stuka, which so demoralised French and Belgian troops. Another eight New Zealanders died on these aircraft in France and Belgium between 14 May and 16 June — Croydon Chamberlain, 30 (Auckland), Jack Edwards, 26 (Auckland), Gerald Bailey, 24 (Gordonton) and Clive Wylie, 26 (Masterton) on Blenheims, and Vern Cunningham, 24 (Wellington), Albert Wickham, 22 (Christchurch), Jim Vernon, 24 (Queenstown) and Ken Rea, 27 (New Plymouth), flying Battles.

Edwards was mourned by Trent as a close friend. They'd gone skiing in Switzerland in February 1939 with other New Zealand pilots. Edwards served with 40 Squadron from September 1938 until his death on 15 May, shot down near Mons, Belgium, attacking German troops.

Vernon died on 7 June, less than two weeks after an action for which he'd won a DFC, the same day Cobber Kain was killed and, in a strange twist, both took off on their last flights from Echemines. A standout athlete at Otago Boys' High School, Vernon was also good academically. He won a flying scholarship, earned his wings at Taieri and Wigram and in mid-1938 sailed for England, with his first and last posting to 150 Squadron.

The odds on long-term survival on Battles were poor. On that late-May day his was one of two aircraft sent to attack a Belgian chateau being used as a Luftwaffe headquarters. The pair became separated during a severe rainstorm but Vernon pressed on, dive-bombing and landing direct hits on the building. He flew through a stream of flak and was attacked by enemy fighters, German fire wounding his observer and gunner. He force-landed his severely damaged Battle, fired the aircraft and ran. The wounded men were rounded up by German soldiers but Vernon managed to evade capture and reach French lines an hour later. He was awarded the DFC for 'outstanding conduct and devotion to duty'. On his final flight on 7 June, Vernon was shot down by flak as he attacked convoys between Abbeville and Poix. All three men on the Battle were killed and buried locally.

Bert Wickham and Vern Cunningham were mates; they trained together in New Zealand, sailed on the same ship to take up SSCs and were destined to die as sacrificial Battle pilots. Wickham worked as a draper's assistant in his hometown Christchurch where he applied for the RAF, Cunningham in a shore-based job for the Blue Star Line. Wickham joined 88 Squadron in France about Christmas 1939 and died on one of the few Battles raids on Germany the night of 23–24 May. The target was Bingen-on-Rhine, a picture-postcard-perfect town on the river west of Mainz. The specific Bingen target, a railway junction or troops perhaps, is still a mystery seventy years after the event. Wickham was the first New Zealander to die in a bombing attack on a mainland German target.

Some New Zealanders survived the agony of France on Battles — and the war. Three who did were Tom Fitzgerald, Jim Hayter and Jack Shorthouse. All distinguished themselves in the following years, commanding squadrons and fighting until the end of the war. Fitzgerald and Hayter were sons of South Island farmers, in Canterbury and on D'Urville Island respectively. Fitzgerald went to Timaru Boys' High School, Hayter to Nelson College. Fitzgerald, first of the three to reach England, was posted to 103 Squadron in mid-1938 and was with the squadron when it flew to France as part of the AASF when war broke out. He was joined there two months later by Hayter, Morton and Cunningham.

In the spring of 1940, as the weather improved, their squadron flew leaflet raids over Germany, practised bombing, flew their own recces and practised formation flying. When the Germans crossed the Meuse at Sedan two days after the blitzkrieg began, 103 Squadron was called into action. Fitzgerald's log shows he flew only two operational flights in France, one on 12 May, the second two days later. On the 12th Fitzgerald, by now a flying officer, led Hayter and another 103 Squadron pilot at low level along the Meuse, bombing a pontoon bridge at Bouillon and blazing away at German troops with their machine guns. On the afternoon of 14 May sixty-three Battles and eight Blenheims launched a 'major' attack from their French bases against bridges, pontoons, strongpoints and enemy troops on the Sedan front. Forty were shot down by flak and fighters — the worst losses the RAF ever had in an operation of this size. Of the eleven battles 218 Squadron dispatched, it lost ten, and 103 Squadron lost four. Vern Cunningham was killed, dying with his gunner when their aircraft took a direct flak hit and exploded over the west bank of the Meuse. Many flights from advanced bases were so short navigators were not needed.

Fitzgerald's Battle, carrying four 250-pound bombs, was among the losses, downed when attacked by two Me 109s in a clear sky at 4000 feet. Wounded in a shoulder and hand by a cannon shell, Fitzgerald force-landed his machine brilliantly in French lines and made it back to his squadron. 'Shot down, both OK, back with French chasseurs' were his laconic log comments. Ken Wynn in *A Clasp for 'The Few'* credits Fitzgerald with shooting down both 109s and while such a feat would have been a rare success by a Battle against Messerschmitts, it never happened. Fitzgerald's log makes no mention of any victories and neither does the squadron diarist who noted: 'F/O Fitzgerald … was awarded the DFC for the conspicuous bravery he displayed in the most successful attack he pressed home from a very low level, and for his subsequent achievement in landing although wounded and regaining his unit together with his complete crew [the gunner]'. Fitzgerald's wounds grounded him and he was evacuated to England.

Chaos in the countryside and in the village outside the Betheniville field between 10 and 15 May is noted in 103 Squadron's diary records. Refugees fleeing west clogged the roads and conditions rapidly deteriorated in the village, built on either side of a main road, where the squadron was billeted. Raiders bombed the airfield constantly and most often inaccurately; electricity and telephones failed. The squadron had to bury local bomb casualties left lying in the open, and retreating French and Belgian soldiers roamed the area in undisciplined mobs. The officers' mess had to be barricaded the night of 15 May and looting spread. The Germans bombed the village where passing convoys laid up at night and smashed the railway station. Late on 15 May 103 Squadron evacuated Betheniville, southwest of Sedan, flying their aircraft south to St Lucien Ferme at Rheges, just short of the Seine. German panzer spearheads streaming west for the coast posed no threat to most of the airfields occupied by the AASF, but bombing and general turmoil made Betheniville untenable.

Jack Shorthouse, born in Portsmouth in April 1920, came to New Zealand with his parents at the age of six. Son of a Foxton pub owner, he was accepted for an SSC and learned to fly at the Wanganui Aero Club and at Wigram. With sixteen other pilots he sailed for England in December 1939, the first draft to leave New Zealand after the outbreak of war. He was posted to France as a replacement pilot for 12 Squadron, mauled over the Maastricht bridges and again two days later when the unit lost another four out of five Battles. Shorthouse flew a night sortie on 24–25 May, his first operation. By that stage Battle losses had become unsustainable and the aircraft were restricted largely to night ops, but some daylight trips were still demanded. When Shorthouse first flew in late May, the squadron had retreated from Amifontaine to Echemines.

Briton Michael Pitt, a 12 Squadron LAC rigger, then 19, now lives in retirement in North Devon. In 2005 he wrote a memoir about his French service on 12 Squadron in which he recalled the pullback. He remembered the flood of refugees on the roads at Amifontaine even as the squadron trucks drove away at midnight on 15 June and regretted leaving the squadron's vegetable garden, which he tended. The trucks covered 120 miles that night but the cooks were in action early.

What a wonderful breakfast the men in the mobile kitchen had prepared for us by the time we stopped. Mugs of the best tea ever … and a dixie full of fried bread, bacon and beans — and second helpings. [They] cooked in steaming cauldrons on a crowded, moving trailer, and there we were like excited boys on a school outing.

The pilots had it much easier, flying to Echemines. The squadron moved again on 3 June, 200 miles further west to the village of Souge, 20 miles past Vendôme.

Pitt noted that the night operations now being flown by 12 were difficult over 'Bible-black' countryside, Battle pilots trying to pinpoint German armour holed up in forested areas and then find their way home. 'In retrospect, these operations were a hazardous, unrewarding burden imposed on aircrew already under great strain.'

Such were the conditions when Shorthouse flew his first op with six others, records showing that five of the seven failed to find their target. He flew another seven completed trips. On one of them Shorthouse force-landed at a French airfield due to engine failure. Because it was L5383 and 'his' aircraft, Pitt was flown to the field with his toolkit the next afternoon to see what he could do. The French mechanics had laboured in vain and the engine wouldn't start. Pitt had already guessed the problem — a sheared off pin in the drive to the starter motor, and proceeded to embarrass the French. He borrowed a ladder, removed one piece of engine cowling, knocked out the sheared pin, substituted an old nail and replaced the cowling. While Shorthouse looked on he had the engine running in ten minutes.

Shorthouse made his last flight in France on 13 June, just three days before the squadron's remaining Battles flew back to England. He and five other pilots were briefed to bomb tanks reported refuelling in the Forest of Gault between Reims and Troyes, meaning a longish flight back towards the area they had left. Shorthouse, who died in Auckland in 2007, left no written record of his time in France, except for a brief mention of the day they were shot down, in a 1986 letter to Dick Copley, his gunner. 'Whatever happened in France in 1940? What staggers me in thinking about it is the total ignorance which we all had and the abysmal lack of training. Maybe it was better that way. I don't think that a few years later that I would have cared to do the same thing again in that way.'

Copley, now in his nineties and living in Canada after migrating from England years ago, still remembers vividly what happened after the Battles took off just before 6 p.m. 'The weather was stormy and in dodging heavy clouds the aircraft were widely separated.' Just short of the target Shorthouse shouted, 'Jesus, Jesus.' Four specks flying towards them materialised as Me 109s. The fighters wheeled around after their prey. Copley saw them suddenly, one, then another and another and a fourth in line astern.

Day after Day

They knew how to attack the Battles by then — from the defenceless rear. We didn't have a chance. I watched them turn and come in slightly astern and below us. We were helpless. I blazed away with my gun but it was pointless. My fire couldn't reach them. They tucked in behind and attacked. I could see the German pilots looking at me. [Cannon shells thumped into the underside of the Battle and machine-gun bullets beat a tattoo.] ... I called to Jack but I never heard another word from him. The intercom had gone.

At the best of times Copley could maybe see the top of the helmeted head of his pilot from his gun position. Now he couldn't see him at all, but one glance down into the fuselage was enough. The plane was burning. He could see that the navigator, Londoner Norm Cotterell, 20, was dead, his head and shoulders enveloped in flames. The aircraft was clearly doomed and Copley jumped.

Wounded in the right foot, he landed, minus his flying boots, in an open field and hobbled away to cover in a ditch. 'I could hear machine guns firing at our planes.' He saw his own aircraft burning on the ground half a mile away and was watching when the bomb load exploded. Shorthouse also reached the ground by parachute, burned by the Battle's flames.

Copley and Shorthouse both evaded capture. The Englishman lay low, received help from the French and made his way to Bordeaux, evacuated with other servicemen fleeing from French ports on the west coast.

Shorthouse was amazingly lucky. He was picked up by a Belgian count driving an ambulance. They stopped at Souge to refuel, by which time the squadron had gone, and suffered strafing several times before reaching St Nazaire. He just missed being loaded on the old liner

Lancastria, sunk with enormous loss of life, before being evacuated on another ship.

Neither Shorthouse nor Copley knew the fate of the other until, quite by chance, they met in the village of Binbrook, site of a big airbase in Lincolnshire, weeks after reaching England.

The following year Copley was on a 12 Squadron Wellington raiding Aachen, Germany, when the aircraft force-landed on an airfield at Antwerp. The crew set their bomber afire, calmly walked away, scaled a fence and made off into the night. Copley and his pilot made it into an escape line, but fell into German hands when they were betrayed in Brussels. This time there was no escape.

Shorthouse, who was badly burned, spent seven weeks in hospital in Plymouth, before flying Spitfires for the Photographic Reconnaissance Unit at high level over Germany for a few months and was posted to Canada. For more than a year he instructed in Moose Jaw, Saskatchewan, where he met and married a WAAF. Ten months in Vancouver followed as a torpedo bomber instructor. After two years in Canada he returned to England, flew a full tour on Lancasters with 44 Squadron, served as a chief flying instructor (CFI) and then formed and commanded Lancaster Squadron 189 from October 1944 until June 1945. He ended the war as a wing commander with a DFC and a Mention in Dispatches.

Postwar he joined TEAL (later Air New Zealand), flying until 1975 and pioneering several new routes. In 1966 in Canada he met Baron Antoine Allard, the man who took him on that long ambulance ride to St Nazaire. The baron, a noted travel-writer and artist, had been long searching for the New Zealander.

Other New Zealand Battle pilots survived close shaves — either to make it back to their own lines or become prisoners. Paul Rabone flew

16 ops in France and was twice shot down on 88 Squadron Battles, but baled out and lived to fly with distinction both in the Battle of Britain and later in the war, before being killed in July 1944 while on operations in a Mosquito. At his death he was a squadron leader with a DFC.

Frank Gill, then twenty-three, and better known much later as Minister of Defence in the Muldoon government, lived through 88 Squadron's horror in France. His worst moments were flying through ground fire that riddled his Battle, and a wheels-up crash-landing at Echemines alongside Cobber Kain's wrecked Hurricane, after his hydraulics were shot away.

Basil Peryman, a 142 Squadron pilot, was shot down and captured on 11 June. Although in POW camps for the rest of the war, he was lucky to be alive as his two crewmen were killed. Peryman attacked a bridge over the Seine in an attempt to delay German forces striking south. The aircraft was hit at low level from the blast of an exploding 88 mm shell, fragments ripping into the petrol tank under him and setting it alight.

Peryman escaped the blazing aircraft at the last moment, his chute opening just before he landed. He came down amid pine trees in a loop in the Seine but was spotted and quickly picked up by German troops. His hands, arms, face and chest were burned but though in shock and pain he took satisfaction in seeing the bridge was under repair when driven past by his captors. It had been hit by one of the other Battles.

Peryman was first treated at a local schoolhouse and then taken to a hospital near Cambrai before beginning his journey into long captivity. Born in December 1919, he grew up in Lincoln and was working as a technician in the Post Office before he applied for an SSC. Son Gerald recalls: 'He wanted a bit of adventure.' He got it in the RAF. Peryman came home with hepatitis and scars on his arms and chest he carried for the rest of his life; fortunately his face was not affected long term.

Peryman's son took his father back to France in 1995, five years before the old pilot died, to see if they could find the bridge and place where he landed. Despite help from the locals they were unable to find them, but did locate the hospital where nurses had cared for him. It was still functioning.

The Battle squadrons still flying south of the Seine continued to take terrible casualties. On 13 June, the day Shorthouse was shot down, his squadron lost two other aircraft, 88 Squadron had one shot down and Peryman's four, while 150 Squadron lost three with another badly damaged and 226 Squadron had one shot down.

Another seven Battles were shot down or written off on 14 June and more were destroyed in enemy raids on airfields. It was the last act and surviving Battles were ordered back to England the next day. Before they went, ground crews torched unserviceable aircraft.

Among other New Zealanders flying in the last stages were Ken Sutton and Ken Rea. Sutton, five days short of his 21st birthday, was shot down uninjured on 13 June, with Rea, 27, killed the following day. Sutton was working as a clerk in Palmerston North Hospital when he was selected for an SSC and trained in New Zealand. He arrived in England in early 1939, and went to France in April 1940 with 98 Squadron, a reserve squadron supplying pilots and aircraft for Battle units. He was then posted on to 142 Squadron, where Peryman was serving. The day Peryman was shot down, Sutton's flak-damaged Battle made it back to base with one crewman wounded. Luck was with him again two days later when three Me 109s ganged up on his aircraft and gunned it down while Sutton was attacking enemy columns. Years later Sutton told a newspaper reporter: 'Fortunately I had a gunner who knew what he was doing. He shot one down and damaged one but I was shot down too. The gunner, observer and I all got out of that all right.'

Sutton was mentioned in dispatches in January 1941 for his flying on 142 Squadron and was awarded a DFC in 1942, the citation noting, among other things, his service in France. He flew night fighters in the Battle of Britain and later Havocs and Mosquitoes. His luck deserted him in April 1943 when his Mosquito was brought down by friendly fire over Hove. He baled out but was hit by one of the props, losing his left arm and lower left leg. He flew again, with a special arm attachment, although not operationally, and ended the war a squadron leader.

Ken Rea, New Plymouth-educated, was among the first group of eighteen New Zealanders selected for SSC training in England, sailing in July 1937. He spent a year with 103 Squadron on Battles, then was transferred to 226 Squadron in September 1939 just after the squadron had flown to France with the AASF. It's not known how many ops he had flown but he survived until the last moments of the squadron's stay in France. His Battle was brought down and crashed during an attack on German armour near Dreux. One of his crew was also killed, the other dying of wounds two months later as a POW.

Exposed as frighteningly vulnerable, the Battles were finished in front-line service as soon they were withdrawn to England, but Blenheims continued to fly in many theatres, proving useful — but not for ground attack. The RAF would have to await the arrival of the destructive Hawker Typhoons and Tempests to fill that role.

Chapter 4

JIMMY PATERSON — AN EXTRAORDINARY YOUNG MAN

Jimmy Paterson missed his ship the night he was due to sail for England in April 1939, but still made it aboard, showing the initiative that was to mark him out in France in May and June of the following year. Paterson arrived at the wharf in Auckland to see Shaw Savill's *Waimarama* disappearing from view. He soon found the skipper of a launch who would give chase, the Harbour Master signalled the ship and at 9.45 p.m. the *Waimarama* stopped in Rangitoto Channel. Ten minutes later a red-faced Paterson climbed aboard.

On the face of it Paterson, son of a farmer at East Chatton, near Gore, didn't have the qualifications when he sought a Short Service Commission. He'd had only two and a half years at Gore High School but must have impressed the perceptive men on the selection panel and was accepted in mid-1938. His 'practical knowledge of motor cars and Caterpillar engines' and his service as a trooper in the Otago Mounted Rifles probably helped, along with his engaging personality. Chosen to train with the RNZAF, in December 1938 Paterson received his wings.

In England he was briefly on a Blenheim squadron but two days before the outbreak of war was posted to command No. 1 Servicing Flight Section (Magister aircraft) attached to 71 Wing of the AASF in France, based at Betheniville. The flight had the task of servicing and refuelling visiting aircraft and squadron Battles. Paterson and his higher-ups invented other jobs — building dummy Battles on the airfield to fool the Germans, camouflaging the base petrol dump by planting fir trees and painting the bright, shiny four-gallon petrol tins dark colours. Paterson flew when he could, mainly Magisters. During the bitter winter the RAF units hunkered down in village billets, the tedium broken by parties and leave.

On New Year's Eve 1940 Paterson attended a 'do' at a doctor's home in Betheniville. He wrote in his diary:

> There were about 15 or 16 of us, mostly young folk, and we had a glorious time in a typically French manner. Instead of singing *Auld Lang Syne* at 12 o'clock, we kissed [the French girls] under the mistletoe. I didn't know, or rather didn't want to know, that it was the custom to kiss their cheeks, not their lips.

On 10 January the Will Fyfe Concert Party performed at Betheniville and Paterson fell in love with dancer Joy Beadell. 'Wizard time. Had supper with Joy in Mess and made date.' The next day he drove his car into Reims to take Beadell to tea. 'Joy is absolutely marvellous and can dance like a fairy. We had champagne at The Cave, tea at the Little Tea Shop, thence to La Couple for a drink … went to the second show at the Opera and met Joy afterwards. Had a wizard party and home very late.'

A week later northeast France was at its coldest. 'Very white and fine snow everywhere, and a cold northeast wind. It is the coldest day I have felt in my life. The temperature ranges between twelve and twenty-seven degrees Fahrenheit below. Had great trouble starting my car.'

On 20 January he was told he would command a party going on leave to England. They trekked across France by train and caught a Channel steamer at Cherbourg. In London, he phoned Beadell, joined up with a pilot from his former Blenheim squadron and met an MP in the Overseas Club 'who sent us to have cocktails with Mrs Handley Page [wife of the aircraft designer] and daughter. Very nice too.' Then he went north to Perth and on to Blairgowrie to stay with the Gibsons, Scots friends of his parents. He was supremely happy in this rural part of Scotland and spent several leaves with the family — who treated him 'like a young king'.

Back in France in early February 1940 he took over No's 2 and 3 Servicing Flights at Champagne airfield, Reims, responsible for two dozen communications aircraft and exchange and replacement aircraft for squadrons. 'Spent the evening [with their pilots] drinking champagne at the Lion d'Or.'

Life in France for RAF servicing pilots, just three months away from the German blitzkrieg, was not unattractive. On 18 February Paterson had a 'very busy day' but still managed to have aperitifs and champagne with a Monsieur Nuiorot and after lunch sampled his liquors. 'The champagne was the best I've tasted. Simply melted on the tongue and liquors were very old and very good.' By the next day the thaw had set in and heavy rain meant no flying was possible, so Paterson spent the morning censoring mail.

A week later Paterson wangled a ride in a DH89 Dragon Rapide to Nantes, overnighting and returning next day. Nearing the city, the aircraft ran short of petrol, force-landed in a chateau's driveway and ran into a moat. Another DH89 came for Paterson and others. 'Seven

DAY AFTER DAY

of us piled in and flew back to Le Bourget, Paris. Had a rest and a beer and thence on to Reims arriving about 1530, after a very good trip. Received some *Free Lances* [magazines] from home.' He flew down to Perpignan where British squadrons were exercising and zipped around the countryside with a Rolls-Royce expert to aerodromes where Whitleys and the occasional Spitfire were down with engine problems.

But war was closing in. On 11 April, Paterson wrote in his diary:

Much air activity. Was woken up by the engines of Dorniers [on reconnaissance] and anti-aircraft guns. Four were shot down near here. Plenty of flap at hangars. Gas clothing, masks and tin hats to be worn generally ... 73 Squadron of Hurricanes moved on to our drome from Rouvres. 20 Hurricanes. A well-organized move. Their transport arrived at the same time.

Paterson flew a Hurricane for the first time on 20 April but strangely made no comment about it. Soon he was often flying Hurricanes, even taking one to Berry-au-Bac, to collect equipment for a Battle.

He woke to the usual sound of anti-aircraft fire from a nearby French battery on the morning of Friday, 10 May 1940, but by the time he reached the aerodrome his warrant officer was in a flap, waving urgent signals. They waited all day for the promised Hurricanes of 73 Squadron, which were back at Rouvres. At 4 p.m. unseen and unheard Dorniers at 20,000 feet caught the field off guard and dropped about seventy bombs, hitting several large hangars and an oil dump. The Hurricanes arrived soon after, landing safely. The Germans, apparently tipped off about the move, had been too early.

Paterson swiftly moved his aircraft to a satellite field already prepared in woods about five miles away, planes nicely concealed, and set to work. 'On the Sunday morning the whole sky was a swarm of activity and I couldn't resist the temptation of getting out of a lovely warm bed to have a looksee. This was as good as any morning tonic, for our Hurricanes were right on the job.' As he watched, the fighters broke up the bombers' attack and forced the enemy to drop their loads in the fields. 'All the local villagers were greatly bucked up about this, and were kissing and cooing us every chance they got; and of course it gave all the old hands some excuse to open up another of those never-ending bottles of champagne, and general celebrations commenced.'

That afternoon he was ordered to deliver a Battle from Reims to an airfield near Chalons-sur-Marne. As he was about to land, the field was bombed.

About 500 bombs all over it, many of them setting alight aircraft dispersed around the edge of the aerodrome. Of course it took me a little time to settle myself down again, for immediately the bombs started I sort of went off in one direction very quickly and flew around until the smoke cleared away enough to let me see a track on which to get down without going into a crater.

By 13 May, German armoured spearheads were beginning to break through in the Sedan area and Paterson was 'not at all happy' when he was asked to fly a Magister to a field quite near Sedan to bring back a Hurricane left there. He carried another pilot to fly the Magister home.

On our way we spotted many Jerry fighters and bombers; they were very high, thank goodness, and I made it my business to make the Magister hedgehop and take advantage of the very good camouflage she possessed. While waiting for the Hurricane to be prepared we could not hear ourselves speak for the gunfire was so intensive; in fact I was quite convinced they were going to come bouncing through the woods in which we were hiding at any moment. I was very happy once again when the Hurricane ran up OK and I was on my way back escorting the Magister.

Paterson had his first taste of action when he was ordered up in a Hurricane to chase a French plane thought to have a German crew aboard. It didn't, but after getting under its tail and following for a while Paterson got tired of 'sitting there awaiting his pleasure' so fired a burst wide of the plane.

The Froggy got such a fright he wandered madly all over the sky, and decided to land at the first opportunity, forgetting about his undercarriage. RAF ground crew were going to pull his crashed machine away with their tractor but the Froggy, who had regained some life, would not have this but insisted on getting some horses belonging to a local peasant. They would be more gentle.

By 15 May the ugly realities of war were pressing in. Paterson watched mobs of refugees — tiny children and old people perched on open wagons on rough roads, women and older children walking — pushing pram loads with their few belongings. 'It made one's blood boil to think this was the second time in a few years that these poor wretches had had to flee from their homes.' He felt for the Battle crews attacking at low level; 'a suicide squad having to face Jerries' best AA fire at point bank range. Many of the chaps never had a chance to drop an egg [bomb], yet they had been two or three years in the squadron flying hundreds of hours in Battles.'

Paterson also witnessed the barbarity of war. He and other RAF men saw three Germans parachute from a stricken bomber in their area and set out in a car to find them, but were too late. French peasants captured the Germans, stood them against a tree and shot them. 'They had dug a shallow grave and were throwing them in when we arrived. They did not have much time for the Jerries.'

Paterson wrote a brief letter to his family on 14 May but it would be another six weeks, by which time he was safely back in England, before he could write again. As he scribbled he could hear bombs landing on the airfield at Reims and said he felt he'd be happier rounding up sheep at East Chatton.

Bombing intensified and Paterson found it hard to get some of his troops out of air raid shelters to refuel and rearm the Hurricanes operating from Champagne. On 16 May he was woken at 3 a.m. with a message to get out, burn anything that couldn't be taken and head south. The great retreat had begun. As 73 Squadron fired five slightly damaged Hurricanes, 226 Squadron blew up similarly damaged Battles. His last glimpse of Reims, flying away in a Magister, was of a sky dark with smoke from aircraft and fuel dumps. He landed at Troyes ahead of his troops in their convoy of trucks and equipment.

A day or so later, the battle situation having quietened in their area, Paterson flew back to Reims to collect things left behind. On the trip his fitter spotted a Battle, down in a field. Paterson landed to find the pilot shot and bleeding and the navigator with a hole right through his body. 'We bandaged them both and gave the observer [navigator] a shot of morphia.' Paterson flew off to a nearby airfield and found a doctor, who organized an ambulance. After taking the medic to the Battle, Paterson and his fitter pressed on to Reims. They landed on a deserted strip to find bullets whining around them, fired from the hangars by a rabble of French colonial troops. The Magister had no guns and Paterson's revolver was taken from him. He was frog marched, bayonets at his back, to a car, driven to Reims and imprisoned for two hours before the French apologised and took him back to the airfield. He arrived to find his fitter had been shot in the arm by a Moroccan, and was so angry, he threatened to shoot the man. Instead he beat him in front of his captain, arguing that while it was not strictly the done thing, it was justified.

On 19 May Paterson and his men, barely settled at Troyes, were ordered on the road again, this time to Boos, near Rouen, about 155 miles northwest. He borrowed trucks and buses from other squadrons and organized his convoy. He flew his Magister to Rouen the next day, stopping en route to make arrangements for his men. 'Slept the night at Rouen — too tired to undress.' They moved again, a bit southeast to Etrepagny, a small field among heavy woods. Paterson set up his HQ in a chateau and dispersed ammunition and fuel oil in small dumps among the trees. His men lived in village barns, where they stayed put for some days. Paterson took mail to Le Bourget and flew dispatches around nearby fields. One night, flying back late to Etrepagny and caught in a rain storm, he landed in a village field. French soldiers arrested him because he had no papers and put a guard on him in the village pub. There, he and his guard 'drank of the cider of the country'. The next morning he woke long before the guard, coolly ate breakfast, said goodbye to the innkeeper and wife, started his aircraft and took off. Then he beat up the village and was pleased to see his guard, now awake, 'running about in small circles.'

Now Paterson was able to fly operations in a Hurricane. There were more aircraft than pilots at Etrepagny and 'I was only too pleased to get into it.' On 7 June enemy aircraft finally found Etrepagny and bombed the village. 'This was just too much for everyone, so two of us tore out to our machines. Mine was the only one to start, so off she went, cold engine and all.' Paterson caught the Heinkels at 14,000 feet and not seeing fighter escort anywhere bored into attack. A couple of strong bursts silenced the rear gunner on one bomber and stopped a port engine. 'About to go in again when a shower of fire seemed to almost burn my ears off. There was a terrific stream of fire from behind and my propeller stopped … the port petrol cock was leaking and the fuel caught fire. Then, with a terrific jar, the propeller dropped right off.' An Me 109 had caught him unaware. The Hurricane went over on its back and straight down. Paterson managed to pull it out at 8000 feet, force-landed and was picked up with slight burns and returned to Etrepagny.

The Germans were reported just two hours away, pouring south from the Somme River. 'We wirelessed HQ that we were going to evacuate and were on the road on our way [southwest] to Dreux in one hour and a half, not waiting approval.' Paterson was using the initiative that was to be so vital to his men in the next few days as they headed for France's west coast and, hopefully, a ship home. To spread the risk he split the convoy — twenty-four trucks, a Hillman tourer, an ambulance, cooking wagon and three motorcycle escorts — into two and sent half one way, the other by a different route. Flying his Magister he saw a huge column of smoke and found some of his trucks had been bombed as they ground up a hill. He landed alongside to find a hideous mess after direct hits on an ammunition truck and another carrying troops. Paterson counted twenty dead and more than sixty wounded. Of the dead he wrote, 'We only had time to wrap them in their blankets and bury them, in one shallow grave. I used the little bible which Dad gave me to carry out the painful business.'

Halfway to Dreux, Paterson was told to head for Caen in Normandy.

DAY AFTER DAY

'The drivers were about at the end of their tether so I refused to go on until morning and let everyone get a chance of a good wash, meal and sleep.' The RAF was still operating Hurricane squadrons in France to protect troops being evacuated from west and southwest French ports and Paterson's convoy with ammunition and petrol was desperately needed.

> In Caen, squadron after squadron of Hurricanes arrived for refuelling and ammunition and all the time my chaps kept them going. I got in seven patrols [on Hurricanes] and had quite a lot of fun chasing dive-bombers ... Unfortunately they would not let me into the front-line patrols on account of my [inexperience], but on three or four patrols I managed to get quite a bit of lead pumped into their tails.

As they retreated from Caen, just a jump ahead of the Germans, they left a fine house they'd taken over complete with strawberry and vegetable gardens, clean white sheets and a WC that worked. The marvellous Hotchkiss car Paterson had commandeered ran out of petrol so he nicked a Morris belonging to an army unit. 'We all refused to listen to the news for by this time we knew only too well what was about to happen, and all the time expected to be told to retire to another aerodrome.' The convoy stopped three nights at the coastal resort of Dinard and then was ordered on to Crozon, an airfield almost on the edge of the sea on a peninsula immediately south of the great port of Brest.

Paterson admired the Normandy-Brittany countryside, ferns, trees and waterfalls along the way, which reminded him of the Eglinton Valley. The convoy reached Crozon late in the afternoon 'very tired and absolutely fed up with travelling'. Infuriated because the French squadron on the base would not lift a finger to help, Paterson retaliated.

> As the end seemed to be approaching I was not so careful with my [the RAF's] 450,000 francs of funds so gave the troops a treat, and also to 'shake' the inhospitable French squadron, arranged to take over the three best hotels in the little town and have them entirely for our own use.

The French airmen were frozen out while Paterson's men, flush with cash, enjoyed wine, women and song.

But he was uneasy. The Germans were not far away and rumours about a French capitulation abounded. He could not contact his HQ and no RAF aircraft arrived. His wireless operator had been killed when the convoy was bombed and he was unfamiliar with the emergency transmitter-receiver. Remembering what he could from Wigram days he somehow got it going and raised an English coastal station, which phoned the Air Ministry and radioed back. 'I was to evacuate as soon as possible by whatever means I could find.' They were on their own.

> [I gave] ... orders to abandon all equipment except small kit and after giving out all the Lewis, K and Bren guns to the troops, we set out for Brest in four lorries leaving everything except enough ammunition to look after ourselves. Actually, we were a very formidable little party, 130 men with thirty machine guns and 100 rifles and every man on top line with the thought of Home or die or something to keep him going.

They had gone just a few miles when a flash followed by an enormous explosion revealed the suspension bridge on the main road to Brest had been blown. South to Nantes or St Nazaire was too far and too dangerous, the roads choked with refugees. 'We turned back on our tracks and headed for the little pier [near] the aerodrome where I had noticed several small boats.' At the head of his men, Paterson marched on to the pier, found a small ferry, strode aboard and woke the skipper.

We told him of our needs but he would not budge an inch. We were ... quite desperate, not knowing how close the Jerries were. The determination not to be caught was very strong so we dumped the captain and his two crew on the pier, [and] all piled on board with rather a crush. The warrant officer managed to get the engine started and with terrific cursing from the old French boy on the pier we headed out into the mouth of Brest Harbour just as the sun rose.

Without enough fuel to reach England and no compass to use with its charts, Paterson steered the little craft well out, but just in sight of land, hoping to be picked up by a larger ship, which is what happened four hours later. A Belgian steamer carrying Army Service Corps troops evacuated from St Nazaire and on its way to Falmouth, Cornwall, stopped for them then cast the ferry adrift. Three Ju 88s attacked the steamer just after she got under way again but the ship escaped serious damage and that night they were home.

After his death in the Battle of Britain (see Chapter 7) James Paterson was awarded a Member of the Order of the British Empire (MBE). The citation noted his 'organising ability of an exceptionally high order' in France and 'outstanding initiative and power of command'. He was three weeks short of his 21st birthday when he died.

Chapter 5

LIFE IN THE PRE-WAR RAF —
WILF CLOUSTON AND DEREK WARD

Life in the pre-war RAF wasn't at all bad, as dark-haired, handsome Wilf Clouston discovered during the last year of peace. Born in Auckland in January 1916 and educated at Wellington College with a final year at Nelson College, he was one who took his chances and went to England under his own steam to try to join the RAF before they started recruiting in New Zealand. While working as a clerk in Wellington in 1935 he learned to fly at Rongotai, and the following year sailed to England, where he was accepted for an SSC. He completed his wings training at Peterborough and in July 1938 joined 19 Squadron at Duxford, in Cambridgeshire.

In a letter to his family just after his arrival, he described what it was like:

Here I am at my squadron — and marvellous it is too ... After Peterborough, the Mess is like a palace. It was only finished in January and everything is extremely modern. In my room, which is as big as the sitting room at 5 Thorby St [his home in Wellington], there is running water, H & C, and all mod cons. Even the lav is just opposite but just far enough away, if you know what I mean … I have struck a marvellous batman — he looks after me like a mother. Wakes me up at 7.30 with a cup of tea and then, if I let him, he would shave, bath and dress me. I am now the proud possessor of one only aeroplane. I only had to sign for it and it becomes in theory all mine. No one else may fly it and I am responsible for everything concerning it except paying for any damage I might do. The bus is a Gloster Gauntlet with a six hundred and fifteen horsepower Bristol Mercury engine. You can't imagine how smart it looks with the squadron markings on the fuselage and the crest on the fin. They are lovely to fly and extremely safe and reliable.

It even had R/T so Clouston could talk to fellow pilots in the air and to the ground 'and if you get lost all you have to do is call up the ground station and ask them where you are. In about two minutes they call back and tell you exactly your position.'

As well as his smart Gauntlet, Clouston had flash new uniforms, acquired when he completed his elementary training, had become an acting pilot officer and was at Uxbridge, learning to be a gentleman, before going on to Peterborough's Flying Training School. The uniforms came from Gieves Ltd, 21 Old Bond St, London, W1. He told his parents:

Though I say it myself, I look very smart — heavens knows they should fit well as we have had four fittings at the tailors and when they are finished the CO here inspects them and if anything is wrong back they go. Mine had to go back, one to have a pocket raised 1/8th of an inch so you can see how fussy they are. The mess kit is rather nice — the same colour as our ordinary kit but the jacket is cut away and the trousers are skin tight all the way down the leg. The shoes are patent leather Wellingtons up to the calf and, incidentally, cost two pounds ten shillings.

Even at the height of the war when thousands of British and Commonwealth airmen were being commissioned, a tailor's visit was an event to be savoured. A man went into a tailor's a sergeant or flight sergeant and came out in his new uniform, an officer and a gentleman.

Only one little thing was wrong with Duxford, Clouston said. It was fifteen miles from Cambridge and there was no bus or train nearby. A car would be nice but he had no money. 'I suppose I will be able to exist somehow — I am definitely *not* hinting in case you thought I was.'

On 4 September 1938 No. 19 Squadron became the first in the RAF to be equipped with Spitfires, to the envy of every other squadron. Clouston had a year to fly them before the outbreak of war and his experience no doubt helped him survive Dunkirk and the Battle of Britain — many other pilots didn't have the same benefit before being flung into battle. Clouston had one big fright on the new fighter. Fellow 19 Squadron pilot George Ball, who was to be his best man, came too close to Clouston in flight one day and chewed up his tail, although both men landed their damaged aircraft safely.

Clouston was married to Anne Hyde, daughter of an admiral, in the village of Little Wilbraham, Cambridgeshire, in March 1940 and given ten days for their honeymoon. He cabled his parents, 'Safely married'.

The day war was declared Clouston wrote home from Duxford where he was still based: 'Well, it's here as expected. It has been expected for so long now all one can feel is a sense of relief. For heaven's sake don't worry about me. I have got a damn safe job — particularly as it is over this country that we'll be working.'

Wrong — for a while anyway. Clouston, by now a flight lieutenant, faced a half-hour flight across the Channel during Dunkirk in May–June 1940 and hostile enemy aircraft on the trip home. He would not be over England. Dunkirk for Britain's fighter pilots mirrored what the Luftwaffe fighter pilots would encounter in reverse during the Battle of Britain.

Derek Ward was born in 1917 in Whangarei, the only son of a popular local GP and his wife. Head boy at Whangarei High School, by the time he sailed for England in April 1938 he had already soloed and flown sixteen hours at the Auckland Aero club's Waikato branch, been selected for an SSC and earned his wings at Wigram with the RNZAF. Ken Newton, a close friend who trained with him, was on the same ship. In June 1938 they were posted to 151 Squadron at North Weald, Epping in Essex, where they flew Gauntlets and then Hurricanes. Newton was to lose his life in June 1940; Ward was killed over the Desert two years later.

Only a few letters from Ward survive, among them a long one to his grandmother, written after he'd been at North Weald for six months, telling her in much detail about station life and training. He said he and Newton had each been assigned a Gauntlet on joining, spent an hour checking out the instruments and controls and then had their maiden flights. 'As they are single seaters we could not do any dual flying in them, so it was a matter of "get in" and "find out for yourself".'

There were no problems first time up in the Gauntlet or in succeeding days, but as he ranged afield Ward found the Essex landscape 'frightfully hard for map reading as there are no prominent land marks and all towns are much alike. There is always a haze and semi fog, and visibility is always hard.' He said the Gauntlet was much

LIFE IN THE PRE-WAR RAF — WILF CLOUSTON AND DEREK WARD

more powerful than anything he'd flown at home and equipped with the wonderful R/T, meaning the pilots could talk to each other in the air and to the ground.

Ward learned quickly, mastering the wide range of skills necessary to become a fighter pilot. He was good enough to be chosen for the squadron's aerobatics team four months after reaching North Weald and soon became a deputy flight commander. A year after joining 151 Squadron he was rated an 'exceptional' pilot and also found himself station fire officer.

This is great fun because I am also in charge of fire equipment on a couple of other secondary [satellite] stations, one of which is at Bradwell on Sea. A fireman and I make monthly inspections of these stations. I generally wait until a good day and then fly there in a two-seater Magister. On arriving I tell the [fireman] to carry on the inspection while I spend a very lazy day eating, sleeping or strolling along the beach.

He had great difficulty finding somewhere to put down one day when fog, 'our great enemy', rolled in extraordinarily quickly and blotted out the land. He looked for somewhere to land and worried about running out of petrol, 'besides I felt like some morning tea. I felt my way down and at 300 feet, I couldn't see a blessed thing — moments like these you need Minties.' At 200 feet he glimpsed trees and flat ground.

Back came the throttle. The machine touched down and rolled to a stop. As luck had it the field wasn't so bad and being slightly boggy, [the Gauntlet] pulled up quickly ... along came the farmers and farmesses. I told them I had dropped in for a cup of tea — I got it — but the farmesses were not of the NZ talent, so I spent a very dry couple of hours telling them what made the propeller go round. By that time the fog had lifted so I took off and 'home James'.

As the German-Czech problem boiled to the Munich crisis in September 1938 the squadron was suddenly recalled from armament training at Sutton Bridge, Lincolnshire. Back at North Weald paint brushes appeared and Ward noted:

In the next few hours our machines had changed from a gleaming silver to a dirty dark brown and green. Our machines were wearing their war paint. Gun belts were loaded and everybody was at readiness. Instructions were issued. We were ready for them. At the last minute when they decided not to have a war there was a vague feeling of disappointment. We had been keyed up and then everything fell flat. But it … looks as though we are to have another 'flap' very soon. If there is another crisis don't worry. Everything is under control.

It was more than eighteen months before the flap in France had Ward winging to Lille/Marcq in May 1940, ferrying planes to hard-pressed 87 Squadron and joining the fray. He was welcomed with open arms.

When he returned to England he remained with 87 Squadron and flew about 170 ops with them. He shot down an Me 110 south of Portland on 15 August, Battle of Britain Day, and damaged a couple of other enemy aircraft. Ward was promoted to flight lieutenant and awarded a DFC in October. Among his ops were a number of night intruder flights over enemy airfields, a new development for Hurricanes.

He flew with 87 Squadron until September 1941, when he was

posted to the Middle East to command 73 Squadron in the Western Desert. He had flown almost 100 ops with 73 Squadron when he was killed in Libya on 17 June 1942, less than a month after he'd been awarded a bar to his DFC. Ward fell victim to the legendary German pilot Hans-Joachim Marseille, who led a group of 109s out of the sun to attack the 73 Squadron Hurricanes as they were about to land after a bomber-escort flight.

Marseille, a brilliant pilot, marksman and tactician who developed and incessantly practised his own combat systems, shot down no fewer than 158 Allied aircraft — seven during the Battle of Britain, the rest in North Africa — the highest score of any Luftwaffe pilot against Western aircraft. The day he killed Ward he shot down two Hurricanes on his first attack. Ward saw what was happening and turned back to protect his two pilots coming down in their parachutes. Marseille swooped again and hit Ward, killing him instantly. The Hurricane crashed but did not burn. The New Zealander, credited with six victories, lies in Halfaya Sollum War Cemetery.

Three months later Marseille was also dead. The engine on his new 109 caught fire and he was hit by the rudder of his fighter as he baled out, never opening his parachute.

Chapter 6

DUNKIRK — A VICTORY INSIDE DEFEAT

Where was the RAF? We never saw a British fighter.' That was the bitter cry of soldiers attacked by the Luftwaffe during evacuation from Dunkirk. Troops, angered by what they thought was the absence of the air force, gave some downed RAF pilots a hostile reception. New Zealand pilot Al Deere, soon to star in the Battle of Britain, ran into a frosty Army major when he tried to board a destroyer about to leave Dunkirk for England. He had survived a crash-landing on a beach not far away. The major barred his way. 'For all the good you chaps seem to be doing over here you may as well stay on the ground.' Deere told the major to go to hell and in the resulting argy-bargy missed the ship.

Some accounts have Deere, an RAF boxing champ, laying out the army man with one blow. Disappointingly, the story is wrong, according to Deere himself. When he finally made it aboard another destroyer he says he was greeted in silence in a wardroom thronged by Army types. He asked a gunner lieutenant, 'Why so friendly, what have the RAF done?' 'That's just it,' the man replied. 'What have they done?'

'So that was it,' Deere wrote in his bestselling *Nine Lives.*

For two weeks non-stop I had flown my guts out, and this was all the thanks I got. What was the use of trying to explain that the RAF had patrolled further inland [trying to get the bombers and Stukas before they reached Dunkirk], often above cloud with the insuperable task of covering adequately a patrol line from Ostend to Boulogne?

The cloud over the RAF's performance at Dunkirk largely evaporated during the Battle of Britain when the RAF stymied and defeated the German air force. By then the public adored the fighter boys, women swooning at the sight of a man in a blue tunic, top button undone, scarf around his neck. But for years soldiers who'd been bombed and machine-gunned on the quayside and beaches of Dunkirk took some convincing the RAF had played a major role in the successful snatch by sea of 340,000 British and French troops.

Which it had. The navy and the little ships carried the men home across the English Channel, but without the RAF's intervention Herman Goering's boast that his Luftwaffe could destroy the British Expeditionary Force locked in the Dunkirk perimeter might have eventuated. Convinced by Goering's promise that the Luftwaffe alone would ensure victory, Hitler called off the panzers. After all, they needed vital maintenance after their dash from the Ardennes to the sea, the canal-laced wetlands around Dunkirk were no place for tanks and he wanted to conserve them for the struggle against major French forces yet to be conquered south of the Somme. Halting the panzers would prove to be a costly mistake.

The Dunkirk perimeter shrank gradually but held long enough, thanks to stout BEF and French resistance against German infantry and

DAY AFTER DAY

artillery, for the troops to be borne back to Britain — 100,000 from the beaches, 240,000 from Dunkirk Harbour. And all thanks to the RAF.

Between 26 May 1940 when the evacuation began and 4 June when it ended, the RAF provided air cover. Not all the time, because Fighter Command didn't have the resources to have aircraft over Dunkirk continuously, but the RAF took a heavy toll on the Luftwaffe — and lost many aircraft itself — and, as Deere noted, many patrols were inland to intercept the German bombers before they reached Dunkirk. In any event, soldiers on the ground couldn't see fighters at 15,000 or 20,000 feet, where most operated. Going low was dangerous — aircraft recognition was poor, 'friendly' ground fire hacked down some RAF planes and the navy fired at anything it could see.

New Zealander Keith Park, a key player at Dunkirk as he was to be in the Battle of Britain, had to carefully juggle his slender resources, weakened as they were by the Battle of France. The only way he could keep constant air cover over Dunkirk in daylight hours was by operating small groups of fighters. As he discovered, wings of two or three squadrons were more effective against the Luftwaffe, but that meant gaps between patrols and these were exploited by the Germans. Whatever the difficulties, and there were many, the RAF fighters — Hurricanes, Spitfires flying in strength in action for the first time and Defiants making their debut — aided by Coastal Command and Bomber Command aircraft, kept the Luftwaffe at bay long enough for the now famous 'Miracle of Dunkirk' to save the Army.

Admiral Sir Bertram Ramsay, the man who planned and organized the evacuation, codenamed Operation Dynamo, sent messages to the air commanders expressing 'a deep debt of gratitude to the Royal Air Force' for its 'support and protection' at Dunkirk. Winston Churchill, distressed by inter-service bad feeling, told the House of Commons on 4 June, '… there was a victory inside this deliverance. It was gained by the Air Force.'

And the cost of that victory? Figures vary, but an Air Historical Branch *Narrative* table says Fighter Command lost 99 aircraft at Dunkirk, while the Luftwaffe lost 132. However, John Terraine, in *The Right of the Line*, notes that when losses by Coastal and Bomber Commands are added, the RAF lost a total of 145 aircraft. Terraine says, 'It was in fact the RAF which suffered most severely at Dunkirk.' Over-claiming by RAF pilots, though understandable for many reasons, was rife as it was to be in the Battle of Britain.

Among New Zealanders who flew at Dunkirk, almost all SSC officers, were Wilf Clouston and Frank Brinsden (19 Squadron, Spitfire), John 'Mac' Mackenzie (41 Squadron, Spitfire), Malcolm Carswell and Harold North (43 Squadron, Hurricane), Al Deere and Colin Gray (54 Squadron, Spitfire), Bob Yule (145 Squadron, Hurricane), Ken Newton (151 Squadron, Hurricane), Falcon Clouston, Geoff Simpson, Vic Verity and Ron Bary (229 Squadron, Hurricane), Hec McGregor (213 Squadron, Hurricane), Noel Mowat, Eric Whitley and Doug Spence (245 Squadron, Hurricane) and Dick Trousdale (266 Squadron, Spitfire).

The two Cloustons were not brothers but there may have been a distant relationship as the Clouston families came to New Zealand from the Orkney Islands and trace their heritage back 1000 years to Scandinavia. Falcon was killed over Dunkirk, the only New Zealand death in those few days. Wilf starred there, survived the Battle of Britain but ended up in 1942 in a Japanese POW camp.

Deere and Gray, two of New Zealand's best-known fighter pilots of World War II and both high scorers — Gray at 25.5 victories topping the list of New Zealanders in the RAF, Deere close at 22 — Christopher

Shores and Clive Williams in *Aces High* says 17 — made their combat debuts over Dunkirk. Gray, his twin brother Ken, and Deere all applied for SSCs in April 1937 with Ken Gray and Deere sailing for England in successive drafts a few months later. Colin failed two medicals, but hardened himself with farm work and finally passed, and in December 1938 sailed as well. By the time he reached 54 Squadron in November 1939, Deere was well settled at the same squadron. (Ken Gray, a bomber pilot with a DFC after only seven operations, died when his Whitley hit a Scottish hill on 1 May 1940 while heading south to meet his brother.)

Spitfires and Hurricanes had been flying patrols over and along the coasts of Belgium and northern France for about ten days prior to the start of Operation Dynamo in support of the Allied ground forces but in these early stages of the war there was no radar control at that distance, individual squadrons used different R/T frequencies, pre-flight squadron briefings were not general and fighter pilots had little idea of the ground situation or how it was developing. Some squadrons clashed heavily with the Luftwaffe, others flew patrols during which they didn't see an enemy plane, even at the height of the evacuation.

Deere flew his first patrol from Hornchurch at 8 a.m. on 16 May in *Kiwi I* as he had named his Spitfire, one of twelve of 54 Squadron's most experienced pilots. They approached the French coast at 15,000 feet and crossed at Calais.

As my eyes scanned the empty skies I was conscious of a feeling of exhilaration and tenseness akin to that experienced before an important sporting event. There was no feeling of fear; how could there be? Like a child who plays with fire my fingers had not yet been burned by the flames of combat.

The fighters cruised up and down for half an hour, saw nothing and turned home disappointed. Questioned by Gray who hadn't flown, Deere said that when nothing happened, 'I was damn bored.'

Later the same day Gray made his debut, and, like Deere, saw nothing. He wrote in his 1990 *Spitfire Patrol*:

> The only excitement was caused by a couple of our own destroyers firing at us — which we soon came to recognise as par for the course. For the whole of the next week the squadron patrolled daily over the Calais-Boulogne-Dunkirk area. By the end of the week I had still not sighted an enemy aircraft.

The situation was about to change. On 23 May Deere participated in the famous rescue of 74 Squadron's CO Frank White and destroyed two 109s as well, his first victories. Sharing Hornchurch with 54 Squadron, 74 Squadron had been in action in the morning and White had force-landed at Calais/Marck with a damaged radiator. German tanks were closing in so a plan was hatched for Prof Leathart, back from France and now 54 Squadron's A Flight leader, to fly to the airfield in the squadron's two-seat Master (74 Squadron didn't have one), land and retrieve White. Deere and Johnny Allen were to fly escort. The low-level flight was accomplished without incident, the yellow-painted Master landing safely. White was there and jumped aboard. As the Master prepared for takeoff a bunch of 109s appeared. One spotted the Master and dived to attack. Allen, flying top escort, shouted a warning to the much-lower Deere, watching over the Master. The little plane had no R/T so Deere frantically waggled his wings as it taxied. The 109 unleashed a stream of bullets at the Master as he plunged down. Fire from Deere distracted him and the New Zealander caught him as he zoomed up, the worst thing the German could have done. He presented a perfect target and Deere's fire fatally damaged his engine. The German stalled and hurtled into the sea off Calais. Leathart realised something was wrong and slammed his aircraft back on to the ground before he and White leapt for a ditch. Deere wasn't finished. After seeing the Master was okay, he climbed to the aid of Allen, now having his own battle with 109s, crossed the path of an enemy machine and shot it down. Allen got another. Fascinated, Leathart watched the three 109s crash, then he took off for England with his rescued passenger. Congratulations poured in that night and Leathart was awarded the DSO.

Gray had his first encounter with 109s the following day, loosing off fire at two enemy fighters inland from Calais, his camera guns showing hits on both. He claimed a probable and a possible. The squadron was climbing to intercept a bunch of bombers escorted by fighters and were ordered into combat with the ringing 'fighting area attack number four!'

These numbered set-piece attacks defined the RAF's outdated pre-war tactics. Developed when the threat to Britain was expected to come from bombers flying from Germany without escorts in the belief that no fighter could reach Britain from German bases, they were still in use. The invasion of France and the Low Countries gave the Germans bases on the Channel coast and knocked that theory on the head. 'They were totally unsuited for the type of combat we now found ourselves engaged in but at that time we did not know any better,' Gray wrote.

Not surprisingly, 54 Squadron heaved out the book on numbered attacks as did other squadrons faced with the realities of combat with Me 109s. The other totally outdated RAF tactic of flying in Vics of three — a leader in front with a wingman on either side a little behind — with four Vics to a squadron, was also gradually abandoned in favour of the Luftwaffe's finger-four formation — two pairs flying together in positions much like the open fingers of a hand. Pilots could watch each other's tails much more easily. The system, developed by the Luftwaffe in Spain during the civil war, was patently superior in both defence and attack, although the Vic held on in some squadrons far longer than it should have.

Gray scored his first victory on 24 May as the squadron escorted FAA Swordfish to dive-bomb Gravelines on the French coast. After watching the Swordfish safely on their way home 54 Squadron ran into twenty-four Me 110s — the first of this type they had seen — and a dozen 109s. As the squadron climbed to attack, the 109s came roaring in. 'I managed to get on the tail of one of them and gave him a good burst that slowed him up,' Gray said. 'He levelled out and I was about to administer the *coup de grâce* when he saved me the trouble by baling out.' One confirmed. But as Gray enjoyed his success, his own aircraft shuddered under the impact of bullets and cannon shells. 'I realised with a shock that I was being shot at. In my excitement I had completely forgotten about the rest of the clan.'

Gray learned a hugely important lesson. Watch your tail all the time and don't waste time gloating. His damaged aircraft flicked into a spiral roll and away and Gray didn't see his attacker again. 'Not that I had seen him in the first place.' Gray nursed his aircraft home with no pitot head giving him his speed, no flaps and no brakes. He made a difficult second-attempt landing and a later inspection revealed the main elevator cables hanging by threads.

A tired and depleted 54 Squadron made one last morning patrol on 28 May — takeoff at 4.30 a.m. — before moving to Catterick in

Yorkshire, for a short rest. Only seven aircraft flew north and seven pilots were missing, although three, Deere among them, made it back to England. On that final sortie Deere's glycol and oil tanks, riddled by bullets from a Dornier he was chasing, forced him to land on a Belgian beach midway between Ostend and Calais. He smashed his head on the edge of the windscreen and when he revived the Spitfire was on fire. Dazed, he scrambled clear. As he walked away with a Belgian soldier he watched *Kiwi 1* burn. He eventually reached Dunkirk after a series of adventures.

Back in England, he flew to Catterick, his tally of enemy planes destroyed up by another three and his total at five — ace status. He and Gray would fight again in the Battle of Britain.

Flying from Biggin Hill and forward field Manston and led by Harry Maguire, who like Wilf Clouston was to be captured by the Japanese at Singapore, 229 Squadron joined the battle above Dunkirk late in May. Falcon Clouston, a flight lieutenant, had downed an Me 109 on 23 May while leading a composite 229/253 Squadron escorting civil aircraft to Merville in France to pick up aircrew and take them home to England. Circling Merville for ten minutes at 9.40 a.m. awaiting the planes' takeoff, he spotted nine 109s coming their way. A dogfight followed at 8000 feet. After damaging one of the Germans he attacked another from the rear. Says his combat report: 'Long burst and white smoke issued from rear. Machine slowed up, stalled and dived into edge of small wood.'

It was a frustrating debut day over Dunkirk for 229 Squadron. They tangled with a group of Do 215s and Maguire, with Falcon Clouston and fellow New Zealanders Simpson and Verity, each forced Dorniers down to near ground level with heavy fire then saw them escape.

Clouston reported: 'Intercepted Do 215 at 8000 feet and remained on [its] tail to ground level giving short bursts of approximately 3 secs. Made several deflection attacks at ground level until ammunition expended. Enemy aircraft appeared still under control although rear gunner out of action.'

Falcon Clouston was killed the next day, 29 May, a disastrous day for 229 Squadron. Along with three other squadrons, 229 Squadron arrived over Dunkirk about 5 p.m., an impressive 40-plane mix of Hurricanes and Spitfires. One remained as top escort over a cloud layer hiding a huge number of 109s, as the others went down. The Germans broke down on 229 Squadron, flying at 10,000 feet. In a few minutes the vastly outnumbered 229 Squadron lost five Hurricanes, among them Clouston and the other flight commander. Only two of the Hurricane pilots survived. Falcon Clouston's body later washed ashore on the German island of Borkum, near the Dutch border. He was buried there but after the war was reinterred in Sage War Cemetery, west of Bremen, where he lies with almost 1000 Commonwealth dead, most of them bomber crew killed over north-west Germany.

The night Falcon Clouston was lost CO Maguire jumped into an aircraft and flew to Farnborough to tell Arthur Clouston his younger brother was missing.

'My brother was holidaying with us when the balloon went up and we never met again unfortunately,' Arthur wrote in his 1954 autobiography *The Dangerous Skies*. 'My next news of his was from his squadron commander, Maguire, who very decently flew over from Biggin Hill to tell me he was missing … I collected my brother's belongings from his station a little later.'

Arthur Clouston was one of a large family who lived in Tasman

Bay and was born in 1908, five years before Falcon. He was running a garage and dealership when he sold up, went to England and in 1930 joined the RAF. He'd learned to fly at the Marlborough Aero Club, his enthusiasm fired by Kingsford Smith's 1928 pioneering trans-Tasman flight. When his SSC ended in 1934, he became a civilian test pilot at the Royal Aircraft Establishment, Farnborough. He made world headlines in the late 1930s, joining in air races and setting record times for flights to and from Cape Town (1937) with woman pilot Betty Kirby Green, and to and from Australia and New Zealand (1938) with newspaper reporter Vic Ricketts, who lost his life in 1942, flying a Spitfire on photo reconnaissance. Clouston rated as a speed freak on the ground as well as in the air; in April 1938 an English magistrate fined him £5 and banned him from driving for two months for speeding, his sixth conviction.

Clouston, recalled to the RAF when war broke, continued test-pilot duties. He flew patrols over and from Farnborough and shot down one He 111 during the Battle of Britain. Later he commanded a Coastal Command Liberator squadron chasing U-boats in the Atlantic. By war's end he was Group Captain commanding an RAF station and had flown more than 4000 hours in 185 aircraft types. Postwar he had a two-year stint commanding Whenuapai, after his appointment as director of Civil Aviation was lost on appeal. In the mid-1950s he was Air Officer Commanding (AOC) Singapore. When he retired from the Air Force in 1960 he was Air Commodore A E Clouston, CB, DSO, DFC, AFC* mid and (bbc).

The three Cloustons, Wilf, Falcon and Arthur, caused problems for the mail people at New Zealand House in London. In June 1937 Wilf wrote to his mother saying he'd 'kicked up a fuss' because he'd just got two of her letters written six months earlier. [New Zealand House] was 'very polite and regretted the delay and explained they had put my mail in with A.E. Clouston's'.

Wilf Clouston was just about as successful as Deere at Dunkirk, claiming four and one shared enemy aircraft in a few days. When 19 Squadron went into action over Dunkirk on 26 May, it was their debut for most of the pilots, but Clouston had already fired his guns in earnest. On 11 May he led a section off the East Anglian coast ten miles east of Dudgeon Lightship that sighted a Ju 88, which the three Spitfires chased for forty miles east, down from 26,000 feet to 9000 feet, playing cat and mouse in cloud layers. According to Clouston's own combat report, the German manoeuvred cleverly at high speed and even though all three RAF pilots fired bursts, the 88 escaped.

Wilf Clouston is given a victory over an Me 109 on 23 May by *Aces High* and Ken Wynn in *A Clasp for 'The Few'*, which is impossible because the entire squadron was back at Duxford on flying training. No patrols were flown that day.

He was immediately successful on 19 Squadron's first Dunkirk patrol when the squadron ran into about twenty Stukas at 10,000 feet and he nailed two. Already aware of the merits of close-in attack, he didn't finger his trigger until his first victim filled his sights at fifty yards, left and astern. His combat report said the Stuka 'turned slowly on its back and dived vertically into the sea. This was confirmed by Red 2.' Then he turned his guns on a second aircraft: 'I repeated the attack on another E/A and after experiencing severe cross fire from [another] E/A I saw several pieces break off, and then it burst into flames. I last saw it diving in a spiral turn towards the sea. Enemy casualties, 2 Ju 87s.'

Frankie Brinsden, recently 21, a Takapuna Grammar old boy and

DAY AFTER DAY

a bank clerk in Auckland before being accepted for an SSC, watched Clouston's first Stuka smash into the sea as he went into attack himself.

> I selected my target and closed to 200–150 yards, fired a short burst. The E/A immediately went down out of control and I broke off the engagement. This action was witnessed by F/Lt Clouston who had turned and was approaching for his second attack. Rounds fired 1000. 1 Ju 87 certain.

Escorting 109s suddenly woke up to the Stuka massacre — the squadron claimed five — and a giant free-for-all developed. The squadron shot down two 109s but lost two of their own, including CO Geoff Stephenson shot down and captured.

Clouston was at it again the next day. He and the other two Spitfires in his flight poured fire into a Do 215 at 15,000 feet but could only claim it as a possible before it disappeared. But there was no doubting Clouston's next victim on the same patrol. 'I encountered [another] Do 215 at 20,000 feet. I made a surprise attack from the sun and the E/A did not see me. I made a quarter changing to astern attack and the E/A burst into flames and dropped to the sea on its back.'

On 1 June at 5.40 a.m. Clouston lifted his tally to four and a half when the squadron mixed it with twelve Me 110s and a dozen 109s two miles northeast of Dunkirk. He and his No. 2 attacked a 110 and watched it fall away, engine stopped. One shared. 'I then climbed up to the cloud base and sighted an Me 109 which I attacked. I closed to approx 50 yards and the E/A stalled and went into a spin with the engine stopped. As engagement stopped at approx. 1500 feet it was impossible for E/A to recover.'

110

Bob Yule of 145 was also successful on 1 June, shooting down an Me 110 northeast of Dunkirk.

Malcolm Carswell of 43 Squadron, poor man, was what you might call an unlucky pilot. He survived but had a tough time — a ditching and near death, two bale outs and burns each time. End of flying. He sailed to England independently in January 1937 and once there the RAF accepted him. By January 1938 he was with 43 Squadron. One stinking cold day in February 1940, flying from Acklington in Northumberland, Carswell joined in an attack on a Heinkel trying to sink a cargo ship off the coast in the North Sea. Suddenly at low level his engine seized. Too low to bale out, he ditched his Hurricane a mile from the ship. Knocked out and concussed, he should have gone down with the fighter but somehow, amazingly, popped to the surface. Almost dead from immersion and cold he was picked up and saved. Three months later he was passed medically fit to fly again, in the nick of time to go south to Tangmere with the squadron for Dunkirk.

Led by Squadron Leader George Lott, later an Air Vice-Marshal, 43 Squadron made its first patrol to Dunkirk late morning on 1 June, tangling with top-cover 109s. Lott, in a manuscript he wrote for a *Blackwoods Magazine* article quoted by Norman Franks in *Air Battle for Dunkirk*, says he spotted the diving enemy just in time and shouted loudly over the radio that 109s were coming down behind and swung into the attack '... I found myself alone amidst what seemed like hordes of Huns and I had a mad struggle for survival.' When he counted noses, they were two short. Sergeant Gough was dead and 'Crackers Carswell, shot down in flames, was burnt quite badly but had been picked up by a destroyer.' Wynn says Carswell watched bullet holes appearing in his chute as German troops fired at him while he floated down, landing near the front lines. French soldiers picked him up and he was taken off Dunkirk, back to England and hospital. 'Poor Crackers,' wrote Lott. 'He recovered and came back for some more in September and was shot down in flames and burnt again. Once more he recovered but this time the medics pinned him to the ground.' Unable to fly operationally, Carswell was posted to fighter control in England and Malta. He ended the war a squadron leader. Lott himself was shot down and lost an eye on 9 July over Southampton.

One of the other squadrons mixing it with the Germans over Dunkirk in the patrol on which Carswell was shot was 245 Squadron, led by Aucklander Eric Whitley. Like Arthur Clouston, he was born in 1908 and joined the RAF on an SSC in 1930, serving in Egypt and Iraq pre-war until 1933, when he returned to England. He was posted to command 245 Squadron when it reformed on 30 October 1939, at Leconfield in Yorkshire. In the Dunkirk action with 43 Squadron, Whitley's squadron claimed four Me 109s confirmed and a couple of probables but lost two of their own. After Dunkirk 245 Squadron moved around a bit, flew patrols, bomber escorts — and raided bases in France newly occupied by the Germans. On one of these, on 20 June, they surprised the Luftwaffe and dealt in a big way to aircraft parked unsuspectingly in rows at Rouen/Boos. While one section circled as top cover the other two, one led by Whitley, the other by Noel Mowat, roared across the field, fire from the eight-gun Hurricanes slashing into the enemy. Accounts of the results vary. Wynn says twenty were estimated destroyed, New Zealand's official history, *New Zealanders with the Royal Air Force,* says four were on fire when 245 Squadron flew away and a considerable number damaged.

Christchurch pilot Doug Spence was also on this raid. He remained with 245 Squadron, flying in the Battle of Britain before a posting in December 1940 to North Africa, where he was killed on a strafing strike. When he was shot down by Allied ground fire in April 1941, he had three enemy aircraft to his credit. He lies in Tobruk Military Cemetery.

Whitley and Mowat also flew in the Battle of Britain with 245 Squadron, based much of the time in Northern Ireland, and both had distinguished later careers, each awarded the DSO, with Whitley ending the war a group captain, Mowat a wing commander. While Whitley died in New Zealand in 1973, Mowat was killed in November 1946, a passenger in an Anson in Germany that struck a colliery chimney then slammed into a second.

Hec McGregor, born in Wairoa in 1910, was only 18 when he joined the RAF. By 1938 he was a squadron leader and CO of 33 Squadron in Egypt and the Middle East. Equipped with Gladiators, squadron detachments based at Lydda (now Lod in Israel) helped subdue rebellious tribesmen and for his leadership role McGregor received the DSO. The then CO of 213 Squadron (Hurricane) was unhappy about McGregor arriving at Biggin Hill to take over the squadron while Dunkirk raged. *Air Battle for Dunkirk* says that Humphrey Edwardes Jones 'remained in full command ... being reluctant to hand over his unit until the Dunkirk show was over'. He adds that McGregor was new to operations and had only flown Spitfires, not Hurricanes. McGregor wanted to participate but Edwardes Jones was apprehensive. However, he finally permitted him to go after doing some circuits in a Hurricane but only as a wingman to the senior flight lieutenant.

In the afternoon of 31 May McGregor made his first flight to Dunkirk, wearing Edwardes Jones' helmet and parachute because he didn't have his own — and was promptly shot down. He baled out, landed in the sea and was picked up by a ship bound for Dover. That afternoon 213 Squadron lost five planes and two pilots. McGregor stayed and led the squadron for part of the Battle of Britain and took out a couple of Germans during several big battles. His talents must have impressed — he was promoted wing commander on 1 September 1940 and became a group captain two years later. His career continued upwards and by 1959 he was AOC Fighter Command and then, successively, Commander, UK Air Defence Region and Commander-in-Chief, Far East Air Force. He retired in 1963 as Air Marshal Sir Hector McGregor KCB, CBE, DSO, mid (7) and was only 63 when he died ten years later.

When notable New Zealand fighter pilot Des Scott was posted to Tangmere in the spring of 1943 to command 486 Squadron, the New Zealand Typhoon squadron, he had a brush with McGregor, then commanding the Tangmere sector. Scott says in *Typhoon Pilot* that before he left his staff job at Fighter Command HQ to take charge of the squadron he'd been given permission by Hugh 'Ding' Saunders, 11 Group commander in succession to Leigh-Mallory, to give the squadron a much more offensive role. When he met McGregor — 'a tall, spare New Zealander … more English than the English' — at Tangmere, he outlined his plans. McGregor bristled.

> He sharply reminded me that he was sector commander and any change in plans would be at his discretion and not at mine. Of course I could not tell him our AOC had given me a free hand, nor would it have been to my advantage to argue. Somewhat deflated, I left his office knowing that our association had not got off to a good start. However, I need not have worried for a week or two later he was posted.

Ken Newton, flying with 151 Squadron at Dunkirk on 29 May, was shot down while leading a section of three. His No. 2, Ron Courtney, quoted in *Air Battle for Dunkirk*, says Newton took the section up to attack 109s above them. Courtney was about to strike at one of them when he was shot down by a 109 he didn't see, and baled out. He was rescued by a corvette. Newton's Hurricane was also downed and he baled out to be picked up by a hospital ship bound for Dunkirk. According to Franks: 'Newton later told his squadron that after he saw Courtney go down with smoke pouring out of his aircraft he saw red, and shot down the offending 109. Then he was hit by others but got away by rolling his machine over and over as though he was finished.'

Newton wasn't followed down and when he saw the hospital ship he glided down towards it and baled out at 3000 feet. He was picked up after only ten minutes in the water.

Newton was shot down again a month later, but this time there was no ship to rescue him. He took off from Manston at 5.30 p.m. on 28 June with two other fighters from his own squadron and other Hurricanes from 56 Squadron as escort to six Blenheims on photographic reconnaissance over the Calais-Boulogne area. They were intercepted by enemy fighters near Boulogne and Newton was shot down. *For Your Tomorrow* says he baled out and a destroyer was dispatched to make a rescue, but it didn't get there in time. Newton was not seen again, and is commemorated at Runnymede.

The Battle of Britain

10 July to 31 October 1940

The Battle of France is now over. I expect the
Battle of Britain is about to begin.
Upon this battle depends the survival of
Christian civilization.

Winston Churchill in the House of Commons,
11 June 1940

Chapter 7

THE BATTLE OF BRITAIN

They flew day after day. From the cold early dawn, until dusk, when they could no longer see. Three, four, even five patrols a day. Sitting in their dispersal huts, awaiting the telephone call from sector control. Scrambling. Lifting off airfields all over southeast England, reaching always for height, seeking the enemy in the sky ahead. Watching as they climbed, looking for lurking 'snappers', the deadly German Messerschmitt 109s, which liked nothing better than to come out of the sun, pouncing in a quick down-and-away dive, picking off stragglers, the unwary, those who didn't yet know how to fight. The easy targets.

When people think of the Battle of Britain today, seventy years on, it's the pilots they remember, Churchill's 'Few', the glamorised young heroes — and they were young, some of them still eighteen — who flew fighters that shot down Messerschmitts, Stuka dive-bombers and bombers — Heinkels and Dorniers. As the days wore on, the Few became grey with fatigue, growing thinner by the day, tiredness etched in their eyes and faces. Flying a fighter in combat was hard physical work. Pilots baked in their cockpits on blue-sky days, sun shining through Perspex hoods, glasshouses some called them, air-conditioning a dream. Pilots sometimes wrung the sweat out of their shirts when they landed; at high altitudes they shivered, heating nonexistent.

But the squadrons kept flying until they were so stretched and had lost so many pilots they simply had to be taken out of the battle, sent north to rest and regroup, taking in new pilots. On 28 July 1940, when 54 Squadron, on which New Zealanders Al Deere and Colin Gray flew, left Hornchurch for Catterick in Yorkshire, only five of their original twenty or so pilots remained. They were back in Hornchurch eleven days later, and back in the fray. Commanders, mindful of the strain on their men, rested them when possible, giving them precious time off. Other than that, only periods of bad weather, when the Germans didn't fly, interrupted the endless aerial scraps and the assault on the southeast — the radar stations, RAF airfields, aircraft factories and then London. The battle was confined largely to the southeast because the 109s couldn't escort bombers much further than that, and bombers without escorts were easy meat. The battle began officially on 10 July with heavy attacks on Channel convoys, although skirmishing had begun before as the Luftwaffe probed the Allied defences. It ended on 31 October when Germany basically cried 'enough' and the approaching winter ruled out an invasion.

Poles who flew for the RAF in the Battle of Britain understandably hated the Germans with an unrelenting loathing after the conquest of their homeland, but most aircrew in the RAF didn't hate their opposites. They believed Luftwaffe pilots were much like them, men with whom they could have had a beer had the war not been on. However, they were angered that the Germans dared to attack Britain, 'intent upon invasion and eventual occupation' as 92 Squadron pilot

Geoff Wellum wrote years later. They regarded the battle as one that had to be won and were confident of victory. Most sensed the future of Britain hung on the outcome.

The RAF defeated the Luftwaffe over the skies of England that summer. It was the first setback Hitler had suffered since attacking Poland and was seen later as a key moment in the winning of the war. Had Hitler been able to invade there is little doubt that he would have crushed the British. But he couldn't and didn't. Doubt now exists that the Germans could have mounted a successful cross-Channel invasion, even had the Luftwaffe swept the skies clear of the RAF, which is what Luftwaffe supremo Hermann Goering boasted he would do. Germany had no experience of amphibious operations and the Royal Navy would have wrecked an invasion fleet even without air cover. An airborne landing involving enough troops and armour and their supply and maintenance was out of the question.

Germany began the Battle of Britain with an overwhelming advantage in the number of aircraft but Fighter Command was given five or six weeks after Dunkirk to make good some of its losses there and those suffered earlier by the Hurricanes in France. During the battle itself British aircraft factories continued to lift their output and enough new fighters arrived at squadrons to replace losses, or at least hold the line. It was the shortage of trained and experienced pilots that was the problem; a problem that became critical. It was the reason so many inexperienced pilots were thrown into the conflict when plainly they were not ready — often at the cost of their lives. Aircrew from the FAA, Coastal Command and Bomber Command volunteered to fly fighters and Fighter Command leader Air Chief Marshal Hugh Dowding scrounged pilots from other sources. Somehow there were enough to see off the Germans, even if it was a close-run thing.

'Stuffy' Dowding, AOC, Fighter Command, was undoubtedly the architect of the Battle of Britain victory. Appointed to his post in mid-1936, he established a chain of radar stations, set up the sector stations and communications network and organized the army of ground observers, key elements of the air defence system. Dowding built Fighter Command from the ground up. From June 1938, New Zealander Air Vice-Marshal Keith Park was his right-hand man.

Dowding and Park (Senior Air Staff Officer, headquarters, Fighter Command, from June 1938 and AOC No. 11 Fighter Group from April 1940) made a winning team. During the battle Park directed the day-to-day fighter operations from the bunker at Bentley Priory, RAF Fighter Command headquarters on the outskirts of London. On his crucial decisions depended the successful deployment of the fighter squadrons opposing the Luftwaffe. He had his critics, notably Air Vice-Marshal Stafford Leigh-Mallory, his opposite at nearby 12 Group, but his tactics won the battle and that's what counted. The unveiling of a Park statue at Waterloo Place in central London on 15 September 2010, the 70th anniversary of the battle, was a fitting tribute. A statue of Dowding stands outside St Clements Danes, the 'RAF church' in central London.

Born in Thames and educated in Dunedin, Park served as an artillery officer in World War I (Gallipoli, the Somme), then flew with the Royal Flying Corps, commanding a squadron and credited with twenty victories, aided by his air gunner. He emerged from that war with a Military Cross and bar and a DFC. He flew his personal Hurricane over Dunkirk to assess the situation and he flew it again during the Battle of Britain. His 11 Group pilots admired him and he often dropped in on squadrons unannounced to have a drink and a chat with the pilots to gain first-hand knowledge of front-line operations. He was also one of the few senior commanders at the time who regularly flew high-performance fighters.

With the battle won, the establishment treated Dowding and Park shabbily — Dowding shunted off to show the flag in the United States before retirement, Park moved sideways to command a training group. Sholto Douglas took over from Dowding and Leigh-Mallory became head of 11 Group. In January 1942 the RAF tapped Park's defence brilliance and he flew to Egypt, and in July took command at Malta. Eighteen months later he was appointed AOC of Middle East Command before his final World War II posting in February 1945, as Allied Air Commander in Chief in South-East Asia. Ironically Leigh-Mallory was posted to the South-East Asia job, but was killed in an air crash on the way out.

One hundred and thirty-five New Zealanders flew in the Battle of Britain — ninety-five pilots, thirty-six gunners and four navigators. The gunners and navigators mostly flew on Blenheims, a good number of them on Coastal Command squadrons attached to Fighter Command at the time. All were entitled to the Battle of Britain Clasp (a campaign attachment to the 1939–45 Star), usually listed as (bbc).

Sixteen New Zealand pilots and four gunners lost their lives during the battle. Of the twenty who died, fifteen were killed on air operations and five in aircraft accidents. Such accidents caused an awful toll during the war years. Another thirty-two of New Zealand's Battle of Britain veterans died later in the war, on operations or in accidents. Eleven became POWs, two during the battle itself — Foxton pilot Maurice Baird and his navigator Doug Burton, Opunake, who were shot down off Norway in their Blenheim in late October and picked up by the Germans. Sixty-three of the New Zealanders entitled to wear the Clasp were alive when the war ended but four of them were killed in postwar accidents, while still serving in the RAF or RNZAF.

The youngest New Zealander in the battle was Aucklander Laurie Rasmussen, a gunner on 264 Squadron (Defiant). He died just a few days short of his 19th birthday, on 4 September, when his aircraft crashed shortly after takeoff on night patrol from a Lincolnshire airfield. The oldest was Eric Whitley, 32 (Auckland), who'd joined the RAF in 1930 and commanded 245 Squadron (Hurricane) in Northern Ireland during the battle.

The only brothers from New Zealand who took part in the battle were Brian and Michael Herrick, members of a well-known Hawke's Bay family. Their parents paid an enormous price in the war. Brian (20), a Blenheim pilot, was killed on 20 November 1940 when his aircraft crashed in the sea during a convoy patrol. Michael (23), by then a squadron leader with a DFC and bar and a US Air Medal, was shot down and killed on 16 June 1944 flying a Mosquito over Denmark. A third brother, Dennis (28), was shot down off Brest on an anti-shipping strike while piloting a Blenheim on 26 June 1941 and taken prisoner. He died in hospital of his wounds four days later. Two other Herrick brothers had distinguished wars in the Royal Navy.

The New Zealanders who flew during the almost four months of the battle comprised 4.6 per cent of the 2900-odd aircrew credited by the RAF with taking part in the battle. Next in strength among the Commonwealth groups were the Canadians (100, including a handful of Americans), Australians (30) and South Africans and Rhodesians (27) — among the last the high-scoring pilot and leader, Sailor Malan.

The relatively high representation of New Zealanders was largely because New Zealand had such a tiny air force pre-war that there were few opportunities for would-be pilots. The RAF's active recruiting here from 1937 was an enormous opportunity for young men, bitten by the flying bug, wanting excitement and adventure. Canada and Australia had much larger air forces with ample chance for at-home enlistment and flying. In early 1937 New Zealand newspapers carried an advertisement for candidates for twelve SSCs in the RAF. Even before the cut-off time more than 2100 applications flooded in — 'an avalanche,' Minister of Defence Fred Jones said. He added: 'The youth of New Zealand is keenly interested in aviation but no one could have realised till now how alluring flying has become and how intense the enthusiasm for it is.' Between 400 and 500 New Zealand pilots were in the RAF at the outbreak of war. Half of them would die.

New Zealand's contribution of fighter pilots was highly regarded because most of them were excellent pilots, tough and resilient. Among 'outsiders', New Zealanders were outnumbered in the Battle of Britain only by the Poles, 146 of whom had escaped from Poland in 1939 and made their way to Britain, most through France. In August 1940, 302 Squadron and 303 Squadron, both made up of Poles led by British squadron and flight commanders, joined Fighter Command strength. The remainder opted to remain in their British units where they felt more at home, according to Stephen Bungay in *The Most Dangerous Enemy*. He notes that although 303 Squadron only entered the battle on 31 August 'they were, with 126 accredited kills, the highest claiming squadron in Fighter Command'. The Poles looked for vengeance when they bored in close to enemy aircraft, machine guns hammering. They were particularly effective.

One of the top-scoring pilots in the battle, Czech Josef Frantisek, destroyed seventeen German aircraft while flying with the Poles of 303 Squadron. He had been with the Polish Air Force after fleeing the German occupation of Czechoslovakia in 1938 and scored his victories

Day after Day

between 2 and 30 September, before dying on 8 October when his Hurricane crashed at Northolt. Eighty-eight Czechs flew in the battle, as did Belgians, Dutch, Norwegians, French, Irish and others.

Compiling lists of victories is an unenviable and unrewarding task — someone always picks holes in them. It's a muddied field because so many different sources give so many different figures. Tables include halves, thirds, shareds, unconfirmed destroyeds, probables. Victory claims by individual pilots and squadrons were often highly exaggerated in the heat of battle. Triumphant Battle of Britain RAF tallies, suspect at the time, were shown by German records postwar to have been far off the mark in many cases.

The well-regarded Mike Spick in *Allied Fighter Aces of World War II* doesn't mess with halves or anything else. He places Yorkshireman Eric Lock (killed in 1941) at the top of the Battle of Britain list with twenty-one, followed by fellow Englishman Ginger Lacey (18), Scot Archie McKellar and Frantisek (17), New Zealanders Brian Carbury and Colin Gray and Pole Witold Urbanowicz (15) then Australian Pat Hughes and Englishman Bob Doe (14). Other lists have different tallies.

New Zealander Alan Deere, a great fighter pilot, provides one example of the problem of counting victories. *Aces High*, by Christopher Shores and Clive Williams, the 'bible' for people seeking victory tallies, credits Deere with an entire wartime score of seventeen and one shared destroyed. Shore says Deere's book *Nine Lives* records twenty-one and one shared destroyed but adds seventeen 'is all that can be found in the record'. He says that Deere's claim for an Me 109 shot down into the Channel on 1 August 1941 was actually a Hurricane of 242 Squadron. 'It is not clear if this claim is included in his total or not.' Shores credits Deere with six outright victories in the Battle of Britain. Many top scorers baled out at one stage or another after being

126

damaged in combat, some more than once and Lacey went out no fewer than three times. Deere is famous for his narrow escapes — bale outs, aerial collisions, crash-landings — the title of his book tells how many times. Carbury and Gray accumulated their high scores without jumping and neither had many bullets or cannon shells in their fighters. Carbury got in quick and away and didn't hang about to slog it out in desperate dogfights, especially when the odds were against him. Yet he still managed a great score and is remembered for his five-in-one day feat during the battle, an achievement matched only by Pole Antoni Glowacki, who immigrated to New Zealand postwar.

The great majority of the New Zealand pilots who fought in the battle were those who had gone to England to take up SSCs, but the RNZAF geared up quickly once war was declared and began to churn out pilots in rapidly growing numbers for the air war in Europe. The first draft of twenty-nine RNZAF pilots for attachment to the RAF sailed on 24 May 1940, reaching England on 9 July — all had their wings but were still novices. They were rushed through cursory extra training and posted to squadrons. Fighter, Bomber and Coastal Commands sorely needed pilots. Those chosen for fighters were given two or three hours on a Harvard or Magister, then presented with a Spitfire or Hurricane and told to fly it. A few hours in the air and they were posted, no time for tactical flying training or gunnery. It was unsatisfactory and brutal but was demanded by depleted pilot ranks. Later in the war pilots were given the luxury of long sustained training before they were allowed anywhere near combat.

The single pilot from the May draft who died in the Battle of Britain was John Priestley. He was sent to a Coastal OTU on 27 July, introduced to Blenheims, an aircraft superior to anything he'd flown in New Zealand, posted to 235 Squadron on 18 August and killed on 30 August, when his aircraft crashed during practice near his Norfolk airfield. He had flown two ops and amassed just 156 hours. Inexperience on Blenheims probably had a lot to do with his death. Thirteen pilots of that first draft were killed during the war. One of the survivors was Bill Sise of Dunedin, a noted Coastal Command pilot who won the DSO and bar and DFC and bar.

Two other RNZAF pilots, Sergeants Bob Holder and Doug Stanley, died in the battle. They sailed in the third draft of RNZAF pilots on 12 July, stayed together in England training on Hurricanes for three weeks before postings to 151 Squadron on 30 September. Less than a month later they were dead, crashing minutes apart during night training in identical circumstances. Stanley took off at 9.30 p.m., climbed to 500 feet, began a gentle turn and flew into the ground, his Hurricane exploding in flames. The impact and fire were seen from the runway and Holder was given the option of staying on the ground but he elected to fly, bravely undeterred by his mate's terrible end. Two hundred feet up, he also dived into the ground, his pyre not far from Holder's crash site. It's probable both relied on feel and instinct rather than trusting their instruments, which gave them a true picture of what they were doing, a fatal practice at night for many pilots. The New Zealanders had each done a handful of convoy patrols qualifying them for Clasps.

Bob Spurdle, Charles Stewart and Neville Cowan (the last destined to be a bomber pilot), the final three SSC New Zealand pilots for the RAF, sailed in June 1940 with an RNZAF draft that included Wally Churches, John Pattison, Mick Shand and Bill 'Hawkeye' Wells. Spurdle should have left earlier but had been in hospital. In his book *The Blue Arena* he notes that of the sixteen on his course who gained their wings, only five survived the war and two of them never saw action. Auckland postman Churches' path in England exactly mirrored Spurdle's. He and Spurdle shared a bedroom at Uxbridge, then the main reception centre, with a third occupant who greeted them on the first night with the words, 'Bloody coloured troops,' climbed out of bed, piddled in the hand-basin and fell back into his bed.

The next day the adjutant asked: 'What aircraft were you New Zealanders trained on?'

Spurdle and Churches chorused: 'Tiger Moths, Fairey Gordons and Vickers Wildebeests.'

Adjutant: 'Good God! Are they still flying?'

Spurdle and Churches did their brief Spitfire training together and arrived at Kirton-in-Lindsey, Lincolnshire on the same day, 21 August 1940, joining their unit as replacement pilots when 74 Squadron was resting out of the line to regroup. They were met by its tough, redoubtable CO, South African Malan, who told them: 'This a famous squadron and I expect you to remember it. Your life expectancy will be in direct ratio to your ability to learn.' They both learned well and did not let Malan down. He added they would soon have plenty of targets. 'I'm sure you will do well.' They did, though they had to put up with the bad side of some Pom pilots, good in the air, bastards on the ground. An effete university-type welcomed them to the mess their first night with, 'More coloured troops! Are we scraping the bottom of the barrel already?'

Spurdle wrote, 'In a subtle way we "Colonials" and the new young British recruits, unless well connected were largely excluded from this kind of old boys' club and felt it keenly.' This attitude was not common but Spurdle obviously experienced it.

The New Zealanders underwent rigorous training taught by veterans — fighter tactics, battle-formation flying, dogfighting, deflection attacks, flying in clouds. They learned on the new and improved Mark II Spitfires, though both had bad moments. A week after arrival, Churches chewed up the tail of another Spitfire in the air. The other pilot jumped; Churches crash-landed in a field.

The squadron moved to Coltishall, Norfolk, on 9 September and six days later to Biggin Hill, the centre of action. On 15 October Spurdle, flying No. 2 to Malan, lost his leader in combat. Back at base he was on the mat.

'Where the hell did you get to?' Malan thundered.

'Sorry, sir, I lost you in a turn.'

'Clot! There were lots of targets! Better pull your finger out!'

A week later Spurdle chased a 109 in a high speed-dive, raced way past the red mark on his 'speedo' and watched his starboard wing rip off. As he drifted down a 109's cannon fire laced at him (guarding Spitfires got the offender) and when he landed in a soft ploughed field a huge farm labourer jumped on him.

'Get off me, you stupid oaf,' Spurdle roared. 'Don't you know your own bloody side?'

The man reared up, fist ready to smash Spurdle. Slowly comprehension dawned. 'Be you RAF, sor?' he asked with a beaming smile.

'No, I'm a fucking angel. For Christ's sake, let me up!'

On 30 October, the second-to-last day of the battle, Churches blew a fleeing 109 to pieces over the Channel and Spurdle claimed a probable. Spurdle got his first victory on 2 November — just too late for the battle scoreboard. His bullets tore into a 109 over Maidstone at 20,000 feet late in the afternoon and the enemy crashed at Ashford. He had chased up behind one of four circling 109s and fired at point-blank range. 'Almost at once white fumes poured out followed by thick black smoke. Pieces of the plane broke off after about one second's firing,' Spurdle's combat report says. That night he celebrated his first confirmed victory and promotion to flying officer, shouted the mess bar and 'drank myself unconscious'.

On 13 April 1941 Spurdle transferred out of 74 Squadron to 91 Squadron and further adventures. Churches stayed on and a week later was killed in a sweep over the Channel. His Spitfire plunged into the cold sea, his body lost. He was still only 19. 'Wally's death was hard to take,' Spurdle wrote. 'We'd flown together some eight months, a long, long time by a fighter pilot's reckoning. No point in ranting against [his] fate — in mute and terrible agony of mind and spirit one could only curse the Hun and promise revenge.' Churches was credited with three victories and two probables.

Shand and Stewart arrived together at Hornchurch and 54 Squadron (Gray's and Deere's unit) on 22 August. Deere discovered Shand had just twenty hours on Spitfires at his English OTU, had never fired the fighter's guns and trained as a light bomber pilot in New Zealand. 'Good grief,' Deere thought. But he knew there was no alternative and no chance of giving Shand more training. A couple of days later Shand and Stewart were both in hospital, wounded. Shand suffered a severe nerve injury and Stewart was shot down into the Channel off Dover by friendly anti-aircraft fire. Some sources say Stewart was a victim of 109s but Stewart's own logbook shows conclusively it was British ground fire. 'Shot down by Ac.Ac. Landed in Channel by chute', it says. Note Ac.Ac (anti-aircraft fire) and not flak, which is what he would have said had it been German fire. He was only fifteen minutes into his patrol from Hornchurch, not long enough to have reached the French coast and the flak.

Shand got his fighter down safely but Stewart had a long cold swim.

He saw a rescue boat coming but it veered away. He must have thought he was a goner but three-quarters of an hour later another boat picked him up. In October 1941 Shand was back in the air with 485 Squadron, but Stewart was dead. After recovering from his icy dunking, Stewart was posted to 222 Squadron on which he did 91 ops before going to 485 Squadron in March 1941 as a founding member. Four months later he was lost without trace, killed as 485 Squadron battled enemy fighters over the Straits of Dover.

A number of New Zealand pilots rose from obscurity, as it were, to make lasting marks in the Battle of Britain; men like Carbury, Gray and Deere.

So did Johnny Gibson. Back from France with three Germans to his credit, Johnny Gibson added another eight to his tally between 13 July and early September, becoming one of the standout New Zealanders in the Battle of Britain and the leading New Zealand Hurricane pilot. Still with 501 Squadron, he operated pretty much non-stop throughout the campaign as the squadron moved successively from Croydon to Middle Wallop, Gravesend and Kenley, often in the thick of the action. Some days the pilots flew from forward bases such as Hawkinge, returning at night to their home fields. Before the Stukas were withdrawn from the battle, with losses too heavy for the Germans to bear, Gibson and the rest of 501 Squadron got among them several times and he accounted for three. He also shot down three 109s, a Ju 88 and a Dornier. In return German fire twice fatally damaged Gibson's fighter and both times he took to his chute.

Gibson got his first Stuka in an action near Dover about 8 a.m. on 29 July, almost certainly saving a Spitfire from destruction. His combat report:

I was leading Red section when I sighted enemy aircraft approaching Dover Harbour. I followed Blue leader into attack and engaged enemy Ju 87 as E/A broke away from attack on harbour. I carried out quarter attack and saw E/A diving steeply with black smoke pouring out. I broke off the attack and saw a Spitfire emitting white glycol smoke with a Ju 87 on its tail. I carried out attack on E/A which burst into flame and plunged into the sea.

Gibson stayed with the wounded Spitfire, accompanying it back to the coast where it force-landed safely in a field. He claimed the first Stuka as a probable. A good morning's work. Late in August he was promoted to flight lieutenant and learned he had won a DFC. During September he was wounded in combat and taken to hospital. Gibson left 501 Squadron in May 1941, instructed for the rest of the year then flew with an Australian Spitfire squadron for a few months. Mid-year 1942 he was back in New Zealand and from January 1944 commanded 15 Squadron RNZAF in the Pacific for six months. Almost as soon as he joined 15 he downed a Japanese fighter over Rabaul, taking his final war tally to twelve.

Gibson returned to England in late 1944, converted to Tempests and flew with 80 Squadron in Europe in the last stages of the war. On 11 March 1945, a couple of weeks after he was awarded a DSO, he was hit by flak during the Army's crossing of the Rhine. He flew his aircraft back into Allied air space but broke a shoulder as he force-landed in Holland. It was the end of his war. Among postwar jobs in the RAF he was personal pilot for both General Montgomery and Air Marshal Tedder.

Another top Hurricane pilot was Irving 'Black' Smith who later earned fame as the man who led in the Mosquito squadrons that blasted open Amiens Prison in February 1944 to free members of the French Resistance and other political prisoners facing execution. His 487 (NZ) Squadron's pinpoint bombing breached the outer walls and 464 (Australian) Squadron followed, smashing the guards' quarters and opening up the prison itself. An RAF backup squadron wasn't needed. Smith was CO of 487 Squadron at the time of the raid, which was under the overall command of Charles 'Pick' Pickard. The group captain lost his life minutes after the raid, shot down by FW 190s as he circled the area to gauge results.

Amiens has overshadowed Smith's great performance in the Battle of Britain, but this early part of his glittering career deserves more recognition. Smith turned up, a fledgling SSC pilot officer, at 151 Squadron (Hurricane), North Weald, an 11 Group field, on 13 July 1940, the fourth day of the battle. He was twenty-three and had finished his training just two days before. Once he'd settled in and learned how to fly in combat, the young New Zealander did extraordinarily well. He clearly knew how to fight and became a Battle of Britain 'ace' with five victories.

He scored his first and second victories, both Me 109s, and damaged a third, on 15 August. In his combat report, he said of the fighter he destroyed southwest of Dover about 7 p.m. on his third sortie of the day: 'Three five-second bursts. I followed the 109 down from about 18–20,000 ft to about 4–5000 ft! I then broke off and pulled out of the dive; when I broke away the 109 was spinning slowly at a speed in excess of 400 mph and going down vertically.' The form asked for the number of enemy aircraft. He wrote: 'Impossible to gauge. A very large No.'

On the 24th he destroyed a Heinkel 111 and later in the month he and two other pilots 'frightened' a 109 into oblivion. The German dived away as the Hurricanes pounced and kept on diving, straight into the ground. The RAF three didn't fire a shot and the 109 was credited to Yellow section. On the last day of August he caught a Dornier east of Hornchurch and shot it down. Smith poured all his ammunition into the bomber at close range. 'The rear gunner ceased to fire shortly after I opened fire. Large pieces of the 215 fell off, one striking my aeroplane.' Out of bullets, Smith flew home. A fellow pilot 'confirms that as I broke away from the 215 the port motor caught fire and the a/c went into a dive.' Two days later Smith was vectored on to a lone-flying 111 and scored again, reaching ace status. The bomber ditched just off a beach near Skegness, Lincolnshire, the crew taken prisoner. (151 Squadron had been based in Lincolnshire, for a month, at Digby, regrouping with a batch of new pilots.) Smith was now a veteran.

As the Battle of Britain ebbed the Luftwaffe's bombing of England intensified and 151 Squadron was one of those converted to Defiants, hopeless as day fighters but given a new lease of life in the dark. Smith, already marked out as a leader, was given command of one of 151 Squadron's three flights and then a larger unit when two flights were combined. He was awarded the DFC in March 1941. On the night of 10–11 that month, one of the heaviest raids on London during the Blitz, he flew a Hurricane (some of which were still on the squadron strength) from Wittering, Cambridgeshire, now the squadron field, and knocked down an He 111 over London, the bomber credited as a probable. On the night of 19–20 February 1942, a few hours after being appointed CO of 151 Squadron, he and his Defiant gunner combined to destroy a Dornier at low level off the Norfolk coast while protecting a convoy — and damaged a Ju 88 that joined in the action.

In March 1943 Smith was posted from 151 Squadron to Fighter

Command HQ. He'd been with the squadron since August 1940, a long spell in RAF terms. He went to a staff job with a second DFC, a new wife and the satisfaction of overseeing the squadron's re-equipment with Mosquitoes, as well as promotion from raw pilot officer to acting wing commander. On the night of 24–25 June 1942 he opened his Mosquito account by downing two bombers off Yarmouth. After his stint at HQ he was given command of 488 (NZ) Squadron, a night fighter unit, but Basil Embry, head of 2 Group, Second Tactical Air Force (later Air Chief Marshal Sir Basil Embry with no fewer than four DSOs) overruled the posting, wanting Smith at his HQ. Smith itched to get back on ops and got his wish in February 1944, taking command of 487 Squadron on intruder raids. The job led to the Amiens raid and others like it. Finally, in October 1944 he became Chief Instructor at an OTU, where he saw out the war. His enemy aircraft tally stood at eight. Postwar he remained in the RAF, eventually promoted to group captain. He was invalided out of the service in 1966, retiring to farm in Devon. He died in 2000.

His son followed the service tradition. General Sir Rupert Smith, KCB, DSO and bar, OBE, QGM, commanded Britain's 1st Armoured Division in the Gulf War (1990–91), subsequently commanded British forces in Northern Ireland, was the UN commander in Bosnia Herzegovina and finished his service as Deputy Supreme Commander, Allied Forces Europe at NATO headquarters. He retired in 2002 after forty years in the army. Three years later his *The Utility of Force: The Art of War in the Modern World* was published to wide acclaim.

Was John Mackenzie a Battle of Britain ace? 'Yes,' say New Zealand sources, 'no,' says Christopher Shores. At issue is a Ju 88, claimed as destroyed by some aviation historians in New Zealand but declared only a probable by Shores in *Aces High*. If it's in the victories list, Mackenzie's total in the battle is five; if not it's four. Mackenzie got another two in November 1940 to lift his wartime total to six — or seven. Of small moment really, but important enough in treasured tallies.

Mackenzie delivered his attack on the 88 on 15 August 1940, when Goering launched widespread raids against Britain. That day Luftflotte 5 (Airfleet 5) flew from bases in Norway and Denmark to bomb targets in northeast England, secure in the knowledge they would be hitting an area undefended by Fighter Command. Luftwaffe leaders were certain they had knocked out so many RAF fighters in the southeast that none remained in the north. Wrong. Dowding maintained squadrons in the north for just such a German adventure and others were on hand, resting. In this case 'rest' meant they still flew patrols and were ready for action. German intelligence was faulty and Luftflotte 5 paid heavily.

The bombers flew without Me 109 escort because the 109s simply could not manage the distance. The Heinkels and Ju 88s were accompanied by Me 110s but in this role the 110s, some burdened by extra fuel and so minus a rear gunner, were no match for the agile Spitfires and Hurricanes that swarmed up. To their cost, the Germans also seem to have not considered the radar stations, which gave ample warning of the streams of enemy aircraft heading in from the North Sea. 13 Group chief Air Vice-Marshal Richard Saul marshalled his forces expertly, scrambling three Spitfire and four Hurricane squadrons to meet the raiders. The first to engage were 72 Squadron Spitfires. The pilots saw the enemy coming — seventy-odd Heinkels and twenty-one 110s. One of the RAF pilots asked his squadron leader if he'd seen them. Ted Graham's response has gone down in RAF lore. Owner of a bad stutter, he finally blurted: 'Of course I've seen the b-b-b-bastards — I'm t-t-t-trying to work out w-w-w-what to do.' He had plenty of time — a clear sky, a few scattered clouds and no 109s. He took his squadron up above the Germans and roared down out of the sun. Other squadrons arrived and, as Stephen Bungay says in *The Most Dangerous Enemy,* 'began the work of execution'.

A big group of Ju 88s headed for Durham and Yorkshire airfields and some bombed Driffield, destroying a number of Whitleys on the ground. They too paid a substantial price. Mackenzie, leading 41 Squadron's A Flight's Red section, latched on to an 88 at 13,000 feet over Seaham Harbour on the Durham coast just before 1 p.m. He heard Red leader call 'Tally-ho' as the Spitfires fell on the Germans. Mackenzie then took his section above the enemy.

> I singled out E/A who was flying a little to the starboard of formation and carried out an attack, closing to 80 yards before breaking away. The ... 88 turned sharply to starboard with smoke pouring from his starboard engine, I last saw E/A entering cloud, smoke still pouring from stbd engine.

Mackenzie did not claim the 88 as destroyed. Conservatively, he wrote in his combat report under Enemy casualties — '1 (Category II)', meaning probably destroyed. In other words, a probable that was so severely damaged it was unlikely to have reached its base, although both *Aces High* and John Foreman in *RAF Fighter Command Victory Claims* list the 88 as no more than a probable.

The RAF squadrons made wild claims of fifty-nine, but the Germans actually lost twenty-three, although it was still a turkey shoot and a crushing Luftwaffe defeat. Several British fighters were damaged but none lost. The Germans never tried such an attack again.

Mackenzie, a South Islander widely known as 'Mac' and on an early SSC draft in 1937, flew non-stop with 41 Squadron until April 1941, his long pre-war apprenticeship standing him in good stead when war broke out. He had his first serious sorties over Dunkirk when the squadron moved to Hornchurch on 28 May 1940. In Norman Franks' *Air Battle for Dunkirk,* Mackenzie is quoted as saying, 'Dunkirk was no doubt a most valuable exercise in introducing the squadron to the realities of war and easing us gently into the big battles which were to follow.' But he was critical of the tight formation flying enforced at the time and said he saw only one enemy aircraft, and that briefly, during a period of ten days and a total of ten offensive patrols.

Relatively ancient for a fighter pilot, he had his 26th birthday during the Battle of Britain. Dowding said he didn't want men 26 and over flying in Fighter Command. Too old, he declared; he required younger men. Despite his age, Mackenzie did extraordinarily well in the battle — four confirmed victories in 41 Squadron's two spells at Hornchurch, three of them 109s, the other a Heinkel. There were no doubts about any of them. They crashed, force-landed or dived into the sea.

He had one horrific victory that must have lived for ever in his mind. A few minutes after 9 a.m. on 17 November he flew in behind three 109s as they did a wide sweep over the sea from Herne Bay, Kent, towards Clacton-on-Sea, Essex. His combat report:

I selected the port Me 109 of the formation and took very careful aim before firing. I thought that I would be able to engage the leading Me 109 after firing at the port Me 109 but he broke away too suddenly after my first burst. I decided to make sure of one Me 109 and gave a second burst and he instantly burst into flames and turned over. I fired a third burst into the Me 109 in an effort to kill the pilot so that he would not burn to death. Aircraft went vertically into the sea.

He had pumped 1190 rounds into his victim, his last fired from just fifty yards.

It was kill or be killed in the air but the New Zealander's feelings for his enemy that day showed the compassionate side of his nature as he tried to prevent unnecessary suffering. That one brief action and Mackenzie's words encapsulate the terrifying violence and personal nature of one-on-one fighter encounters.

Mackenzie's final combat victory, over an Me 109 at 23,000 feet on the Maidstone patrol line over Kent mid-afternoon on 27 November, surprised him. He singled out the German fighter from a scattered group and gave him a very short burst. The 109 half-rolled before going down almost vertically.

Got slightly below and about 200 yards behind and gave him a very long burst into fuselage. A few seconds later flames started licking out of his tail. This is the first time I have noticed the tail catching alight. The flames slowly crept up the fuselage until he was blazing from stem to stern. He crashed beside a farmhouse in the hills north of Folkestone, and blazed for quite a while. I landed at Hawkinge as my fuel was getting low.

Steve Brew, in his forthcoming history of 41 Squadron, *Blood, Sweat and Valour*, records the dead German pilot as Adolph Benzinger.

Brew says Mackenzie, and fellow New Zealander Hawkeye Wells, his No. 2 that day, plunged down on a group of scattered 109s spotted while the rest of the twelve-strong squadron, led by CO Don Finlay, attacked another six 109s from out of the sun, a loose group flying in from Calais in pairs. Mackenzie and his Green section had been acting as lookouts for the other Spitfires. The entire squadron was at 30,000 feet on the Maidstone line homebound to Hornchurch to refuel when the fun started. In fifteen minutes the Germans lost seven fighters, with no losses to 41 Squadron. Brew notes that afternoon's victories were 41 Squadron's last successes until 30 March 1941, action slackening off as winter began.

Wells shot down one of the seven. Brew records he chased the Me 109 out over the coast as it fled 'flat out for France'. Closing gradually, Wells began firing at 250 yards. His first burst appeared to have no effect but after his second, glycol and smoke poured out. Now the 109 started a steep dive and pieces of the aircraft, the hood among them, blew off. The pilot failed to bale out as the fighter continued straight on into the Channel.

Wells would have been taken under Mackenzie's wing during his time at 41 Squadron and was lucky to have his wise, battle-hardened countryman as a tutor. Wells' victory on 27 November was his third and final of the year, all 109s. He got his first on 17 October as the Battle of Britain waned and his second on 2 November, as his reputation as an excellent newcomer began to build. He left 41 Squadron not long before Mackenzie, to join the new 485 Squadron.

Wells was blessed with two great attributes — superb marksmanship and remarkable eyesight. He was accustomed to firearms and shooting birds on the wing and ranked as a champion competition claybird shooter in New Zealand. Fellow New Zealander John Pattison said Wells had the 'most marvellous' eyesight. 'He would spot German aircraft and report … long before anybody else could see them. That was a tremendous advantage.' Johnnie Johnson, the RAF's top World War II scorer over Britain and occupied Europe with at least thirty-eight to his credit, called Wells' eyesight 'amazing' in his 1956 book *Wing Leader* and said the New Zealander was generally acknowledged among fighter pilots to be the finest shot in the air.

Mackenzie, awarded the DFC in November, remained with 41 Squadron until April 1941, when he was rested and posted for fighter control duties. He had flown 245 ops. Six months later he was appointed a flight commander of 488 Squadron, formed in New Zealand and on its way to Singapore. He went to the island 'fortress' with Wilf Clouston, named to command 488 Squadron. In Singapore, Clouston's future was decided by a fateful posting. The squadron's hopelessly outperformed Buffaloes were no match for the Japanese when they attacked in January 1942. Later that month Clouston was posted to RAF HQ in Singapore and Mackenzie was given command of 488 Squadron. The remnants of the squadron, Mackenzie among them, were withdrawn to Batavia (Jakarta) in February and then evacuated to New Zealand.

In New Zealand Mackenzie headed 14 Squadron as it formed, then had six months as CO of the fighter conversion unit at Ohakea. He returned to England in mid-1943 and after several postings was appointed in April 1944 as CO of 64 Squadron (Spitfire). He was repatriated to New Zealand later in the year but postwar rejoined the RAF and served until 1957. He died in Balclutha in 1993.

Poor Wilf Clouston. Captured as Singapore surrendered, he faced almost four years behind wire, prisoner of the barbaric Japanese. He spent most of those in a notorious camp in Palembang, Sumatra, but was transferred not long before the Japanese surrendered to Changi in Singapore. To the end of his life in 1980, a life shortened by war, he kept a 1946 letter from a friend in Singapore, noting the trials and hangings of nine Japanese from the Palembang camp plus long sentences of hard labour for others. 'I feel we have done a little to square off the accounts of Chief Petty Officers Eden, Fench, Devis, gunner Williams and all the rest of the good chaps,' his friend wrote. What suffering is hidden behind those names?

Clouston, awarded a DFC in June 1940 for his glowing record over Dunkirk, had added another four successes in the Battle of Britain with 19 Squadron. The squadron returned to Duxford from its French blooding but then moved to Fowlmere, a Duxford satellite near Cambridge. Here the squadron remained until November — in 12 Group as an integral part of the Duxford Wing. This group of three, later five, squadrons, known as the 'Big Wing', was the pet project of Leigh-Mallory and his offsider, Douglas Bader. They resented the major role of 11 Group in the southeast and Leigh-Mallory and Park cordially disliked each other. Friction on tactics caused major problems and arguments. The Big Wing, and the Leigh-Mallory/Bader team's theory that it could inflict major losses on the Luftwaffe, have been debated endlessly in the seventy years since 1940, mostly adversely. But the fact is Park's tactics, generally launching attacks with one or two squadrons and adding reinforcements and later operating two pairs, worked seamlessly most of the time. They won the Battle of Britain.

Park was backed to the hilt by Dowding. The commander-in-chief, however, let the wrangling go on for far too long and postwar admitted he should have acted to rein in Leigh-Mallory and Bader. History shows the big unwieldy wing took too long to form up and often missed the action. Leigh-Mallory was slow in responding to Park's urgent calls for help, unlike the admirable South African, Quintin Brand, who headed 10 Group in the southwest and was always ready with prompt aid.

Stephen Bungay notes Park reported to his boss in November that the Duxford Wing had been used on every possible occasion in October but in ten sorties it had managed to intercept only once and had shot down only one German aircraft. Some of the wing's own pilots were critical. Frank Brinsden, who flew with Clouston, is quoted by Derek Palmer in *Fighter Squadron*, his history of 19 Squadron, as saying he was never a fan of the Big Wing. He thought it was 'time wasting in assembly and cumbersome in operation. In any case the formations fragmented when battle was joined, so why waste precious time assembling them?' He said there was no doubt the clash of personalities at group command level, combined with giving way to Bader on the tactical use of the Duxford Wing, inhibited the skills of some first class and experienced pilots.

The Big Wing of three squadrons made its debut late afternoon on 7 September, the day of the first invasion alert (Attack Imminent) and the first big daylight bombing attack on London. It performed with mixed results against an enormous bomber stream, protected by an impressive escort force. Stephen Bungay says 19 Squadron was strung out on arrival in the North Weald area, behind the wing's two Hurricane squadrons, and Clouston returned without firing his guns.

With other squadrons in the Big Wing, 19 Squadron were based behind the centre of action in the southeast, with their chances of action diminished by their location. Clouston, an above-average fighter pilot, would likely have compiled a much higher score had he been in the thick of it, with a squadron at Hornchurch, Biggin Hill, Croydon or Tangmere. The squadron was also plagued during some

Above and left: To war — May 1940. Two rare photographs.

Above: A crane hoists Hurricanes of 46 Squadron onto a barge for the trip downriver on the Clyde to the ill-fated fleet carrier HMS *Glorious* for its voyage to Norway. JOHN JAMESON

Left: New Zealander Jamie Jameson (background left) listens as Flying Officer Mike Mee talks to another man (obscured) on the deck of *Glorious*. Mee was one of 1500 lost when the carrier was sunk off Norway on 9 June. Jameson was one of a handful of survivors. JOHN JAMESON

Below: Jameson later in the war. JOHN JAMESON

Cobber Kain.

Right: Kain in the cockpit of his 73 Squadron Hurricane. Air Force Museum

Above: A plate number souvenired from the wreckage of Kain's initial 'kill' — a Dornier 17. Peter D Cornwell

Below: The German bomber crashed in a French village and Kain wrote on the back of this photograph: 'Looking a little sobered after viewing my first victim, Do 17, which is scattered about me burning in the trench it has dug.' Air Force Museum

```
NEW ZEALAND POST OFFICE TELEGRAPHS.           Date-stamp.
    (If prepaid in stamps, affix in this space.)
                                              5/2/1000
                                                      No.

Code :_____  Time :_____  Words :_____
Instructions :_____  Charges :_____
        (For conditions of acceptance see over.)
                                    FOR OFFICE USE ONLY.
ADDRESS.   Dr. S H Ward             Sent_____  Checked.
           Whangarei                To_____
                                    By_____
                                    Ackgt.

    Deeply regret to learn that your son Squadron Leader Derek
    Harland Ward DFC and Bar has been killed in action. The Prime
    Minister desires me to convey to you on behalf of the
    Government his deepest sympathy with you in your great loss.

                            F Jones
                            Minister of Defence.


                    FILE.
                    25/6/1942       Initials.

Note.—The name and address of the sender if not to be telegraphed must be written on the back of the form.
```

Top left: Derek Ward points to the unlucky symbols he painted on his Hurricane to show he wasn't superstitious. WARD FAMILY

Top right: Ward climbs aboard his fighter carrying Scottie, the little dog that flew with him many times on non-operational flights. The dog was lost in France in 1940. WARD FAMILY

Above: The dreaded wartime telegram that hundreds of New Zealand families received telling them of the deaths of loved ones. This one announced Ward's loss in combat in North Africa in 1942. WARD FAMILY

Jimmy Paterson, a genuine number-eight-wire New Zealander with huge initiative, served with distinction in France in 1940 but was killed during the Battle of Britain.

Above: In a tin hat, worn on the ground in France to protect against bullets and shell and bomb fragments. The photograph ran on the front page of a London daily. JIM DILLON

Below left: Paterson in uniform with the inevitable RAF moustache. JIM DILLON

Below right: Paterson fell in love with Joy Beadell, a talented dancer and lifetime dance and ballet teacher. In 1988, a widow by then, she migrated to New Zealand to be near a son and daughter and set up a dance school on arrival. She died in Auckland in 2007 aged 87. JIM DILLON

Death in the Battle of France.

Above left: 15 Squadron pilots. The three standing at the back are, left to right, New Zealanders Tom Bassett, Len Trent and Bill Frankish. Bassett and Frankish died on 12 May 1940 in the suicidal operation to try to destroy canal bridges at Maastricht, Holland, in a vain attempt to halt the German invaders. Somehow Trent survived. He won a VC in 1943. Martyn R Ford-Jones Collection

Above right: Frankish married Marjorie Townend just a week before his death. The bride had travelled from New Zealand. Mrs Marjorie Prendiville

Below: The burned, mangled wreck of the rear section of Frankish's Blenheim in a forest near Maastricht. Martyn R Ford-Jones Collection

Right: Len Trent, in white flying overalls, survived the disastrous Maastricht raid. MARTYN R FORD-JONES COLLECTION

Middle: The shattered remains of New Zealander Edgar Morton's 103 Squadron Battle lie in a Luxembourg-Belgium border-area field, shot down on 12 May 1940. Morton and his gunner died. PETER D CORNWELL

Below: 15 Squadron's Operations Record Book records the six of twelve aircraft lost on the raid. MARTYN R FORD-JONES COLLECTION

Right: Handsome Tom Fitzgerald outside A Flight's commander's office, 103 Squadron.
Mrs Clare Hornibrook

Below: Fitzgerald flies his Fairey Battle PM-K (PM was 103's squadron code). Note his gunner, muffled up in a white scarf, in his open gun position above the letter K — the individual aircraft's ID. Fitzgerald, wounded in the Battle of France, ended the war a wing commander. Mrs Clare Hornibrook

Above: Wilf Clouston alongside his 19 Squadron Spitfire in 1939, its tail 'chewed up' by a fellow squadron pilot who was to be best man at his 1940 marriage. The squadron was the first in the RAF to be equipped with Spitfires. RICHARD CLOUSTON

Below left: Clouston, now CO of 258 Squadron, talks to a ground crewman in the summer of 1941. RICHARD CLOUSTON

Below right: Clouston, in the cockpit of a 258 Squadron Hurricane, has said something that amuses his brother John, serving in the same squadron. Wilf was captured by the Japanese in Singapore in 1942; John, a recent POW, was killed by strafing American aircraft in June 1944. RICHARD CLOUSTON

Jimmy Paterson and fellow 92 Squadron pilots Brian Kingcome and John Bryson intercepted a Ju 88 over Porthcawl, South Wales, pursued it and shot it down.

Above: Paterson begins to cut out the swastika for the squadron mess. Bryson (left) and Kingcome accompany the New Zealander. JIM DILLON

Below: Paterson still at work on the swastika as the crashed, overturned aircraft smoulders. JIM DILLON

Right: This recent memorial stone at the crash site remembers Paterson's Battle of Britain death in Kent. JIM DILLON

Extraordinarily good New Zealand pilot Brian Carbury shot down an astonishing fifteen German aircraft during the Battle of Britain, one of the highest scores.

Left: The lanky Carbury with his ever-present long-stemmed pipe. DAVID ROSS

Below: Carbury astride a biplane, nose down after an unhappy landing. From the smiles, no one is too worried. DAVID ROSS

Opposite: Carbury's combat report for his last sortie on 31 August 1940 when he shot down his fourth and fifth victims of the day, both Messerschmitt 109s. Only one other pilot scored five in a day during the Battle of Britain. UK NATIONAL ARCHIVES

F/O CARBURY

h27/117

95

S E C R E T.

FORM "F"

C O M B A T   R E P O R T.

Sector Serial No.	(a)	
Serial No.of order detailing Patrol.	(b)	
Date.	(c)	31 . 8 . 40
Flight, Squadron.	(d)	'B' 603 Squadron
No. & Type of enemy aircraft	(f)	2 ME 109's
Time attack was delivered	(g)	0825 hours *(1751-1900)* 1825 hours
Place attack was delivered	(h)	North of Southend
Height of enemy	(j)	25,000 feet *probably correct*
Enemy casualties	(k)	Destroyed 2 ME 109
		Probable --
		Damaged --
Our casualties. Aircraft	(l)	--
Personnel	(m)	--
Searchlights	(n) (i)	--
A.A. Guns Assistance	(ii)	--
Fire from fighters	(p)	Range opened 150 yards
		Length of burst 3 seconds
		Range closed 50 yards.
		No. of rounds fired.

Catalogue Reference:AIR/50/167

Image Reference:4

96

Enemy aircraft sighted over London and we attacked. 3 of us attacked 9 ME 109's, the first went down straight and burst into flames; attacked 4 e/a which were in pairs, slipped up a beam attack, hit the glycol tank of one and he rolled over and went straight down hitting a wood. An ME 109 got on my tail, received one cannon shell and the air system punctured so came home.

BJ Carbury P/O

Left: England bound. New Zealanders chosen for Short Service Commissions in the RAF on the deck of the *Rangitata*, December 1938. John Gard'ner at right, back row; Colin Gray, second from right, middle row. JOHN GARD'NER

Middle: Group photograph — Elementary training at De Havilland's airfield at Hatfield, Hertfordshire. Almost half this group were New Zealanders. Among them, back row: John Gard'ner (extreme right), Ron Bary (third from right). Front row: Colin Gray (second from right). JOHN GARD'NER

Below left: After success at Hatfield course, Acting Pilot Officer Gard'ner, 1939. JOHN GARD'NER

Below right: The senior officers of 488 (NZ) Squadron in 1942 — CO Dick Trousdale flanked by his flight commanders, Paul Rabone (left) and John Gard'ner. JOHN GARD'NER

Boulton Paul Defiants were hopeless as day fighters but operated more successfully at night.

Above: Defiant in flight. JOHN GARD'NER

Below: John Gard'ner at the controls of his Defiant, his gunner behind him. JOHN GARD'NER

Above: These pilots, course 9 at Wigram, passed out with their wings on 11 February 1940. One of the successful course members, Bill Finlayson, was not present for the photograph. The others are: (back row, left to right) Herbert Ballantyne, Allan Bridson, Clive Saxelby, John Bickerdike, Charles Miller, Eric Orgias; (front row, left to right) Bill Hodgson, Noel Pettit, Peter Sigley, Bill Krogh, Herbert Newman, George Fitzwater and Peter Robinson. Krogh and Fitzwater were retained in New Zealand to be instructors. The other twelve sailed for England later that month to take up Short Service Commissions in the RAF. Ten of them were killed. The two survivors, bomber pilots Newman and Saxelby, became POWs. Krogh was killed in an aircraft accident in Canterbury on 22 July 1940, the same date Bickerdike died in England. Fitzwater ended the war as CO of 25 Squadron in the Pacific. He died in New Zealand in 2002. THE PRESS, CHRISTCHURCH

Right: Hodgson. TONY EYRE

Below left: (left to right) Aubrey Breckon, WAAF Rosemary Ross and Hodgson, the day the men received their DFCs at Buckingham Palace. TONY EYRE

Below middle: Ross. MICK HOLLYER

Below right: Memorial to Hodgson in Shotgate, Wickford, Essex. PETER NUTT

Left: South Islander Mindy Blake, back from a flight, explains what happened. A top pilot, Battle of Britain survivor and inventor, Blake was shot down at Dieppe in August 1942 and captured. He was about to become a group captain.
ALISON WALFORD

Below: This Messerschmitt 109 crash-landed and flipped in Windsor Great Park during the Battle of Britain. New Zealand pilot Frank Gill, driving past the scene at the time, hopped out of his car and raced across the fields to capture the dazed pilot. Princesses Elizabeth and Margaret came from nearby Windsor Castle to see the wreck.
AUTHOR'S COLLECTION

Top left: A farmer's son, Cecil Hight celebrated his 21st birthday and 'bon voyage' with family, and friends from the New Plymouth Aero Club, where he learned to fly, before working his way to England in late 1938 to join the RAF. He died during the Battle of Britain flying a Spitfire with 234 Squadron. HIGHT FAMILY

Top right: Hight in flying rig. RAY STEBBINGS

Middle: Hight's funeral procession in Bournemouth, the south coast town where his body fell, parachute unopened. The flag- and flower-covered casket is on a bier pulled by airmen. RAY STEBBINGS

Left: Fellow New Zealander and fellow 234 pilot Pat Horton in his cockpit, a swastika crossed by a Spitfire painted on the door. Horton died in November 1940 when his out-of-fuel Hurricane went down in the Mediterranean while heading for Malta from an aircraft carrier. RAY STEBBINGS

parts of the battle by constant problems with their guns. They were guinea pigs, the first RAF squadron to be equipped with the Hispano cannon. Stoppages were frequent and devastating for pilots. Promised improvements didn't work. Eventually the cannons were replaced and the squadron went back to its eight machine guns for a time. Brinsden, quoted by Palmer again: 'I remember being elated when we received the first cannon Spitfires, then bitterly disappointed when they proved unreliable under combat stress. I got myself into several good astern firing positions only to find my guns jammed.'

Clouston scored his four battle victories in September: an Me 109 on 9 September, plus a 109 probable the same day, an Me 110 and a Dornier 17 on 15 September and a Ju 88 on 18 September. He had already shared in the destruction of two enemy aircraft, when he led the squadron into action over the north of London to the Thames Estuary on 9 August. The nine fighters climbed to 23,000 feet to attack a group of 110s and as they did so two Me 109s cut across in front. Clouston opened up. The first burst into flames and the second glided down 'in apparent distress'. Clouston, out of ammunition, took no further part as the other Spitfires went for the 110s.

Brinsden, leading Yellow section, tangled with an Me 109 after the attack on the 110s and then 'after watching the general action for some minutes, I joined up with a Hurricane in destroying a He 111 … after firing off all my rounds, I passed quite close to the E/A and noticed that his flaps and undercarriage were "out" and both his engines had stopped.' The Heinkel was on its way down to a forced landing.

Brinsden flew with 485 Squadron as one of its two flight commanders from March 1941 for four months and then, after promotion to squadron leader and ground jobs, was given command of 25 Squadron, flying Mosquitoes on night sweeps in support of

Bomber Command. On the night of 17–18 August 1943 when the bombers raided Peenemunde, the V-weapons research and testing station, Brinsden was blinded by searchlights after a low-level bombing pass over Sylt, off the coast of North Germany. The Mosquito touched the water and both props snapped off. Brinsden successfully ditched but he and his navigator were blown ashore in their dinghy next morning — into captivity. Postwar Brinsden remained in the RAF, retiring in 1966 as a wing commander.

Clouston, appropriately enough, had his best day on 15 September, now Battle of Britain Day. Just after midday he destroyed an Me 110 as the Big Wing attacked German bombers and fighters over London and flew again in the afternoon when the best Duxford could do was put up forty-nine aircraft, among five squadrons, according to Derek Palmer. The wing by now included the Poles of 302 Squadron and the Czechs of 310 Squadron. Palmer says 19 Squadron CO Brian Lane was asked to estimate in his combat report the number of the enemy. 'Whole Luftwaffe,' he wrote.

Clouston led Blue and Green sections into the attack on a formation of Do 17s, picking out his own target. He set his victim's starboard engine afire, then played cat and mouse in cloud gaps. He waited for the Dornier to emerge and made a savage beam attack, stitching hundreds of bullets into the German. 'About 10 feet of port wing fell off,' Clouston's combat report says. 'One of the crew then baled out over a convoy 15 miles east of Burnham-on-Crouch [Essex]. I continued to attack until aircraft went down towards the sea, rolling over and over to port.'

On 18 September the squadron patrolled over Hornchurch, above the clouds at 20,000 feet. No fighters about but AA flashes through the clouds indicated action and 19 Squadron dropped down to find Ju 88s and Heinkels with scattered Me 110 support. Clouston, leading the squadron on its third sortie of the day, bored in on an 88, guns winking as he fired almost all his ammunition. The German's starboard motor burst into flames and the crew baled out, the 88 crashing behind houses west of Deal.

In November 1940 Clouston was named commander of 258 Squadron, a World War I unit reforming with Hurricanes at Leconfield, Yorkshire. It soon became known unofficially as the New Zealand squadron, because more than a dozen of its pilots at the time were New Zealanders and painted fern leaves on their fighters. One of them was the CO's younger brother John, who began his training in New Zealand in mid-January 1940 and arrived in Liverpool, a sergeant, on the last day of September. He joined 258 Squadron in December 1940, clearly the work of his brother, and was commissioned the following May. When he was transferred to 403 (RCAF) Squadron four months later he had flown 146 ops with 258 Squadron, convoy patrols from the Isle of Man and cross-Channel sweeps from Kenley.

The brothers said their goodbyes, Wilf to take Command of 488 Squadron in Singapore and be captured by the Japanese, and John off to the Canadians. They were never to see each other again. By mid-1944 John was a squadron leader flying with 165 Squadron (Spitfire). He was shot down by flak on D-Day on his 330th op, then tragically killed two weeks later by strafing American fighters while a POW.

Three years later Allan and Vi Clouston learned precisely how their son had died. Their long search for answers led to an American who was able to tell them. Billy Cross, living in Coshocton, a small town in Ohio, told them he'd been a POW with Clouston and had learned that the New Zealander's petrol tank had been punctured by flak just

DAY AFTER DAY

off the Brest Peninsula on 6 June, forcing him to bale out. He'd been picked up by a German patrol boat and taken to Rennes by train, the train attacked on the way by Spitfires, which killed several POWs but left Clouston unharmed. Cross met Clouston in Rennes jail and journeyed with him by stages to Tours where they stayed for a week, the group growing larger as the Germans added other POWs. On the morning Clouston died the prisoners were put in a truck headed for Chartres. They were within four miles of the cathedral city when the vehicle broke down:

> Two of the guards were trying to fix it and we were all sitting wondering what was going to happen next when they let out a call of P-38s [American Lightnings]. The 15 of us in the back of the truck all tried to get out of the two exits, our first thought being the protection of the ditches at the side of the road. [Cross couldn't make it and dived under a seat near the cab.] After the third P-38 had made its pass … I jumped out and as I ran for cover I saw John lying in the road. I stopped to help him but it was too late. He had been killed instantly.

Two other POWs were killed and several wounded. John Clouston left a widow and two young daughters. He lies in Pont-du-Cens Communal Cemetery in Nantes.

Tom Fitzgerald and Jim Hayter, lucky to survive on the wretched Battles in France, remained with 103 Squadron for some time after getting back to England. Fitzgerald then volunteered for transfer to fighters, among a number of Bomber Command pilots who did the same when Fighter Command was desperately short of aircrew. He joined the mauled 141 Squadron (Defiant), now on night fighter duties, as a flight commander in early August, and took his flight south to help defend London on 13 September. The mix of day and night fighters at Biggin Hill didn't work and the flight was shuffled to nearby Gatwick, now a major London airport, but then just an aero club's short grass strip alongside Gatwick railway station, until the whole squadron reunited at Gravesend in November. Fitzgerald stayed with 141 Squadron until April 1941 and a posting to 23 Squadron's Havocs, to once again become a night fighter.

Years later Fitzgerald wrote about his first night at Biggin Hill and an unexpected visitor, none other than Sir Archibald Sinclair, Secretary of State for War, who questioned the New Zealander closely about the capabilities of the flight and said heavy raids were expected. 'He wished to know how many hours I had flown at night. To comfort him I trebled my total and the figure of 120 seemed acceptable. We were the first to engage in this form of London's defence and as I took off for the first solo interception of the gathering armada, I too was greatly impressed by the gravity of the situation.'

To aid night landings Gatwick had nothing more than six 'glim' lights, small, low intensity, battery-powered units invisible until the runway was lined up at about 500 feet. As well there was a lead-in light that Fitzgerald, with the 'connivance' of the railway station master, had personally strapped to a pole on a railway wagon carefully sited and parked as a fixture on a siding 300 yards from the first glim lamp. Came the night when a railway newcomer shunted the wagon to East Croydon, pole and all. Fitzgerald, flying home from a patrol couldn't see a trace of the lead-in light. Although he had by then learned to use the hooded railway signals on the Brighton to London line as a guide to Gatwick in the blacked-out countryside, he had a devil of a job getting down safely. Once parked he strode over to the station, spending the night there, making sure the missing wagon was shunted back again and parked.

Jim Hayter, Fitzgerald's friend and fellow Battle pilot in France, was another who volunteered for Fighter Command in the summer of 1940. He flew Hurricanes with 615 Squadron briefly, then 605 Squadron from Croydon. He damaged Me 109s on 15 and 26 October but on 26 October was hit by a 109 he didn't see and baled out. Hayter was to become expert at saving his nine lives with jumps, crashes and crash-landings — almost as good as Deere. He landed by chute on 26 October in the grounds of Great Swifts, Cranbook, Kent, the country home of Colonel Victor Cazalet, World War I soldier, godfather to Elizabeth Taylor and well-connected Conservative MP. He was also Polish wartime leader General Wladyslaw Sikorski's liaison officer and died with him in July 1943, when their Liberator crashed on takeoff from Gibraltar. In 1940, Hayter, not much the worse for wear, was quickly gathered up and given several stiff drinks at a cocktail party taking place at Great Swifts. Then he made a 'come-and-pick-me-up-darling' telephone call to his wife, living not far away.

Between December 1940 and August 1942, Hayter shot down four 109s and was awarded a DFC before a posting to the Middle East in March 1942. He was flying a Hurricane II on 1 December 1940 when he overtook a pair of 109s at 32,000 feet. 'I fired approximately 2 second burst from below and behind at about 50 yards. He pulled up and fell on his back [in flames] and dived vertically.' The German crashed near Canterbury.

Vic Verity was another New Zealander who flew in France, and Dunkirk, where he shot down an Me 110 on 31 May, the same day he baled out into the Channel to be picked up by a paddle steamer of the Little Ships. He shot down a Heinkel 111 and a Ju 88 in the Battle of Britain with 229 Squadron and later, flying 96 Squadron Defiant night fighters, he and his gunner downed a Heinkel and two Ju 88s in May 1941 plus two 88 probables, for which he was awarded the DFC and his gunner the DFM. He later served in the Middle East before returning to England. His end-of-war tally was eight.

Southlander Bob Yule was a good choice for that 1938 scholarship, as he proved throughout the war. He was not a high-scoring fighter pilot — his tally was three victories, five shared destroyed, a couple of probables and another which crashed on its return to base across the Channel. But he clearly had great leadership qualities and talents as a staff officer and was involved in planning fighter operations for the invasion. He was CO of 66 Squadron (Spitfire) by June 1942 and later led several wings. By war's end he was a wing commander with a DSO, DFC and bar. Flying with 145 on Hurricanes, he got his first German over Dunkirk, an Me 110 which crashed northeast of the town on 1 June. The second, a Ju 88, fell to his guns on 12 July over the Channel, finally crashed on reaching its base. His next, and last, was three and a half years later, on 7 January 1944, when he shot down an FW 190 while leading 15 Wing over France.

But Yule's combat reports and his high number of 'shareds' show he was very much a team player, not haring off in search of his own quarry but happy to work with other pilots around him to make sure of the enemy plane they were attacking. Such was the case on 1 July when his section chased a lone Dornier from 23,000 feet down to sea level in the Channel from Brighton to Beachy Head. Yule fired one burst into the bomber after his leader attacked and as the third Spitfire

DAY AFTER DAY

attacked 'the enemy aircraft blew up and fell into the sea'.

Yule, who remained in the RAF postwar, died on 11 September 1953, while leading a wing in rehearsal for a Battle of Britain Day flypast. During a sudden manoeuvre by several planes to avoid a Hurricane which had appeared in front of the wing, Yule's Meteor was hit by another jet, lost its tail and crashed.

At 6.15 p.m. on 30 August 1940 nine Ju 88s swept over Biggin Hill dropping bombs, part of the Luftwaffe's sustained late-summer assault on airfields in southeast England. Six raids had been mounted on Biggin Hill, 'the bump' as it was known to pilots, in the previous three days but the 30 August attack was the most devastating. Bombs scored a number of direct hits. One blast destroyed an air-raid shelter and a number of WAAFs huddled in a nearby slit trench died. In all thirty-nine personnel lost their lives.

Among the dead was Tasmanian-born Aircraftwoman 1st Class (Edna) Lena Button, 39, who had spent twelve years of her life in New Zealand before sailing to Britain. She arrived here in 1927 to work for the Methodist Church after studying at the church's Ladies' College in Launceston. When she left New Zealand in 1939 she was Deaconess at Auckland's Methodist Mission.

Button joined the WAAFs as a medical orderly after war broke out and was stationed at Biggin Hill when she was killed. *For Your Tomorrow* says that when the raid began she had taken all her patients from the sick bay to shelter and was following them in when a bomb fell nearby and caught her in its blast. She is buried at Orpington, Kent. In December 1942 the Sister Lena Memorial Ward at Dunedin's Children's Home (health camp) was dedicated to her memory.

In mid-September 1940, after six weeks in hospital and another six on sick leave after the loss of the carrier *Glorious* off Norway, Jamie Jameson became CO of 266 Squadron, now in 12 Group, at Wittering, Cambridgeshire. The squadron had suffered heavy losses in earlier stages of the battle in the southeast. Jameson wrote about it years later:

> Replacement pilots I was getting … came straight from the training system with usually only about five or six hours flying in Spitfires. They hardly knew how to fly the aircraft, let alone how to fight [with] it. When the squadron wasn't on patrol over the Thames Estuary we set about an intensive operational flying training programme. [266 became part of the Big Wing of which Jameson was no fan.] The enemy could see our large tightly packed unmanoeuvrable formation long before we spotted him with the result that before we reached the target area he had gone. The only time that we had any success during these operations was when we left the wing and operated as a squadron, as in fact the 11 Group fighters had been and still were doing so successfully under Keith Park.

Jameson made no claims during the battle but shot down three German aircraft in the April-May period of 1941, when 266 Squadron was playing a night-fighter role during the London Blitz. He became wing commander flying at Wittering in June 41, another step on his upward path.

BRIAN CARBURY — A WASTED TALENT

On 27 August 1940, Royal Auxiliary Air Force Squadron (RAuxAF) 603 Squadron (City of Edinburgh) flew from RAF Turnhouse, an airfield on the outskirts of Edinburgh, to Hornchurch, a sector station in Essex on the eastern edge of London, to join the scene of the real action. For weeks the pilots of 603 Squadron, stuck up north on convoy and other routine patrols, had itched to join the fight taking place in the southeast. Now at last they had been called into 11 Group and the front line. Among those flying south was the squadron's only New Zealander, Flying Officer Brian John George Carbury.

No one had an inkling that 22-year-old Carbury was to emerge as one of the top half-dozen scorers in the Battle of Britain, shooting down fifteen German planes, remarkably most of them Me 109s. He and Polish pilot Antoni Glowacki, later to fly with the RNZAF in New Zealand, were the only pilots credited with the destruction of five enemy planes in one day and Carbury was one of only a handful of men awarded a DFC and bar during the battle.

It was all so astonishing. Carbury, a shoe salesman from Auckland, became a Battle of Britain hero overnight. He damaged an Me 109 the day he arrived at Hornchurch, then went on a shooting spree that ended on 10 October when he scored a pair of 109s, one over the Channel, the other north of Hornchurch. His tally also included a couple of 'probables' that are not counted in his fifteen confirmed victories.

What he might have done had he continued in combat can only be conjecture but it's hard to believe he would not have been among the RAF's top scorers had he gone on. He didn't. 603 Squadron remained at Hornchurch until early December when it went to Rochford and then back to Scotland. A few more patrols up north, during which he damaged a Ju 88, then months of instructing; that was the end. Carbury never flew operationally again. On 21 October 1941 this notice appeared in *The London Gazette*:

Flg Off. B.J.G. Carbury, D.F.C. (40288), to be dismissed the Service by sentence of General Court-Martial. 1st Oct. 1941.

It was a sad ending for a wonderful flyer and combat pilot. Some mystery is attached to it all, but put simply it seems that Carbury was court-martialled for bouncing cheques, perhaps because of bills he could not pay, run up by an extravagant wife. Writing cheques for which there were no funds was an offence punishable by jail in those days and was certainly considered a serious breach of RAF law, particularly by an officer. Carbury and his wife eventually divorced and he remarried, happily, a second time.

New Zealand pilots of the calibre of Colin Gray, Alan Deere, Hawkeye Wells, Bill Crawford-Compton and Johnny Checketts had enormous publicity during and after the war and remain fixed in the public mind. Carbury, because he was so good, should be just as well known and it is unfortunate he's not. His New Zealand family has been reticent to talk about him, probably because of his court martial for what are now minor offences but were then considered serious. Perhaps as a result little has been written about him; a pity because he was one of New Zealand's wartime greats in the air. One might also wonder about RAF minds who trained him to kill but threw him out because of a non-violent, civil crime. Aviation writer David Ross in his history of 603, *The Greatest Squadron of Them All*', quotes a 603 Squadron ground crewman: 'We needed his experience after the Battle of Britain ... what a waste.'

Brian Carbury was born 27 February 1918 in Wellington. His Irish-born father Herbert (Paddy), a veterinarian, had migrated to New Zealand in 1913 and worked with horses during World War I at the Wallaceville Research Station. He later moved his family to Auckland

DAY AFTER DAY

where he pioneered the treatment of small animals. The Carburys sent their son to King's College for three years but the youngster went no further with his education. He took a job selling shoes with the Farmers Trading Company in Auckland but decided that wasn't for him and in June 1937 he sailed independently for England. Accepted for an SSC in the RAF, he began training in September that year. In July 1938, when he had his wings, Carbury was posted to 41 Squadron at Catterick, Yorkshire.

When he arrived 41 Squadron was still flying the Hawker Fury biplane, but in January 1939 converted to Spitfires. Because he'd had plenty of experience on Britain's best fighter as war started, Carbury was attached as a training officer to 603 Squadron, a temporary appointment which soon became permanent.

One of the thirteen auxiliary squadrons formed pre-war — in 603 Squadron's case as early as 1925 — from volunteer part-timers, their pilots flew mostly at weekends or in the evenings with annual 'camps'. They drew their members from various cities and counties, their numbers associated with those places. Thus 600 (City of London) Squadron, 602 (City of Glasgow) Squadron, 605 (County of Warwick) Squadron and so on. When war broke out they were mobilised at once and treated as any other RAF squadron.

On 16 October 1939, 603 Squadron had the honour of gunning down the first enemy plane over British territory in World War II; the squadron went into action mid-afternoon against Ju 88s attacking naval shipping in the Firth of Forth near the iconic Forth Bridge. A 603 Squadron section downed one of the bombers and fifteen minutes later 602 Squadron Spitfires, based at Drem, got another off Fife Ness, on the Firth's northern entrance. Four of the eight men aboard the two aircraft survived to be taken prisoner. After the war 603 Squadron learned another 88, badly damaged, crashed in Holland, killing the crew. Carbury was in the air that afternoon with his section, flying his personalised Spitfire *Aorangi*, but had no contact with the enemy.

Ross says the raid, first of the war on Britain, showed early signs of faulty German intelligence. '[The chief of Luftwaffe Intelligence] Beppo Schmid had told the raid leaders there were no Spitfires in Scotland, so it was a nasty shock that scouting He 111s had seen Spitfires earlier [that] day.' Ross adds the scrap 'was the first test of Fighter Command's systems ... they did expose some flaws but it was such experiences that honed the system that was so effective in the Battle of Britain.'

Ross also says the squadron learned lessons that day. Their firing and aim were poor and tactics outmoded. Pilots had to learn to compensate for the downward 'kick' of the guns when fired, as the recoil caused the nose of the aircraft to drop a few degrees. The lessons of 16 October were learned well and 603 Squadron was drilled hard in the months that followed. It was ready for the struggle in the southeast.

Carbury first saw swastikas just after midday on 7 December, as he bored in for an attack on an He 111. Three of the Germans ran into a section of Spitfires flying patrol from Montrose, midway between Dundee and Aberdeen, where there was a 603 Squadron detachment protecting the aerodrome's flying training programme. It was one-on-one as the three Spitfires picked out a target. Carbury damaged his 111: 'Carried out frontal attack. White smoke issuing from port engine enemy aircraft,' he wrote in his first combat report. He fired five bursts at a distant 400 yards, exhausting his ammunition. It was probably the last time he would open up so far away, but just the first of his many head-on attacks. Flying directly at an enemy was a dicey business; a

DAY AFTER DAY

pilot needed skill and aggression to be able to judge precisely when to break away and which way, and fly into enemy fire. Ross quotes an unnamed author who said of one of Carbury's head-on exploits: 'By some extraordinary manoeuvre, Carbury had put himself into a position to make a frontal attack ... such attacks were sometimes made in the Battle of Britain by very experienced pilots cool enough to fly through the concentrated fire of the enemy formation's front gunners. It needed fine judgment ...' On the same subject Ross also quotes Paddy Barthropp, a noted pilot in the battle and later: 'Bloody dangerous. There [were] one or two lunatics who revelled in it.' The practice became a common combat tactic later in the war.

In the bitter winter of 1939–40, with ice in cockpits, frigid winds and snow from the North Sea, 603 Squadron kept up its patrols and constant training, carrying on into spring and summer. Carbury shared in the destruction of an He 111 on 7 March 1940 and likewise a Ju 88 on 3 July, both off the Scottish coast. A flying officer since April, he led the section that attacked the 88 accompanied by Ron ('Raz/Ras') Berry and South African Gerald ('Stapme') Stapleton. Outstanding fighter pilots, both survived the war, Berry eventually reaching air commodore rank. Stapleton was the man who shot down Me 109 pilot Franz von Werra during the Battle of Britain. Werra is remembered as the only Luftwaffe member to escape back to Germany from a POW camp in Canada. His exploits were marked by the movie *The One That Got Away*.

Carbury, lanky at 6ft 4in and addicted to a long-stemmed pipe, was friendly and talked with everyone, regardless of rank, breaching the traditional divide between officer-sergeant pilots and ground crew. Ross quotes a sergeant pilot from 41 Squadron: 'Not like other officers, he used to chat freely with the sergeant pilots and airmen [ground crew]; there were a few others from overseas, who also disregarded the "class barrier" — a couple of Canadians and another New Zealander [John "Mac" Mackenzie].' Ross quotes others, including an officer in Turnhouse's ops room: 'A really terrific chap, so easy to get on with ... tall, slim, warm, charismatic, a genuine character, no airs and graces', and an NCO: 'Brian had no time for ... senseless class distinction and fraternised with the NCOs and other ranks, probably to the consternation of his seniors — it certainly surprised me.'

He was also at ease with intellectuals. On 7 July Richard Hillary of *The Last Enemy* fame arrived at 603 Squadron, accompanied by Peter Pease, his close friend from Oxford University. They met Carbury on their first evening with the squadron. 'He greeted us warmly and suggested an immediate adjournment to the mess for drinks,' Hillary wrote.

Carbury and other 603 Squadron pilots spent some of their leaves hunting and fishing from a lodge on the Dalhousie estate northeast of Dundee. The Earl, like many other landowners, was a generous host to aircrew. Carbury, a sharpshooter in the air, was just as good on the ground. Ross quotes a letter Carbury wrote home in early August 1940: 'Last week I got me a young stag, 24 rabbits and four trout. It is marvellous getting away up there away from it all and not having to worry about dress or anything.'

The squadron continued to fly patrols but they were now at full strength, well trained and impatient to go south to hunt the Luftwaffe. Finally they were called in to the action zone. When the news broke, Hillary remembered: 'Broody [Noel] Benson was hopping up and down like a madman, "Now we'll show the bastards! Jesus, will we show em." Stapme was capering about shaking everyone by the hands and Raspberry's [Berry's] moustache looked like it would fall off with the excitement ... "I've had just about enough of bulling about up here"!'

603 Squadron replaced the battle-shattered 65 Squadron and was to share Hornchurch with several squadrons including 54 Squadron (with Deere and Gray) for a few days before that squadron flew to Catterick for a rest. The station commander, the splendid Group Captain Cecil 'Daddy' Bouchier, met his new squadron on the tarmac. Three years later he wrote:

> the CO [George Denholm] ... meandered towards me with bent shoulders, hands in his pockets, followed by, what seemed to me then, to be the motleyest [sic] collection of unmilitary young men I had seen in a long time. I was not impressed. Good heavens (I suddenly remembered) it's an Auxiliary Squadron. Ah, I thought, that explains it. But what have I done to deserve it? How could they possibly cope with what they were up against ... How could they acquit themselves in the same manner as my long line of regular squadrons ... how wrong I was ... how I was made to eat my words.

Bouchier, who was to call 603 Squadron 'the greatest squadron of them all', said it was composed of a collection of quiet and serious young men from the city desks of Edinburgh and the fields of the Lothians. And, though he didn't say it, an ex shoe salesman from New Zealand.

The squadron made its bow the next day, taking off at 12.27 p.m. to patrol over Chatham, Carbury one of the twelve. They ran into Me 109s but the Germans scattered. The New Zealander flew again that afternoon, tangling with Me 109s over Hawkinge near Dover. His first Battle of Britain combat report says: 'Fired short burst at one Me 109; smoke emitted from front of cockpit and carried on at about

45 degrees in dive for France, so left him. Sighted another Me 109; gave a full deflection burst but lost him in cloud. Lost rest of squadron, so returned to base.' He claimed a probable but someone has circled the written comment: 'Operations Record Book says damaged' and that's how it's been recorded.

For the rest of the squadron the afternoon was disastrous — three Spitfires down, three pilots dead. One of them, says Ross, 'was an only child. His mother never recovered from his loss and took her own life.' Another was 21-year-old Benson, whose flaming fighter crashed in a Kent field.

This also was the afternoon when Al Deere was forced to bale out, hit by fire from behind by another Spitfire. Deere was chasing 109s in line ahead, trying to close to firing range when friendly fire cut his rudder control cables and seriously damaged the port elevator. Deere clearly saw the RAF roundels on his attacker as it banked steeply to come in behind. The offending Spitfire was never identified but Stephen Bungay in *The Most Dangerous Enemy* says it's possible that newcomers 603 Squadron were responsible.

Carbury now began to line up Germans and shoot them down as if he were born to it, his superb flying and shooting at close quarters too much for most of his opponents. Ross quotes a ground crewman in 603 Squadron: 'The "Carbury Trick" was the expression we gave to his tactic of getting in very close to the enemy before firing. He didn't mess around with firing from a distance.'

Never shot down and only once suffering damage, he wasted no time in starting his tally. He took his first victim, a 109, over Manston at 27,000 feet in the early evening of 29 August, attacking from the front with slight deflection — especially difficult with the small target presented by a fast-moving fighter. 'A long burst and the e/a smoked

DAY AFTER DAY

and then blew up.' He took another the next day north of Canterbury when he mixed it with three 109s. This time Carbury closed in to fifty yards on one of them and fired for two seconds. 'I got a good burst in and the propeller of the rear enemy aircraft stopped, started and finally stopped, with white vapour coming out behind. [It] went into a glide for the east coast. I veered off as other enemy aircraft were closing in on me.'

Carbury's tactic of getting away fast and not staying to fight if he was outnumbered or in a difficult situation preserved his life. 'You don't have to look for them,' Carbury told Hillary. 'You have to look for a way out.'

Ross quotes him as once saying, '… it was a matter of fighting your way out and knowing when to break off — "He who turns and flies away, lives to fight another day." It was often a case of flying full tilt through the formations and shooting at anything in range.'

Hillary got his first victory when he was flying No. 2 with Carbury. The New Zealander attacked an Me 109, then broke away, presenting Hillary with a perfect target. When Hillary was shot into the Channel in flames, burned beyond recognition, he had five German planes to his credit. On that last flight he was so busy chasing an aircraft he had damaged he didn't see the fighter that got him. A cardinal error.

It seemed as if Carbury couldn't miss and his tally mounted swiftly. On 31 August, at the height of the battle, he achieved his jaw-dropping five. The squadron was flying three and four times a day. Raz Berry told Ross years later:

Half a dozen pilots would sleep at dispersal in readiness for surprise dawn attacks. This entailed being up at 4.30 a.m. with the Spits warmed up by 5 a.m. The first sortie was usually about brekky time, the last

162

about 8 p.m. We had eggs, bacon and beans for breakfast which was sent over from the mess. Other times we ate whenever we could. Some didn't even live to enjoy brekky.

Carbury scored his five victims on three successive flights. First a 109 at 9 a.m. — '... the Me 109 turned over and spun in, the pilot jumped out'. Victims two and three were He 111s at 1.40 p.m. The first 'went straight down ... and crashed into the ground', the second 'went on his back, pilot jumped out ... and e/a crashed and burst into flames in a vacant bit west of Southend'. Finally he gunned down a brace of 109s north of Southend. '... the first went straight down and burst into flames'. Carbury attacked the second and hit the glycol tank. '... he rolled over and went straight down hitting a wood'.

Carbury also had a narrow escape that day. 'An Me 109 got on my tail, received one cannon shell and the air system punctured so came home.'

Bungay says of Carbury's brilliant achievement: 'Brian Carbury claimed no less than five, which, coming from most pilots, would have been dismissed as exuberance. However, it was already clear that Carbury was a man to take seriously, and, unlikely as the total might be, all were confirmed.'

During the Battle of Britain many pilots hardly fired their guns, let alone destroyed an enemy plane. Carbury took seven in his first four days of combat. His other eight and two probables were spread over the period 1 September to 14 October. Most of those victims got the Carbury treatment — heavy concentrated fire at close quarters, some in frontal attacks. One day he closed to within 10 yards of his victim.

As the Battle of Britain waned in October the pace grew less frenetic and combats fewer, and in December the tired squadron flew back to

Scotland. Before they went, the station padre shouted the squadron a fancy dinner at the Dorchester in Park Lane where they celebrated the 100 German aircraft they had claimed and toasted in remembrance the thirteen 603 Squadron pilots killed in the battle.

Carbury was gazetted with the DFC on 24 September, the citation noting his five in one day. His bar on 25 October applauded his 'outstanding gallantry and skill' and 'cool courage'.

His combat reports, no words wasted, are fascinating documents. Take his report on the double victory, his last, on 10 October over the channel:

I was leading Green section when E/A (Me 109s) were sighted heading for France. Squadron went into line astern and I remained at 33,000 feet, saw two Me 109s and sent a burst into the last one. He went on his back and dived straight into the Channel. I sighted another E/A trying to climb over me, so I climbed after him to 31,000 feet. He rolled on his back and I gave him a burst. The E/A went down vertical, so I followed, but he crashed on the beach at Dunkirk. One wing flew off and the rest shot along the beach. No parachutes were seen, and I returned to base to refuel and re-arm. [One aircraft he didn't claim was a 109 that exploded as he neared it.] ... I followed one down at approximately 25,000 feet. Suddenly he blew up in front of me and I saw no other aircraft near enough to cause the explosion. I was still out of range and had not fired a shot when this occurred. I circled about and had to come lower as the oxygen was running out.

Carbury never visited New Zealand postwar, remaining in England, where he died on 31 July 1961, aged 42, of bone marrow cancer. He was survived by his second wife and one son, also called Brian.

BILL HODGSON — MY LITTLE HEART WENT PITTER-PAT

Fate was particularly unkind to the twelve young men who sailed from Wellington on 25 February 1940, bursting with pride and enthusiasm, having been chosen for SSCs in the RAF and trained in New Zealand. They were a talented bunch, carefully selected from many applicants. Five were dead within seven months, another five were killed by September 1942 and just two survived the war, both in bleak prisoner of war camps. Many drafts suffered high casualty rates, but that of February 1940 paid an astonishing price.

Of the ten dead, no fewer than six died in aircraft accidents and of the four killed on operations two died in crashes near their bases. Only two lost their lives facing the enemy, both skilled and experienced bomber pilots. Charles Miller, 24 (Blenheim), was on his 20th op when he and his entire 97 Squadron Lancaster crew perished the night of 11–12 July 1942, raiding U-boat yards at Danzig, Poland, victims of flak.

Two months later Peter Robinson and his 158 Squadron Halifax was lost over the North Sea. His body washed ashore in Belgium and was buried in Ostend. Robinson, 22 (Hawera), was already a squadron leader on his second tour, and both men had won DFCs.

John Bickerdike (21), Bill Hodgson (20), and Eric Orgias (25) flew in the Battle of Britain. Hodgson was the only one of them alive when it ended but was killed in an aircraft accident the following February. Bickerdike and Hodgson went to the same Flying Practice Unit (FPU) on arrival in England then to the same OTU to convert to Hurricanes. Both were posted to 85 Squadron at Debden in inland Essex, south of Cambridge, arriving there the same day, 25 May. They were among replenishment pilots for 85 Squadron, back two days earlier from a mauling in France. Both men worked on radio stations before enlisting,

Bickerdike as an announcer on 3ZB, Christchurch, and Hodgson as a technician at 4YA, Dunedin.

Throughout June the squadron, led by the urbane and charming Peter Townsend, best known for his postwar romance with Princess Margaret, trained its new men hard for the coming conflict. Every day, sometimes four times, they were in the air practising — formation flying, attacks, air firing, flight formation, air combat, section reconnaissance, aerobatics, R/T work — all honing their flying. They were lucky to get this essential exposure.

On 7 June Hodgson flew his opening operational sortie, first a patrol up the Essex-Norfolk coast to Lowestoft and back, followed by a dusk patrol. These routine patrols, plus cover for convoys, continued through June, July and into August, as the squadron languished in 12 Group, back from the front-line action and bored with non-combat flying. Bickerdike, like Hodgson, did the patrols, tasting brief success before his death. On 12 July, he was in a section of three that tangled with Germans attempting to bomb a convoy. In his first action, Bickerdike blasted a Heinkel 111 and watched it plunge into the sea. Ten days later he was killed. Returning from an op, he spun off a half roll at 2000 feet while approaching Debden and crashed.

The war changed for 85 Squadron on 18 August, a day of tough battle against hordes of Luftwaffe aircraft described as 'the hardest day' by Alfred Price, in his book of the same name. The squadron was ordered in to attack large formations of German fighters and bombers, and free-for-alls swirled around the sky. For the first time an excited Hodgson began writing exuberantly in his logbook.

Battle over Channel. Sqn attacked one mob of 200 Huns, one mob of 110 and one of 150 Huns. Destroyed one Me 109, damaged one Dornier

17, damaged one Me 109. Nigger [Plt Off James Marshall] had wing tip taken off but got back. CO [Townsend] gets bar to DFC. F/Lt [Richard] Lee DSO, DFC (Dickie to the boys) missing. [He is commemorated on the Runnymede Memorial, his body never found.] Ruddy huns won't stay and scrap. Chased home out of ammo by 30 Me 110s. My little heart went pitter-pat.

The next morning the squadron flew to Croydon, their base until they withdrew, exhausted, on 3 September. Several days of bad weather when the Germans more or less stayed home gave Fighter Command and 85 Squadron a breather, though on the night of 24 August the airfield was bombed and two Hurricanes destroyed. The struggle soon resumed and in his second patrol on the 26th Squadron Hodgson and other pilots combined to down three Dornier 215s while he damaged another and an Me 109. 'Squadron bagged six.' Of the scrap on the south coast, Hodgson again wrote of the Germans' apparent reluctance to mix it. 'They wouldn't stay and fight. They had fingers well up. Their fighters would not come down but stayed up and watched bombers shot to hell … chased main formation to France and had to beat it home with 109s after my blood.' That flight lasted an hour and thirty-five minutes. Up again for another hour-long patrol the squadron ran into fifty bombers and 100 fighters. 'Bagged one Do 17 (with Red section).'

His next patrol, lasting just thirty minutes, ended with an astonishing 'capture', of a Gotha Go 145, a small German trainer-communications aircraft with a top speed of 180 mph. Hodgson and his flight commander spotted the twin-engined job meandering along on the south coast and gave chase. The Gotha, no match for two menacing Hurricanes, was forced down on Lewes racecourse, near Brighton,

DAY AFTER DAY

without a shot fired. The German pilot had lost his way while heading for Germany with his Bordeaux fighter wing's mail. Ouch. As one aviation historian later commented: 'Tootling around over southern England in the middle of Battle of Britain action in one of those. Scary!' And did the Hurricane pilots shout out in triumph, 'Gotcha Gotha!?'

It was a satisfying day for Hodgson. He was in the air no fewer than five times, landing from his final flight at 8.15 p.m., having flown a total of four hours ten minutes.

Some sources suggest Hodgson didn't fly on 29 August but his log shows otherwise and he makes a claim for another Me 109. But the reality of the life and death encounters and the terrible toll exacted by the battle shows in one log entry that day: 'A bunch of Me 109s came out of the sun and shot the flight commander down; (my mate "Ham"). [Flt Lt Harry Hamilton, 23, a Canadian] He was killed. Chased them to France but could not catch them. Took pot shots at one or two.'

If you were a half-decent pilot, and Hodgson was more than that by now, you couldn't miss scoring. The skies over southeast England were filled with flocks of Jerries. On 30 August: 'Big scrap over Maidstone. Shot down 3 Me 110s, came back, refuelled and rearmed and was in the air again within three minutes. Nigger bailed out. Damaged one He 111.'

The next morning started badly. Townsend's Hurricane was hit and he baled out. He lost a big toe and was off the scene for several weeks. Scrambling again and patrolling the Thames Estuary on their third sortie of the day, Hodgson was shot down for the first, and only, time. His log:

Damaged one Do 215, bagged one Me 109. Was shot down with engine on fire. Three Me 109s followed me down trying to finish me off but S/L Leathart, a Spitfire boy of 54 Sqn, kept them off. I managed to land without baling out at Wickford [Essex]. A major of the 2nd Glasgow Highlanders got me tanked. Boy they treated me well. Hank's machine [was the one] I lost. He is still mourning over it. [Hodgson elaborated in his combat report.] ... I did a head on attack on a Do 215. I saw pieces fall off the nose and starboard wing but could not see whether he went down or not ... I then attacked a He 111 but owing to an Me 109 being on my tail I broke away and engaged it. I out-turned him and got on his tail and gave him a long burst. I saw him stagger and I then noticed five 109s diving onto my tail so I gave another short burst at 200 yards. White and black smoke burst from it and he rolled over and went down with smoke billowing from the engine. I immediately pulled around steeply to engage the two 109s on my tail but unfortunately there was a 109 under my tail that I could not see and he hit me at close range with an explosive cannon shell which blew up my oil lines and glycol tank. This was over the oil tanks at Thameshaven so I presume my Me 109 down in approximately the same spot.

At 20,000 feet, his engine stopped. Hodgson glided away from the enemy, unstrapped and prepared to bale out. But because he was over the oil tanks and a built up area he changed his mind and stayed with the fighter, keeping the flames away from the fuselage by side slipping. The fire eventually died down, though white glycol and black smoke still streamed into the cockpit while a thick jet of oil spurted from the engine.

James 'Prof' Leathart, 54 Squadron's CO, had won an immediate

DAY AFTER DAY

DSO for the daring rescue of 74 Squadron's CO Frank White in Calais at the time of Dunkirk. Now, barely three months later, Leathart spotted vulture 109s near Hodgson. He nosed down, flying protective circles around Hodgson, defying the German fighters to have a go until Hodgson made a successful wheels-up landing. The Germans flew away.

The New Zealander came down in a field at Shotgate, a village a mile from Wickford. He was proud the fighter was still in fair condition, flyable again after repairs. 'The tail, fuselage and main planes [wings] are OK. Guns, instruments are also OK. I have approx. 100 rounds of ammunition left in each gun, 15 gallons fuel in the each of the wing tanks and 25 gallons in the centre tank.'

A nearby unit of the Glasgow Highlanders posted a guard on the machine to deter souvenir hunters while Hodgson drank the usual cup of tea offered by a villager who'd watched the combat. Then he went off with the major for a stiff one, or two.

Hodgson doesn't say so, but it's a fair assumption he drove to Hornchurch, where 54 Squadron was based, to thank Leathart personally for looking after him over Essex, for the next day his log records he flew back to Croydon from Hornchurch in a Magister.

He did not fly operationally on 1 September but his log reports a bad day for the squadron pilots who did:

F/O Woods-Scawen went west; Sgt Ellis went west; P/O Gowers baled out, in hospital burnt; P/O Worall baled out, in hospital full of shrapnel; Sgt Booth in hospital, baled out, chute caught alight, broken collarbone, leg and arm; Sgt Goodman landed with tail badly shot up; P/O Lewis crashed on aerodrome.

The result depressed everybody — four Hurricanes lost, two pilots dead, two in hospital — though some records say the squadron claimed six enemy aircraft in return. The death of Patrick (Paddy) Woods-Scawen, 24, was a particular blow. Hugely popular, he was irreverently and widely known as 'Rabbit' because that is exactly what he looked like. His big circle of family and friends, numbed by his loss, were shocked anew the next day when his brother Tony, 22, flying with 43 Squadron, was also killed. Both died when they baled out too low for their parachutes to open. They were in love with the same girl and she accompanied their widowed father to Buckingham Palace when he received their DFCs from the King.

The spirits of the gloomy squadron, now short of experienced pilots, were heartened on 2 September when Sammy Allard, a veteran of the French campaign, was awarded a DFC and a bar to his earlier DFM. Tattered and weary, 85 Squadron was taken out of the line on 4 September and flew north for rest and regrouping.

Hodgson learned on 20 September he had won the DFC, the citation praising his performance and bravery in the ongoing battle and noting that staying with his Hurricane the afternoon he force-landed had undoubtedly saved civilian lives. He would have been pleased but commented offhandedly in his log, 'Got DFC slung at me.' Hodgson certainly celebrated when he went up to London to receive his decoration from the King at Buckingham Palace on 25 February 1941.

He must have invited New Zealander Rosemary Ross serving in the WAAFs to attend the investiture, as Assistant Section Officer Ross wrote home in a letter:

I got off duty at 3 p.m. [on 24 February], rushed up to town, checked in [to the Strand Palace in Piccadilly, a favourite hotel for Commonwealth airmen] and dashed off to get my hair done. Got back fairly late and very weary so decided to do without food and go to bed early; just got there when the phone rang — Bill — 'see you downstairs in half an hour.' Instantly felt unweary of course. When I met him he had just discovered two other NZers — Aubrey Breckon (plus wife) and Duncan McArthur. They were such nice folk and we all stuck together that night and next day. We found we were all staying at the Strand.

Rosemary Ross was the granddaughter of Scots-born John Ross, joint founder in 1860 of Dunedin-based company Ross and Glendining. By the end of World War II the company was the largest manufacturer of clothing, footwear and woollen goods in New Zealand, with 2500 employees. Miss Ross was in Britain when war broke out and joined the WAAF, where she worked in intelligence.

Both the other men were also getting the DFC, as was 'Mac' Mackenzie, a Battle of Britain survivor and, like Hodgson and McArthur, SSC pilots. Breckon had joined the RAF in 1935 and became a Group Captain in the RNZAF postwar. McArthur had flown tours with 75 Squadron and was killed over Tripoli in May 1942, piloting a Liberator. He lies in an unmarked grave and is remembered on the Alamein Memorial.

The investiture went swimmingly, though Ross said that when the orchestra played a few bars of what everyone thought was the start of *God Save the King* the guests stood up awaiting the King's entrance. 'However, as it then broke into the *British Grenadiers* we all sat down again. After a bit, he did come in and we did stand up and the orchestra did play *God Save the King.*' At one stage the King dropped the medal he was about to pin on someone. The recipient picked it up and pinned it on himself.

New Zealand High Commissioner Bill Jordan, popular with New Zealand aircrew, also attended and after the ceremony drove them all away in his official car. Ross: 'We sailed merrily along with the NZ flag flying from our radiator. After photographs and a lot of fuss being made of us, Mr and Mrs Jordan took us all to lunch at the NZ Services Club where we had a very happy NZ time.'

They then all went to a pilots' club in Piccadilly and later to a night club. At least some of them did. Mackenzie wrote years later he couldn't remember if Hodgson was with them at that stage. 'My memory of later events that day is hazy.'

Just over two weeks later, Hodgson was dead. At the end of the Battle of Britain 85 Squadron was designated as a night-fighter squadron, flew Hurricanes without success (except for one German Townsend shot down) and marked time waiting for the new American-built Havocs to arrive. In January 1941, after shuttling around several airfields, 85 Squadron was back at Debden. Hodgson had flown a few quiet patrols from Gravesend in the December and on one chased an Me 109 over the Channel, claiming it as a possible: 'Hunted unofficially down over Dungeness, saw Me 109, gave chase down to sea level, saw top of rudder and fin shot off and then lost him in fog.' Townsend, who called Hodgson 'Ace', wrote below that entry: 'Good effort. I don't suppose he got back to Deutschland.'

Hodgson had been grounded in December, declared unfit to fly operationally, his eyes damaged by glycol, probably from the action above Thameshaven. On 16 December, after a night flying exercise, he wrote: 'Eyes packed up and had to come down.' For the next month or so he did mainly short local flying.

On 13 March he took off in a Havoc from Debden with good friend Allard at the controls, he and fellow 85 Squadron pilot Frank Walker-

Smith as passengers. Hodgson is said to have been hitching a ride to a nearby airfield to visit a WAAF he'd met there; the others were to go on to another field to pick up a Havoc that Walker-Smith would fly back to Debden. The aircraft lifted off at 4.20 p.m. but almost immediately a top gun panel flew off and jammed against the base of the tail fin. Uncontrollable, the Havoc pitched up, climbed, stalled, spun and crashed two miles from the airfield. The three men perished in the resulting explosion and fierce fire.

They were buried side by side in Saffron Walden Cemetery. The RAF Cranwell Band headed the procession from the airfield to the cemetery. Townsend and the entire squadron saluted their dead comrades as their coffins were lowered into the ground. Hodgson Way, a street in Wickford, is named after him. He is credited with five victories, two shared destroyed and one probable.

The two survivors of Hodgson's draft were, ironically, bomber pilots whose chances of living, especially as early starters in the war, were extremely slim. Bert Newman, who came from Ashburton, skippered a 75 Squadron Wellington, four of whose crew were New Zealanders, shot down the night of 29–30 December 1940, raiding the railway yards at Hamm on the northern edge of the Ruhr Valley. The crew of six were taken prisoner to face long years in German camps. Newman returned to England in May 1945 and a few months later married the widow of another bomber pilot. He remained in England and in 1996 he died in Norwich.

Southland-born Clive Saxelby came out of POW camp to fashion a brilliant postwar career in the RAF. Like Newman he flew with 75 Squadron, completing his tour and winning the DFC, the citation noting his exceptional feat of twice bringing home badly damaged

Wellingtons from raids on Germany. Flying his second tour with 103 Squadron and now a squadron leader, Saxelby's Halifax was shot down the night of 6–7 September 1942, while raiding Duisberg. He was not quite twenty-one. Taken prisoner, he was held at Stalag Luft III, Sagan, where in the spring of 1944 he took part in the Great Escape. He was 82nd in the break-out order, close to the ladder that took the escapers from the tunnel to the surface when shooting broke out. He crawled back and survived.

Within a few weeks of returning to England in 1945 he was flying again and then commanded 617 Squadron, the Dambusters. He qualified as a jet test pilot in 1948 and was given charge of the testing of the Victor, the second of Britain's nuclear V-Force bombers. Later, as a staff officer, he played a major role in the controversial mid-sixties restructuring of the RAF. He retired in 1969 as Group Captain C K Saxelby, CBE, DFC, AFC and bar. He died in 1999.

The deaths of Cecil Hight and Terence Lovell-Gregg

Cecil Hight's death in a 234 Squadron Spitfire late in the afternoon of 15 August 1940 is baffling. One minute the young pilot from Taranaki was flying with a section of three, attached to the rest of the 234 Squadron, the next he wasn't. Neither were the other two. Fellow pilot and Englishman Bob Doe looked back and couldn't see the three fighters. They vanished near the Isle of Wight as the squadron turned to battle enemy aircraft, probably bounced and knocked out of the squadron ranks. Hight was likely mortally wounded in the attack. It's known the pilots of the other two survived, as prisoners. One baled out into the Channel to be picked up by the Germans. The other landed his Spitfire at Cherbourg in France in puzzling circumstances. But Hight? All that's certain is that his damaged fighter appeared over the south coast city of Bournemouth. People below heard it, saw him get out of the cockpit at about 5000 feet, then watched appalled as his parachute didn't open. The Spitfire nosed over and plunged down about a mile from the town's business centre at an intersection on the edge of a golf course. Hight's death occurred on 234 Squadron's first patrol after it was called into the front line the previous day, flying into Middle Wallop, Hampshire, from St Eval in Cornwall at the height of the Battle of Britain

Sirens blared as German bombers crossed the town, apparently followed by Spitfires. Everyone could hear machine-gun fire and then they saw Hight's fighter. Witnesses said the plane stalled, reared up and then went down. 'I was cycling close to where the plane crashed when I heard the rat-tat of machine guns almost over my head,' one man said. 'Looking up I saw the plane nose diving to earth.' Another: 'I saw this body come out and I can remember jumping up and down shouting, "He's out!".' And a woman: 'We expected to see a parachute open but there wasn't one and we were stunned when we realised the pilot was dead.'

Police, ambulance staff and air-raid wardens poured into the area looking for Hight's body. It was found quite quickly, in the kitchen-garden behind a two-storey dwelling close to the spot the Spitfire crashed. Local reports at the time said the New Zealander had suffered grievous wounds and had probably not opened his chute because he was unconscious. Somehow he got out of his cockpit in a last despairing effort.

Hight, born in September 1917 on a farm near Stratford, attended the town's technical high school. Mad keen on flying, he had aero club lessons and soloed before he was 20. After working his passage to England he was chosen for an SSC. He finished his training at Little Rissington, Gloucestershire, received his wings just days before war broke out and on 6 November 1939 was posted to 234 Squadron.

Also ordered to 234 Squadron the same day were two other New Zealanders, Keith Lawrence and Pat Horton. They'd trained together after arriving in England on 15 March in a draft of eighteen that included Jim Wilkie (killed in Norway), Bob Trousdale and Vic Verity. Lawrence was working in a bank in Invercargill and Horton with the Mines Department in Wellington when they were accepted for SSCs.

234 Squadron had a short life in World War I and didn't have happy beginnings in World War II. Reformed at Leconfield, Yorkshire, on 30 October 1939, its first squadron leader was injured in a car crash before he could take up the job; the second was a no-hoper who was eventually sacked. One flight commander was distant and suffered from asthma.

The real leader was the other flight commander, Australian Pat Hughes, who was to become a top scorer in the Battle of Britain before his death in combat. The gentle, diffident, self-confessed slow learner Bob Doe, who was to become famous and another high scorer, said Hughes taught him everything he knew in the air. John Willis in *Churchill's Few* quotes Doe: 'We respected him, listened to him … he was one of the lads as well. He was the real power behind the squadron.'

Leconfield was a bomber base and it seemed 234 Squadron might become a bomber unit. Some pilots posted to the squadron had trained on twin-engined Ansons and imagined they'd be flying multi-engined planes in action. Someone finally decided, however, it would be a fighter squadron and in March 1940 Spitfires were delivered. The Dragons, as 234 Squadron called themselves, after the dragon on the squadron crest, moved to Church Fenton, also in Yorkshire, then in mid-June on to St Eval, one of a cluster of RAF stations on Cornwall's southwest coast. Until the move to Middle Wallop the squadron played a fringe role, its task looking for enemy shipping in the Channel and flying patrols over British convoys.

On 8 July southwest of Lands End, Hughes, Lawrence and a sergeant pilot shared 234 Squadron's first victory, claiming a Ju 88 that had been nibbling at a convoy. Lawrence bored in close, loosing off all his ammunition in six bursts as the others attacked. Four days later Lawrence and a second pilot chased another 88, which had the temerity to drop a stick of bombs on St Eval and got off bursts before their intended victim escaped into low clouds. Horton chimed in on the 28th as he, Hughes and a third pilot jointly hacked down another 88 five miles south of Plymouth. Horton followed the enemy aircraft from 4000 feet down to sea level 'firing short bursts at 200–250 yds all the way. When my ammunition was exhausted I broke away to allow Blue 2 to attack ...' The German crew tried hard to shake off their tormentors, return fire coming from the front and rear of the 88. Horton kept up dummy attacks, attempting to turn if off course or force it lower. Eventually 'the starboard engine caught fire and the E/A turned to starboard and struck the water, sinking in 10 seconds. I consider it unlikely that any crew escaped,' he said in his combat report.

Hight flew his full share of ops and is credited with more than seventy, although no combat reports from him have been found and no letters home survive.

When Fighter Command ordered it in to Middle Wallop, 234

Squadron was still without a new CO. The Dragons flew into their new base on 14 August and were in action next day — the day the Germans called Black Thursday and what Stephen Bungay calls the Greatest Day in his absorbing study of the Battle of Britain, *The Most Dangerous Enemy*. A series of raids and five major actions developed throughout the day. At about 5 p.m. 234 Squadron, with Hec McGregor's 213 Squadron and 87 Squadron, both at Exeter, were scrambled to intercept forty-seven Stukas escorted by about sixty 109s and forty 110s heading for RAF Warmwell in Dorset.

RAF attacks diverted the Germans from Warmwell to their secondary target, the naval base at Portland, and fighting swirled over a wide area. The Luftwaffe suffered grievous losses as the RAF smashed into them — 234 Squadron apparently first to meet the enemy. Despite the loss of Hight and his section the squadron performed well. Doe, who had been certain he was going to die when he took off that afternoon, landed back at Middle Wallop with two 110s to his credit. Hughes downed another two and at least two more fell to the squadron guns. Doe was a good shot in the air, and remembered shooting the heads off of flowers in his back yard as a child. Perhaps that was when he first learned the art?

Bungay totals German losses for the day at seventy-five, against the RAF's thirty-four aircraft and eighteen pilots dead or missing. Among the casualties were Hight and fellow New Zealander, Terry Lovell-Gregg.

'Shovel' Gregg was born in Wanganui in 1912, and was a top scholar at Nelson College. He learned to fly in New Zealand and paid his own way to England in October 1930 to join the RAF. Said to be a brilliant pilot, he served in Iraq, flew float-planes and then spent several years

DAY AFTER DAY

as an instructor before five months in early 1940 on operations room duties. Baptised with Lovell as his second given name, at some stage he added a hyphen to his name and became Lovell-Gregg. He grew a wonderful thick, dark moustache and was chafing for action when he was posted in mid-June to 87 Squadron and made CO less than a month later, taking over from Johnny Dewar, who became station commander at Exeter. But expert flyers don't necessarily make fighter leaders or even good fighter pilots, especially on debut. The majority of 87 Squadron's pilots had been battle-tested in France while Lovell-Gregg had never flown operationally. He was apparently aware of his shortcomings and *A Clasp for 'The Few'* says he allowed the more experienced pilots to lead the squadron until he felt ready to do it himself. On 15 August Lovell-Gregg led the squadron into the German hordes, Roland Beamont in *My Part of the Sky* noting the squadron was not in good shape, having just lost both flight commanders in action (Hughes on 7 September).

New Zealander Derek Ward, who had flown in the Battle of France, filled in one gap, promoted to lead A Flight, Beamont writing: '... to everyone's satisfaction'. He said 87 Squadron saw the Germans over Lyme Regis at 12,000 feet, and described them as a 'gigantic swarm of bees all revolving around each other in a fantastic spiral from about 8000 feet up to 14,000 feet'. As the distance closed and the little group of Hurricanes approached, 'Shovel called "tally-ho" over the R/T ... and the next minute Shovel wagged his wings and we were diving ... the air was thick with aircraft, dark grey 87s, dark green 110s with sky-blue bellies, pale green and silver 109s; a black swastika'd horde.'

Beamont used up all his ammunition in the frantic struggle, claiming one destroyed and a probable. 'Our attack apparently upset the whole organization for it was no longer a well-ordered armada filling the sky with tier upon tier but a confused dogfight stretching from Portland to Dorchester, Warmwell to Lyme Regis.' When he landed back at Exeter 'the CO was missing and then came a message that he'd died trying to force land at Warmwell'.

Lovell-Gregg must have been still alive as he tried to reach Warmwell, but probably fatally wounded because, according to witnesses, his flaming Hurricane changed direction a couple of times before flying low over a field and plunging to the ground among trees. He was thrown clear but was dead when found, clothes smouldering.

That day 87 Squadron scored well in the battle over Portland, Ward among them. Ten miles south of Portland, at 5.45 p.m. he bagged an Me 110:

I had several short bursts and then got three effective full-deflections shots into a 110. He climbed sharply with black smoke apparently streaming from his fuselage. He rolled on his back and dived vertically down ... I didn't have time to watch him as I was attacked by Me 110s from behind.

Ward was awarded the DFC in mid-October.

Altogether 234 Squadron claimed seven German aircraft for the loss of three of their own, 213 Squadron nineteen and 87 Squadron thirteen. Even allowing for over-claiming it had been an enormously successful action and 87 Squadron was on a high on its return to Exeter, despite their CO's death. Lovell-Gregg was the only pilot killed, the others missing reported safe, one in hospital. Beamont wrote: 'All these stirring events gave just cause and vast thirst for, as the boys put it, a ginormous party at the "Rougers" that evening.' It was how

DAY AFTER DAY

fighter pilots reacted and celebrated — and how they blanked out the continuing deaths. Entirely normal.

A couple of days later Ian Gleed was promoted from within the squadron to take over command and he, Ward and fellow New Zealander Ken Tait donned best blues and flew their Hurricanes to Warmwell. 'It only took 15 minutes. England was looking her best in the hot August sun,' Gleed wrote in his slim little 1942 volume *Arise to Conquer*. At Warmwell Gleed was given a small white bag containing the contents of Lovell-Gregg's pockets — slightly burnt letters, a wallet with several pounds in it, a bunch of keys and a car key on a half-burnt rubber holder. Then they joined the RAF funeral cortege for the short journey to the cemetery — two lorries, one carrying the flag-draped coffin, the other with the pilots, the casket-bearers, an RAF firing party, a bugler, a padre. Each of the pilots carried a wreath, one from the squadron, one from the station and a third from RAF Warmwell. They buried Lovell-Gregg in the churchyard cemetery of Holy Trinity, Warmwell, under the shade of tall trees. Gleed wrote, 'You would love your graveyard if you could see it; it is very peaceful. Perhaps you can see it. I wonder if you are smiling at us now.' A brass plate on the coffin carried Lovell-Gregg's name. The padre read the burial service, a volley of shots cracked out and the pilots threw dirt into the grave. The Last Post sounded. 'I walked round to the head of the grave and saluted. "Au revoir, Shovel"; you leave behind happy memories.'

Cecil Henry Hight was buried the same day at Bournemouth East Cemetery, the service conducted by Canon Hedley Burrows, vicar of St Peter's. It was a similar ceremony to the one at Warmwell with fellow officers on hand. But there was a large gathering, and flowers sent in tribute by local people. Hight has a Bournemouth street named after him and flowers are still laid on his grave to honour the only Allied flyer killed over Bournemouth in World War II.

On 7 April 1943 a memorial service for him was held in St Peter's. The church was packed again, among the mourners squads of New Zealand, Australian and Canadian air force personnel stationed temporarily at Bournemouth, awaiting postings. New Zealand High Commissioner Bill Jordan unveiled a plaque of kauri, carved by students at Stratford Technical High School in the form of air force wings. On it were the words, 'In memory of Pilot Officer Cecil Hight of Stratford, New Zealand, who died in defence of the Empire, at Bournemouth. 15th August 1940.' Two days later a 14-minute radio programme of recordings made at the service with commentary by Auckland-born Noni Wright was broadcast in her wartime BBC service *Calling New Zealand*. National stations throughout New Zealand carried the programme.

JACK FLEMING — GUINEA PIG

Two quick-thinking doctors at a cottage hospital in Kent saved Jack Fleming's hands and plastic surgeon Archie McIndoe saved his legs. The 25-year-old New Zealander was one of the early Battle of Britain pilots McIndoe cared for in 1940 with his pioneering saline-bath burns treatment. A Hurricane pilot on 605 Squadron, Fleming was shot down on 8 September, the day after the unit arrived at Croydon. Just before midday the following day, a Sunday, 605 Squadron scrambled to meet an incoming raid by Dorniers and Ju 88s escorted by Me 109s. They were joined by the Hurricanes of 253 Squadron from Kenley and clashed with the Germans over Kent.

DAY AFTER DAY

Fleming, flying as a weaver behind the squadron, suddenly spotted 109s streaming down from behind. He shouted a warning over the R/T: 'We're being bounced, break, break.' Then he added he'd 'go back and look at them'. He turned his Hurricane to face the oncoming attack and said later, 'we had a private party', getting in some damaging shots before he was overwhelmed. German fire knocked the tips off his wings, ripped into the radiator and started a fire below him. More bullets smashed through the cockpit and ignited the fuel in the reserve tank in front. Flaming gasoline poured into the cockpit well and onto his legs. 'There was a big whoomph and I couldn't open the hood.' Twice he turned the plane over but still the hood wouldn't budge. The third time upside down he desperately shoved himself off the floor. 'I was thirteen stone ten and very fit so the hood came straight off the runners and I went out wearing it around my neck.'

Fleming floated down in his chute. Then he was on the ground in a field, clothing burnt off, stitching on his parachute webbing pretty much burned through, his face, hands and legs badly burned. Farm labourers pulled a gate off its hinges and carried him across fields to a road where home guard troops took over. At Wrotham Cottage Hospital, filled with maternity cases, two local doctors did something remarkable. They recognised that if they didn't act quickly his cruelly burned hands would curl over as the skin tightened, leaving the young man with club hands. Their ingenious solution — putting tennis racquets under his forearms and tying his fingers to the mesh in a spread-out position so they were straight, flat and couldn't fuse. Fleming never lost the use of his fingers, as he might well have done had it not been for the doctors' quick thinking.

After initial care at Wrotham he was transferred to the RAF hospital at Halton, near Aylesbury in Buckinghamshire, where his third-degree burns were swathed in bandages. He was given morphine every four hours while doctors decided what to do. Eventually they recommended his legs be amputated at the hips. Fleming refused, and was fortunate to be found by McIndoe, who was visiting Halton. The surgeon thought his new saline bath treatment might suit Fleming better than the tannic acid then in vogue and Fleming was transferred to McIndoe's care at Queen Victoria Hospital in London's East Grinstead.

Fifty years later Fleming told a reporter he initially screamed from the pain of handling every time he was put into the bath and taken out two hours later. Miraculously the treatment worked; new skin began growing in just ten days and sight returned to his burned eyeballs. But his recovery was long and tortuous, and he remained at East Grinstead for almost a year. An extended convalescence followed and in 1942 he needed to return to McIndoe's hospital for two months. Fleming, a guinea pig in every sense of the word, was a founder and lifelong member of the Guinea Pig Club, the exclusive band of servicemen restored by McIndoe. He was the club's No. 2 for some time and served on its committee for many years.

Fleming never flew operationally again but remained in the RAF, appointed chief armament instructor at an OTU in 1942. He served in Canada and returned to Britain in the spring of 1945 to join teams tracking V1 and V2 sites. He remained in the RAF postwar until 1958, when he retired as a wing commander. While the scars on his face had long since disappeared, he always wore support stockings on his legs, from toe to hips.

Born in 1915 in Scotland, Fleming arrived in New Zealand as a three-year-old with his parents, who settled in Wellington. His widow Joy says her husband never talked much about his family or life in New Zealand or why he wanted to become a pilot but always said he had believed war was inevitable and wanted to play his part. It is known he attended Lyall Bay primary and Rongotai College, and perhaps little planes buzzing in and out of nearby Rongotai airfield sparked his interest in flying.

Fleming earned a B.Com from Victoria University College in 1935 and a Masters a year later. In 1938 he was awarded one of the rare direct entry permanent commissions offered each year to British and Empire university graduates, and in May 1939 he sailed for England.

While he visited Wellington postwar, Fleming decided he wanted to live in England, where he died in 1955.

MINDY BLAKE — PILOT AND INVENTOR

Mindy Blake was an extraordinary character — and extraordinarily lucky. Just after war was declared he survived a horrendous crash, blamed on hay of all things, and a couple of ditchings. Above all, he was a man of enormous and varied talents.

Born in Eketahuna in February 1913, Blake was an outstanding academic, going to Southland Boys' High School and then on to Canterbury University College where he graduated at 21, with a Masters degree in science and honours in maths. While he took up a university post there as a physics lecturer, there was far more to him than academic brilliance. Universities champion gymnast for three successive years, he also excelled at the pole vault and in 1935–36 was New Zealand national champion.

Blake was also an inventor. His father bought him a small chicken farm in Christchurch where Mindy could live and make money while he studied at Canterbury. Between lectures and books, he hatched chicks, milked a cow, cooked his own meals — and invented an automatic egg-weighing machine widely used in New Zealand both before and after the war.

In late 1936, after just missing a Rhodes Scholarship, he gave it all up for the RAF and sailed for England. He was granted a permanent commission the following year and after learning to fly was posted to 17 Squadron.

There his progress was swift and by March 1939 he was a flight lieutenant. The squadron converted from Gauntlets to Hurricanes in mid-1939 and the day before war was declared moved to Croydon.

Five nights later he wrote off his Hurricane but suffered only minor injuries and was soon back flying. The blackout was in force and the grass runway lights were switched on only briefly as he came in to land. Blake saw he was too high and gave the Hurricane full throttle to go around again. Without warning the engine cut and Blake braced. Short of the runway the Hurricane smashed into a chimney on a nurses' home, flipped over and smashed down into the foundations of a new hospital. Blake made it out shaken but unhurt, except for a cut on his head. An investigation revealed that hay, lying around the cut-grass runways and surrounds, had been ingested into the air intake, causing engine failure. Rolls-Royce moved swiftly to provide a fix.

After instructing and a Hurricane refresher, Blake joined 238 Squadron as acting CO at St Eval, Cornwall, in mid-August while the Battle of Britain raged. The squadron moved to Middle Wallop, Hampshire, the following month. He scored the first of his ten victories off the west coast of Cornwall on 21 August and another two the following month, both in the southeast. The squadron had been called in from 10 Group to help attack the waves of bombers over London. At the end of September he was given command of 234

DAY AFTER DAY

Squadron, returning to St Eval again, and in December was awarded a DFC. His score mounted as he led 234 Squadron on Channel sweeps in the summer of 1941, his fine performance eventually leading to the command of the Portreath Wing in Cornwall, the DSO and his capture during Dieppe.

On 10 July 1941 Blake's fighter was damaged over Cherbourg while 234 Squadron escorted Coastal Command Blenheims attacking the docks. The Spitfires were attacked out of the sun by 109s as they turned for home. A fierce scrap developed and Blake shot down two of the Messerschmitts. As the engagement ended he was hit by fire in the radiator and the engine temperature began to rise. He got on the R/T and told his squadron: 'I've got a bullet in the cooling system. I reckon I have nine minutes before the engine seizes up. When you get back tell them I'm putting down in the sea about seven miles off the coast.' His men urged him to bale out. 'No, I think I can manage it,' he replied.

Writing an introduction to one of Blake's books in the 1970s, writer and friend Harry Weaver claimed that at that time nobody had successfully put a Spitfire down in the sea. That's not so but emerging alive from a ditched Spitfire, or a Hurricane for that matter, was extraordinarily difficult. The fighters didn't float long, if at all, and many pilots went straight down with their aircraft in seconds.

Blake's inventive mind had planned a couple of different ways of ditching, and according to Weaver, he put one of them into effect on 10 July. He believed the G-forces on a pilot's body were in the order of five to seven when a fighter hit the sea, knocking the pilot out or killing him. He thought he could reduce the Gs to about one and a half by sticking a wing into the water and cartwheeling, and that's exactly what he did. He made it out of his sinking Spitfire unhurt and was soon paddling his dinghy away from the French coast, picked up by the ASR twelve hours later after paddling to within two miles of the Isle of Wight.

A Clasp for 'The Few' has this story too, but Eddie Walford in his 1985 book *War Over the West* (the west of England) says Blake simply tightened his straps, jettisoned the hood and waited for the crash. The plane began to sink immediately but after a struggle and what 'seemed an eternity' Blake got out and into his dinghy.

His second idea, altogether different, also proved effective. Blake worried about being blinded and then trying to exit a fighter. He decided if that happened to him he'd slide the hood back, undo his straps, disconnect his microphone and oxygen tube, sit back, put his feet on the control column and dive the plane straight into the sea, calculating he'd be catapulted from the cockpit. He got the opportunity to test his theory when he was hit over Dieppe on the ill-fated raid in August 1942 (see Chapter 11). Shattered cockpit Perspex smashed into his face (his goggles were pushed back on his head) and temporarily blinded him in one eye. He dived the aircraft and at 200 feet was ejected.

'He proved quite correct,' wrote Weaver. 'He described a graceful parabola through the air, his parachute opened a split second before he hit the water, and, within a few minutes, had his K-type dinghy inflated and was paddling again.' This time the outcome was not so good — a German E-boat picked him up short of Dover.

Whether other pilots tried these techniques isn't recorded, but there are countless reports of fighters cartwheeling into the sea, pilots and planes disappearing forever in a huge flurry of foam. While opening a chute at 200 feet was hardly to be recommended, mathematician Blake had worked it all out, and for him it worked.

Blake led the Portreath Wing with distinction from September 1941 until he was shot down at Dieppe. His squadrons on the Cornish coast flew long-range patrols down as far as Cherbourg and Brest. Norman Franks in *The Greatest Air Battle — Dieppe* says that Blake should not have been flying that day. 'He had just been notified of a posting to Operations with a promotion to Group Captain in the offing.' But he wanted to fly because he had developed a gyroscopic gunsight — his inventive streak again — and wanted to test it in battle.

After his capture at Dieppe, Blake spent several weeks in hospital outside Paris where the Germans repaired his eyes before he was put on a train for interrogation at Dulag Luft, near Frankfurt, and then sent to a POW camp where he worked on more inventions. He made a bold bid for freedom before the train reached Paris, breaking through a toilet window and flinging himself off as the train slowed. He suffered a broken hand and other injuries and was in poor shape when he finally received help at a French farmhouse. Because his presence there was widely known, the family gave him up for fear of reprisals. Blake wrote to his station commander from POW camp about his capture and adventures, ending with the words 'I tried to get back, but I couldn't make it.'

Blake visited his family in New Zealand after his release, met and married Christchurch woman Molly Seldon after a chance meeting and a whirlwind romance, then returned with her to England and the RAF. He also resumed his pole vaulting and was RAF champion again for several years. He quit the RAF in 1958 and worked for several companies before golf took over his life. Apart from playing the game and eventually becoming club captain at Wentworth, a famous course, the ever-inventive Blake spent hundreds of hours in his backyard workshop designing golf clubs which are still sold today, including one permitting golfers to practise in their living rooms. He also talked about golf and wrote about it, including several books that sold thousands of copies. 'To understand golf,' he said in *The Golf Swing of the Future*, 'you need the kind of mind which is good at mathematics and physics. Golf is purely a matter of technique.' Together with his good friend Weaver, he also wrote a book about what he saw as the evils of socialism. Blake died in 1981.

On a final note, Blake's young brother Doug, then 16, made headlines in May 1942 when New Zealand newspapers revealed he had fooled his parents the previous October by running away to sea to get to England in an attempt to join the Army. He told them on a Friday he was going to stay with a friend in Christchurch for the weekend but instead signed on the crew of a ship about to sail from Lyttelton, saying he was 18.

His father received a note from his son on the Sunday night confessing all, but by then the ship was long gone. Cables flowed between Wellington and London and the youngster was met in Glasgow when the ship docked.

Mindy Blake intervened and his brother was sent to school in England to complete his education before being returned to New Zealand. A third brother, Nelson, served in the Royal Navy in England and in February 1942 the three brothers enjoyed a reunion in Portreath.

'WE GOTCHA, WE GOTCHA'

The November 2009 issue of *Flypast* headlined its backward look at 141 Squadron's disastrous 19 July 1940, just after the start of the Battle of Britain, as the 'Slaughter of the Innocents'. The English magazine was not exaggerating. Nine Defiants of 141 Squadron took off from Hawkinge, near Folkestone on the south coast, at 12.33 p.m. on a Channel patrol. An hour and a quarter later they were attacked out of the sun by Me 109s. They had no chance. In a matter of minutes four were shot down into the sea. Seven of the eight aircrew aboard were dead, two of them New Zealanders. The sole survivor was New Zealand pilot John Gard'ner. Another of the Defiants, fatally damaged, fell in a street in Dover, killing its two crew. A sixth Defiant was written off in a crash short of Hawkinge. Only three of the two-seat 'fighters' landed safely, one without its gunner, who had baled out to his death. It was a massacre in the true sense of the word, the surviving Defiants saved only by the timely intervention of 111 'Treble One' Squadron Hurricanes, which destroyed two 109s.

Four 141 pilots and six gunners died. New Zealand pilots John Kemp, 25, and Rudal Kidson, 26, were among the dead. Gard'ner was injured and escaped death by a slim margin, gasping for air as he burst to the surface after struggling clear of his sinking aircraft with great difficulty, to be dragged out of the water by exuberant rescuers.

Kemp, who grew up in Timaru, was working in Wellington when he was locally selected for an SSC in the RAF. On 16 December 1938 he was among a group of eighteen, who sailed from Auckland on the *Rangitata*, including Gard'ner, Colin Gray and Ron Bary, a wing commander killed tragically over Italy three weeks before the war ended, his Spitfire's bombs exploding as he dived at a target. Only seven of the eighteen would survive the war.

Gray and Kemp became particularly good mates on the voyage, according to Gray's *Spitfire Patrol*. When the draft reached England half, including Gard'ner, Gray and Bary, were posted to Hatfield in Hertfordshire, where elementary flying training was given at the de Havilland flying school, which was under contract to the RAF. There, in pre-war days, they were considered civilians and addressed as 'Mister' for two to three months until they had soloed, mastered their elementary training — appropriately enough on de Havilland Tiger Moths — and considered up to RAF standard. Those who passed went to Uxbridge for a couple of weeks, appointed as acting pilot officers (APOs) on probation, then on to Shawbury in Shropshire for six months of more intensive flying training before gaining their wings. Promotion to fully fledged pilot officers was normally conferred one year after entering flying school.

Kemp's group did their initial training at White Waltham, Berkshire, and then went on to Drem in Scotland. Training completed just a few days before war was declared, the young pilots anxiously awaited postings to begin real life in the RAF. First, though, those chosen to fly fighters went to St Athan, Glamorganshire, where they flew Hurricanes 'before being let loose on a front-line squadron', according to Gray. 'This was a wise precaution, because by then all front-line squadrons were equipped either with Hurricanes or Spitfires and the transition straight from an ancient old biplane to one of these may well have caused problems.' The New Zealanders from Drem also ended up at St Athan 'and I was delighted to meet up with Jack Kemp once again'.

At the end of November Gray and Kemp were pleased to find they were both off to 54 Squadron at Hornchurch, where they would be on Spitfires. Their reunion was short-lived. Kemp's original posting to 141 Squadron at Grangemouth, Scotland, surfaced and he left 54 Squadron.

Gray's provisional posting to 145 Squadron never turned up. 'Someone seemed to have lost sight of our original posting notices, but unfortunately for Jack his eventually caught up with him ... to his cost.' Gray discloses another twist. A couple of weeks before Kemp's death, a Pilot Officer J L Kemp arrived at Hornchurch to join 54. Gray says the squadron needed replacement pilots after Dunkirk and he had suggested his mate Kemp to Prof Leathart, the CO, because Gray knew Kemp was unhappy about his posting to 141 Squadron. 'Leathart remembered Kemp and thought this was an excellent idea, but unfortunately someone along the line sent the wrong Kemp: J L instead of J R. My friend was killed a fortnight later.' Kemp might not have been killed had someone in the RAF done his paperwork properly.

Kidson, born and educated in Wellington, was sheep farming when he decided to join the RAF and sailed independently for England in 1938, earlier than the others. After receiving his wings he spent some time as a staff pilot at an air observers' school and was then posted to 141 Squadron in October 1939, two weeks after it reformed.

John Gard'ner (known as Johnny G in the air force) now lives in retirement in Tauranga, still playing golf at 92 and one of three Battle of Britain pilots still alive in New Zealand in the spring of 2010, when this book was completed. He cast his lot with the RAF in 1938 'because I wanted to see the world and it just seemed a marvellous thing to do. I had no idea then there was going to be a war.' He dates his interest in flying to the day when he was ten or eleven and saw three planes land on Dunedin's St Kilda mudflats.

I lived on Queen's Drive at St Kilda with the beach at one end, the mudflats, solid at low tide, at the other. A friend and I leapt on to our bikes and went off down there to see these aeroplanes. They seemed to me to be terribly big things, all wires and things like that and these chaps dressed in white got out of them. I have the impression there were guns on top of the wings. From that moment I was always interested. Then my father died and we went to Nelson.

There Gard'ner had a ten-shilling joyride over the town and was totally hooked. He was the first from Nelson to apply for the Civil Reserve of Pilots scheme and had done a couple of hours on a Puss Moth (a three-seater, high-wing monoplane designed and built by de Havilland) before seeking an SSC. 'I'd been at college with a chap called Alan Boxer [later Air Vice-Marshal Sir Alan Boxer] and he got one and I thought, "If he can go, I can try for that too."'

After finishing his training in England, Gard'ner was posted to 141 Squadron at Grangemouth, Edinburgh, where the squadron flew Blenheims until the arrival of Defiants in April 1940. The Defiant was one of the worst aircraft in the RAF's World War II lineup — at least in its role against German fighters. A low-wing monoplane of all-metal construction and powered by a Rolls-Royce engine, the same as the one in Spitfires and Hurricanes, it was far slower than the other two, its performance degraded by the power-operated turret with its four machine guns. Designer Boulton Paul and the RAF believed the lack of forward-firing guns, under control of the pilot, would give the pilot freedom to concentrate on flying. It was a fatal flaw — the heavy turret created drag and the wings, rudder and tailplane restricted the gunner's arc of firing.

Only two Fighter Command squadrons were equipped with Defiants during the Battle of Britain — 264 Squadron, which received its first aircraft in December 1939, and 141 Squadron. Making its operational debut over Dunkirk, 264 Squadron achieved momentary success — and made exaggerated claims — especially when it got among the

DAY AFTER DAY

Stukas. The Me 109s were surprised when they came in from above and behind to be met by a hail of fire from the four-gun turret. But the Germans learned swiftly that the Defiant was a dead duck when they attacked frontally or fired into its belly, and 141 Squadron's suffering off Folkestone signalled the beginning of the end. They suffered brutal losses and were immediately withdrawn from day action, with 264 Squadron pulled out of the battle in August, after similar heavy losses.

On 11 July 1940, 141 Squadron, with Gard'ner, Kemp and Kidson among them, flew south to the grass strips of West Malling, formerly Maidstone Airport. A fourth New Zealander, Don Wilson, 23 (Wairoa), was also with the squadron but did not fly on the fatal 19 July (he was one of the *Rangitata* eighteen who survived the war). For the next few days they flew patrols, some on 18 July from Hawkinge, without sighting Germans. Next morning the entire squadron flew to Hawkinge and at 12.33 p.m. took off to patrol the Channel at 5000 feet. Nine planes lifted off. According to *Flypast*, Me 109s sighted the Defiants at 1.43 p.m.

Hannes Trautloft, leading the Germans, heard a cry from one of his pilots: 'On the right below, several aircraft.' Trautloft squinted, saw the nine aircraft in three Vics. 'With the sun behind them the 109s swooped.' Flashing down, they swung up to fire from below, aiming for the vulnerable bellies.

Kemp was apparently first gunned down, falling on fire into the sea, followed by another and then, in quick succession, by Kidson and Gard'ner. It's been written that all four were 'flamers' but Gard'ner's certainly was not. He saw a little smoke but no flames in the cockpit and smelt oil and cordite. In an interview in 2009 he recalled the squadron patrolling quietly on a sunny day with a bit of cloud and a flat sea.

Then we were hit completely unawares. Suddenly thudding sounded on my aircraft and I saw white streaks going out in front of me, machine-gun fire I think. I realised later the thudding was probably my gunner [Sergeant Dud Slatter, an Englishman] getting off a few shots. I said to myself, 'God we've been hit, got to do something, got to get out of here.'

Gard'ner called to his gunner, whom he barely knew, on the difficult-to-hear intercom, but there was no answer and he never saw or heard from him again. He slammed the Defiant hard over and down, diving to sea level to evade further attacks. The 109s didn't follow. On the way down Gard'ner realised there was no power from the engine and the prop was windmilling. He pulled the plane out of its dive and headed towards a small naval vessel he could see. The Defiant was going too fast and shot past the vessel. Gard'ner now discovered his rudder was useless but somehow turned around. He pulled back the hood, undid his straps — 'The most stupid thing to do'. When the aircraft stalled and plonked on the water, an unrestrained Gard'ner was thrown forward and knocked unconscious. He must have recovered his senses quickly but remembers little except that the water was black and getting blacker. The plane was sinking. 'I thought, "hell, I've got to get out", so I kicked my way out of the cockpit and got myself to the surface just about bursting.'

He heard a voice shouting, 'We've gotcha, we've gotcha. Are you alright, are you alright?' He'd been fished out by the crew of a motor torpedo boat, which happened on the scene. Bleeding from a gashed forehead from his collision with the cockpit and with skin hanging down and the back of his head also smashed about, Gard'ner began to feel ill. 'I must have flaked out because the next thing I recall is waking

DAY AFTER DAY

up in hospital at Dover, swathed in bandages. There was an air battle going on overhead and I started to get up to have a look.' A nurse told him sharply to get back to bed.

Kemp, Kidson, their gunners and Slatter went down with their Defiants. Both New Zealanders are remembered at Runnymede.

Gard'ner spent ten days in hospital and then went on extended recuperation leave. At the end of October he rejoined 141 Squadron, now flying its Defiants as night fighters. He flew operationally for much of the war, mostly on night fighters with 141 Squadron, 409 (RCAF) Squadron on Beaufighters, and 219 Squadron and 488 Squadron on Mosquitoes. At war's end he was a squadron leader and flight commander on 488 Squadron. He got his only victory one night in November 1944 operating from Amiens/Glisy, France, when he shot down an FW 190 while he was with 488 Squadron. He regarded that 'kill' with distaste then and still does. 'That was plain murder as far as I was concerned. I was put on to him by control. He was flying straight and level, made no effort to move anywhere. I went up behind him and fired a short burst, eleven shells I think. He went straight down.'

Gard'ner rejoined the RAF postwar and served until 1965, his last post as British Air Attaché in Brussels and his final rank group captain.

92 SQUADRON— A WILD BUNCH

On the ground 92 Squadron lived by their own exaggerated rules; in the air they were determined, disciplined and effective. How could it have been otherwise, with Britons like Brian Kingcome, Bob Stanford Tuck, Tony Bartley, Geoff 'Boy' Wellum, Don Kingaby, Wimpy Wade and, until he was killed, New Zealander Jimmy Paterson? They drank seriously at night in the White Hart Hotel, seven miles up the road from Biggin Hill, and at the nearby Red House. Installed there, when they weren't at the hotel, were the tall, gorgeous, elegant and identical twins Sheila and Moira Macneal, daughters of a wealthy industrialist, one a young widow, the other married to an RAF officer serving in the Middle East.

' "Come on, chaps, let's get up to the Red House," pleaded someone [at the White Hart]', Bartley wrote in his entertaining book *Smoke Trails in the Sky*:

We piled into the station wagon like sardines again, and after a short drive, arrived in front of a fine old red-brick manor house. The twins had gone ahead, and were waiting for us at the door. I was shown into the drawing room, and a very large whisky thrust into my hand. Someone put on the radiogram and John Bryson grabbed one of the twins and started to dance her around the floor. He was the only one taller than her. Several hours, and three bottles of Scotch later, I suggested that we should be getting back to the airfield. Geoff Wellum had been sick in the garden. Brian said that he was staying for a while, but I couldn't figure which twin was the attraction. I wondered how we were going to make dawn readiness ... My batman called me at 4.30 a.m. with a cup of tea. I struggled into my clothes and bumped into Wimpy Wade in the corridor. He had thrown on his uniform over his pyjamas. It was cold and dark outside. The boys converged from various rooms of our barrack block, dressed in polo-necked sweaters, corduroy trousers and flamboyant scarves.

The squadron went through a succession of COs, one setting himself afire, lighting a cigarette while his uniform was still soaked in the fuel

DAY AFTER DAY

he used to clean it of oil. At times when the squadron was without a CO, they were led by the incomparable Kingcome. 92 Squadron raised eyebrows with its off-duty antics, running their own show, doing their own thing, until late in the conflict when a tough Canadian hauled them into line and the RAF, battle won, decided order and dignity needed restoring. But they were the sort of squadron vital to Britain's fate in the dark days of 1940, and their behaviour was forgiven in the heat of the battle because they were so good in the air. Winston Churchill stopped off from time to time to see them at Biggin Hill on his way to Chartwell, his home in Kent. Bartley: 'He would burst into our crew room, unheralded, and sit and chat with us while he puffed on a huge cigar … we were proud to think of him as a friend as well as our leader.'

Four New Zealanders flew with 92 Squadron while it was at Biggin Hill at the height of the Battle of Britain — Howard Hill, Jimmy Paterson, Maurice Kinder and Johnny Pattison. Hill and Paterson died; the other two survived the war, Pattison becoming the third-to-last commanding officer of 485 Squadron (Spitfire). Hill, a 92 Squadron veteran, having joined in 1939, was killed on 20 September 1940, hit in the head by a cannon shell. He was found in his cockpit after his death, his shattered Spitfire lodged in high tree tops near the Kent coast. Exactly a week later Paterson went down in flames. Unable to get out of his cockpit, he plunged to his death in a Kentish field. Remembering his incomparable leadership qualities in France, his loss was severe. What might he have accomplished postwar had he lived?

Kinder had only two and a bit weeks with 92 Squadron before the Battle of Britain ended but soon after had plenty of excitement.

The squadron, which saw brief late service in France in World War I, reformed at Tangmere in October 1939 and flew Blenheims until

200

March 1940, when it received Spitfires. Among its new pilots were Hill and Bartley who had trained together. The squadron shifted around several fields in 11 Group then, on 18 June, after being shattered over Dunkirk, they moved to Pembrey, near Llanelli, for the best part of three months, to regroup and fly defensive patrols.

The squadron made a disastrous operational debut over France on 23 May — two pilots dead, two shot down and taken prisoner and two seriously injured. One of the POWs, CO Roger Bushell, became the leader of the Great Escape from Sagan and was callously executed after recapture by the Germans.

The other was John Gillies, son of New Zealander Sir Harold Gillies, London-based pioneer plastic surgeon, relation, teacher and mentor of Sir Archibald (Archie) McIndoe, who became even more famous for his work on burned and maimed RAF aircrew. John Gillies, born in August 1912, who had a privileged early life, was educated at Winchester and Cambridge. A brilliant squash player, he represented England and in 1935 reached the final of the amateur championship. In the summer of 1932 he joined the Royal Air Force Volunteer Reserve (RAFVR), his urge to fly fired by a flight at Winchester. 'Cambridge University did have an air squadron but it cost quite a lot to belong, and so the decision to learn as a budding member of the RAF as I had very limited funds in those days … was an easy one.'

Gillies went solo after about ten hours dual on Tiger Moths. He read law at Cambridge and after graduation spent three years in London, becoming a chartered accountant but still flying at the reserve's annual camp. As war loomed in 1939 Gillies joined 604 Squadron RAuxAF at Hendon, London, so he could fly at weekends. The RAF called up reservists on 23 August 1939 and that night Eileen 'Smiff' Galloway

DAY AFTER DAY

accepted his proposal of marriage. The next day Gillies donned uniform and reported to Hendon. He was pressed to join the RAF's accounting section but declined, not prepared to become chair-borne. He married on 24 February 1940 and soon after his honeymoon was posted to 92 Squadron at Croydon. On 23 May Gillies was on leave at Northolt, another London-area field where 92 Squadron was based at nights, waiting for his wife to join him for a day or two. The squadron had flown patrols over London but on the morning of the 23rd operated over Dunkirk for the first time. In a family memoir Gillies wrote in late life he said:

Just before lunch I was asked to fly a Spitfire from Northolt to Hornchurch. Not long after I landed at Hornchurch 92 Squadron came back from its morning sweep over France only eleven pilots strong, one having been lost in an air battle there. So I was asked by ... Bushell to take his place and subsequently achieved the dubious honour of being shot down on leave! We had done one or two sweeps over the Calais-Boulogne-Dunkirk area without seeing anything and then suddenly we were attacked by a circus of about fifty Me 110s ... In the course of the ensuing battle, when I was attacking one of them head-on, my engine was hit and started missing badly. Being as a result a lame duck, I went down to low level and as the engine did not pick up, had no alternative but to crash-land the plane with wheels up ... I somehow managed to miss trees and other obstacles and came to rest, with no more than a cut nose, on the edge of Boulogne, expecting to get a ship back to England the next day.

Gillies soon found the Germans had encircled Boulogne, with fighting going on in the harbour area. After spending the night huddled in a cellar with refugees, he managed to get inside the town citadel, already under artillery fire. The French then surrendered and Gillies was marched out with them into long captivity. The next day he spotted Bushell, shot down on the other side of Boulogne, in a field packed with POWs. The two became close friends as prisoners.

Gillies began an activity that was to prove invaluable to British intelligence, interviewing new POW airmen and sending home valuable information he and others gathered from aircrew and other sources, in coded letters. Also involved in this work was New Zealander Bob Stark, a 75 Squadron navigator from Invercargill, shot down over Germany the night of 29–30 December 1940. An accountant, he and Gillies shared a growing friendship and Stark was soon urging Gillies to shift Down Under postwar.

Gillies and his wife did just that in 1949. The two men worked together in an Invercargill accountancy firm, eventually as partners. In December 1946 both received the MBE for their work as prisoners. In 1986 Gillies was awarded the Queen's Service Order for more than thirty years' work with the Save the Children Fund and for his drive in the establishment of new squash courts in Invercargill (as a player he won the national squash title 1951, 1952 and 1953). Gillies died in 1993.

Jimmy Paterson, back from France, leave and a Spitfire conversion course, joined 92 Squadron in Wales, on 15 July. He did his first patrol three days later over the Pembroke area. 'Went on scramble in afternoon but saw nothing over Cardiff area. Received 3 Auckland *Weeklys* [*New Zealand Weekly News*] from Mum.'

On the afternoon of 24 July Paterson shared in the destruction of a Ju 88 that he, John Bryson and Kingcome intercepted near Porthcawl at 12,000 feet. They poured fire into the aircraft. 'I went in on his tail

DAY AFTER DAY

giving a short burst at 300 feet and following him through cloud found him larger than sights would take, so gave him all I had until his engines seemed to slow up,' Paterson wrote in his diary. The three of them trailed the Ju 88 down as it landed on a moor, one engine flaming. One crewman jumped by chute as the plane was about to touch down. The 88 crashed through a stone wall and burst into flames. As the Spitfires circled one crewman pulled two others out.

The three RAF pilots returned to the scene in Magisters souvenir hunting, cutting off the plane's swastikas for the mess and collecting the captured crew's mae wests (Paterson: 'miles better than ours') and helmets. Paterson also snaffled an expensive Leica camera and a Mauser automatic.

> The local hotel gave us free lunch and fine bottles of hock after we had had many beers. A truly marvellous time was had by all. We set off back across the Bristol Channel from Ilfracombe to Pembrey in rain and low cloud, but despite the drink we made it.

The squadron flew patrols by day, and by night, even though the Spitfire was an unpopular and difficult aircraft for night flying. When the weather was fine and they were on stand-down or leave, the pilots went yachting, fished and swam on the long, beautiful beach near the airfield, barred to the public because the army was busy driving steel stakes into the stand, an anti-invasion measure. Paterson sometimes went to the movies with other pilots in Llanelli, and partied along with them all.

> [On 7 August] Came back from fishing to the hotel about 2am with a very nice trout and some eels. Had breakfast of several fish I caught

yesterday. Set off for Carmarthen at 1545 hours with mailman. Arrived after many stops. Bought Hillman Minx Tourer at Evans Motors, £25, and drove home.

He must have been dissatisfied with the car because five days later he returned to the garage and swapped it for an Austin 14.

He wrote one letter to his parents asking them to mail his photograph album from Wigram training days. 'My CO doesn't believe we have mountains in NZ.' He wrote again after the squadron was scrambled to the south coast and mixed it with a large force of enemy aircraft over Portland.

What a time; the greatest fun going. Bags of Ju 88s, 87s, Me 109s and 110s all together, but the funniest thing of all was that the 109s, instead of protecting the Ju's, nearly always 'protected' the 110s, making the bombers 'cold meat'. After 'cleaning up' the bombers, the practice is to chase the fighter escort, even if you have finished [your] ammunition. After they have seen one or two of theirs going down they beetle home; and it is then we generally catch them, for a few squadrons generally manage to sneak behind and intercept them, and it's then the dog fights begin. I don't know how many machines I've actually accounted for, for it is far too dangerous to hang on to one and watch him go down. The idea is to give him a good rattle and then go like h ... to avoid something else on your tail.

Paterson and Wade shared in the destruction of another Ju 88 on 19 August, catching it over Portsmouth and watching it flop down in the Solent and disappear. At 3 p.m. the 88 had bombed and machine-gunned the field at Bilbury, Gloucestershire, where Paterson, now

DAY AFTER DAY

a flying officer, had been detached with his section for a few days. Paterson and Wade raced to their Spitfires and took off, chasing and eventually nailing the enemy.

On 8 September the squadron moved to Biggin Hill and the big action. Paterson was shocked by the state of the bombed airfield. 'Hardly a building standing,' he wrote, 'and aerodrome full of holes.' Three days later the Luftwaffe launched more than 300 aircraft on London in an afternoon attack and Paterson claimed an Me 110. He attacked the aircraft head-on and as he turned away saw the fighter climb, stall and dive away, black smoke pouring from the port engine. But on a later patrol the same afternoon Paterson was shot down himself.

> Rather clumsy of me for I saw one coming a fair way off and was getting in a good position to fox him into a trap, when another blighter came out of the sun and put a cannon shell right through my wing and punctured the petrol tank at the same time. The end of the wing began to bend slowly up and then with a mighty tearing sound the whole wing blew away. I opened my roof for petrol was pouring all over me, but immediately the airflow got into the cockpit a huge sheet of flame came up in front of me and the machine went into an inverted dive. It was a rather worrying moment … for I began to realise I'd have to jump for she wouldn't fly with one wing, and besides, things were getting pretty warm. … [As he struggled out of the cockpit the slipstream blew his goggles away and the flames] burned my face and eyes somewhat … [He free fell for some thousands of feet, pulling the ripcord at 6000 feet.] … It was indeed a beautiful sight to see yards and yards of beautiful white silk cords holding me up to the mushroom of cloth, but what was even better, a Spitfire was circling round and round

206

me … and I went floating peacefully down and landed with a somewhat rude jolt in a paddock.

The following day he was promoted to flight lieutenant and went to London to see an eye specialist. The problem wasn't too serious but he was ordered to take a week's leave while his right eye healed. He went north to Scotland again to stay with his parents' friends. One day he attended a sheep and cattle sale at Perth and was astonished by high prices, then was taken shooting, his party bagging fifty pheasants and grouse. Another day he stalked deer on an Earl's estate and shot three stags. Paterson got back to Biggin Hill on 26 September, his eyes given the okay for a return to flying. In his short time away he found Bryson, Hill, Norman Hargreaves and Gus Edwards were dead and seven others in hospital. The next day Paterson was killed, shot down by an Me 109.

He never made it out of his cockpit, his Spitfire tumbling to the ground in flames. Tony Bartley wrote: 'I saw him spin down quite close to me, having been hit and struggling to get out of his cockpit. A burned offering to the God of War.' Bartley remembered that just before Paterson was killed a new pilot spotted him in the crew room with 'terrible bloodshot eyes' and a 'crimson face' and thought he looked a real booze hound if ever he saw one and hoped he was not in his flight. 'He … learned later that the pilot was New Zealander [Jimmy] Paterson who had been shot down in flames a few days previously, but refused to take a rest because of the shortage of pilots.'

Paterson's fighter, X4422, crashed in a field on the edge of Sparepenny Lane, Farningham, Kent, just north of Shoreham, where today there's an aircraft museum.

The museum is in the process of building memorials to Battle of

Britain pilots who fell in the county. The first, dedicated in Sparepenny Lane at midday on 27 September 2006, remembers Jimmy Paterson. As the RNZAF flag (filched by Paterson the day he received his wings in New Zealand and kept by his family after he was killed) was pulled away to unveil the stone cairn, a Spitfire roared low over the field in tribute.

Bartley put Paterson's and other deaths into perspective:

From an hour before dawn until dusk we lived at our dispersal point on the airfield, and fought until we ran out of ammunition. At night we drank and played and made love like there was no hereafter. I can't remember all the pilots who flew with us. Some came in the morning and were dead by nightfall. I swore never to hate anyone again after I'd seen one of our team I loathed blow up alongside me when caught by a 109 ... Some days, we could only field five serviceable aircraft out of twelve ... we lived for the present and dismissed our future. The battle would be won, of course. We had no doubts about that. Meanwhile the casualties mounted but no one grieved as we knew it was inevitable. I found myself secretly watching the others, searching their faces for who would be next, and I thought I saw them looking at me the same way. But we never revealed our thoughts about fear. They were locked up as tight as the straps on our parachutes.

It's often been written that Howard Hill's body was discovered in his wrecked aircraft in the trees a month after he was killed. Errol Martyn has corrected that story in Volume 3 of *For Your Tomorrow*. Hill was in fact buried at Hawkinge just five days after he was killed on his 45th op. He was 20. Hill's parents, like many others, suffered the loss of a second son when Howard's younger brother Peter, then aged 22 and a bomber navigator, was killed in January 1945 when his aircraft crashed on a night exercise.

Howard Hill took off on his last sortie about 10.30 a.m. on 20 September, the squadron sent to intercept a major raid. He and another pilot were victims of famous high-scoring German, Werner Molders. His Spitfire was hit by cannon shells 27,000 feet over Dungeness and was seen gliding steadily down but the pilot couldn't be raised on the R/T and vanished. *Battle of Britain — Then and Now* says the missing fighter, partially hidden by dense foliage in the tree tops, was spotted by an Anson pilot but repeats the story of the plane not being found for a month. Long ladders had to be used to recover his body and it was clear he had died during the attack. The plane fell in woods near West Hougham, Kent, many miles from Dungeness.

Maurice Kinder, who died in Auckland in 1988, remembered 92 Squadron in his memoir as a 'rough lot'. He wrote: 'No ties were worn in those days, instead we tied our girl friends' silk stockings around our necks.' Pilots had quickly discovered the stiff detachable collars of the day rubbed their necks raw as they twisted their necks, constantly on the lookout for enemy fighters behind, and also restricted movement. 'We stuck our maps and revolver in our flying boots and left the top brass button undone on jackets.'

Kinder paused in his narrative to recall Keith Park.

What a wonderful inspiration to all fighter pilots it was when Park flew in his Hurricane to all the different squadrons which were fighting for their lives and that of the world … He saw the pilots after patrols when they had seen their best friends go down in flames. He would have a cigarette and drink with them and he was, in return, looked on as one of the boys.

Another pilot remembered Park walking into a squadron mess one night, dressed in his trademark white overalls and standing alone at the bar with a drink. The pilot walked over to Park and said, more or less, 'Who are you?'

Park replied, quietly, 'I'm your AOC.'

Park endeared himself to 11 Group pilots and without exception they admired him. There was no support among them for the whingeing criticism of Park and his tactics by Leigh-Mallory and Douglas Bader.

Geoff Wellum, interviewed by English writer James Holland in 2001, said of Park: 'Brilliant. Would have done anything for him. Park was wonderful. Absolutely wonderful. You had great faith in Park. He used to turn up in his Hurricane and have a chat ... I was very upset when he and Dowding were pushed out by that other bastard Leigh-Mallory.'

Kinder, like Bartley, also remembered Churchill with affection.

He invited the whole squadron to stay [at Chartwell]. It was a lovely old place, with [its library], wooden parquet floors and lovely gardens. We saw a lot of Churchill ... an inspiration to everyone he met with his cigars and 'V' sign which he copied from the RAF (but which meant a very different thing to us). I don't think he knew the original meaning.

The New Zealander acted as a weaver on 92 Squadron, scudding about the sky, watching for enemy aircraft attacking. The practice lapsed eventually because too many weavers were lost and it wasted fuel. He says New Zealanders and Australians were often picked for the job because, coming from 'clear air' countries, their eyesight was acute. Kinder's fighter was often shot full of holes. On one patrol a cannon shell ruptured his main petrol tank, the fuel poured through the cockpit and fumes nearly overcame him. He contacted Control, asking for a fire tender when he got down. 'As I landed and slowed, Control called and said, "You are on fire, get out as soon as you can."' Kinder dived out while the Spitfire was still rolling. 'I rolled over and over but wasn't hurt apart from a bit of skin here and there because I still had my gloves and helmet on.' The tender doused the flames in the tail which had been fed by the gushing petrol. 'I was very lucky not to have been roasted alive.'

On another patrol, short of petrol because of his all-round-the-sky weaving, Kinder put down in a field across which stretched anti-invasion wires, smashing through four until the fifth bent his undercarriage backwards so the fighter slid along on its nose, bending back the prop blades. It stopped, nose down, tail in the branches of a large oak. Kinder clambered out, walked with his heavy parachute to the nearest house with a telephone and found himself talking to family-planning pioneer Marie Stopes, who gave him a drink of warm goat's milk. He declined a brandy, wondering about the squadron medical officer. 'He might have thought I'd been drinking.' Kinder must have been the only downed RAF pilot who said no to alcohol after a force-landing.

On 1 November, the day after the Battle of Britain ended, Kinder knocked down a Stuka and almost immediately was shot down himself. His radio malfunctioned in the air and he didn't hear the order to leave Ju 87s alone and head for the 109s. 'I attacked the 87s and went for the leader, shooting him down. I didn't know it at the time but another pilot was also on the job and between us we made Jerry drop all his bombs in the water.' Suddenly the 109s came to the aid of the Stukas. Cannon shells blew off his port wing tip, knocked out a port gun and

DAY AFTER DAY

hit the side of the cockpit. 'I felt a bang on both hips and buttocks like a hammer blow … then no pain. My right wrist was broken with a severed artery.' Groggy from loss of blood, Kinder put down alongside the Ramsgate to Canterbury road.

> Australian soldiers came over and thinking I was dead because of all the blood in the cockpit, removed all my buttons, helmet and gloves for souvenirs. Nice types. While they were at work I came to and said something rude. With an astonished 'he's alive', they helped me get out of the wreck. A doctor [arrived], ripped off my trousers with a knife to survey the damage, bound up my wrist to stop the bleeding and said, 'You'll live.'

Chatham Hospital sent a message to 92 Squadron saying, 'Aircraft damaged, pilot repairable at base.' In February 1941, a repaired Kinder was posted away.

John Pattison, born in 1917, was one of the handful of RNZAF pilots who arrived in England in time to take part in the Battle of Britain. He joined the Civil Reserve of Pilots and learned to fly while managing his parents' farm just west of Waipawa. He remembered his nervous solo flight in an interview with author and historian Alison Parr, from the Ministry for Culture and Heritage, not long before his death in 2009.

> I came in and did what I considered a very decent landing … and taxied up to my instructor with a big smile on my face. He said, 'John, that wasn't a bad landing considering you landed down wind.' Fortunately there wasn't much wind. I had forgotten about the windsock I was so pleased to find the aerodrome again.

212

Pattison enlisted on 26 October 1939, trained at Bell Block and Woodbourne, was awarded his flying badge on 23 April 1940 and commissioned as a pilot officer a month later. He sailed from Auckland in the *Rangitata* on 7 June 1940, one of twenty-thee RNZAF pilots for attachment to the RAF (thirteen were killed), the second such group to leave New Zealand. The ship was not short of liquor and Pattison recalled a 'pretty jolly trip'. He said they got Bob Spurdle plastered one night and shaved off half his moustache. 'He was furious. Didn't see the joke at all.'

The ship steamed into the Firth of Forth in late July as the Battle of Britain warmed up. The RAF, desperately short of pilots, rushed the New Zealanders to training units, half, including Pattison, chosen for fighters. Pattison went to Hawarden in north Wales. 'We were given an hour's dual in a Master … three hours solo flying in that and then straight into a Spitfire. We were shown the knobs and taps and what have you, and told, "There you are, take it off." ' On the Mark 1s they were flying, the undercarriage retraction was not automatic and pilots had to pump the wheels up by hand. Tyro pilots were always obvious. They had not yet learned the knack of doing two things at once and as they pumped, one hand on the pump the other on the stick, their Spitfires went up and down in unison with the pumping, wallowing along after takeoff. Older pilots loved watching.

Pattison worried about his early flights. The last thing he wanted to do was break a Spitfire and possibly be grounded. 'They were difficult for a greenhorn but later on, a lot later on, getting into a Spitfire was rather like putting on your favourite old sports jacket.' Pattison was proud of never breaking or bending a Spitfire other than on ops. Later, as an instructor, he once did the forbidden, roaring under the Severn Bridge at the cost of a court martial and three months' seniority.

Pattison made his first operational flight a few days after his posting to 266 Squadron on 27 August, barely a month after arriving in Britain — and got himself lost before running out of petrol and making a forced landing. Told to stick close, as No. 2 to an experienced pilot, Pattison became separated as the other pilot turned up and into the sun. And then he was alone in the sky, 'stooging around and feeling foolish'. Losing R/T contact with the ground, he went down, petrol gauge showing low, and realised he was lost. Spotting a lone Hurricane he tagged on, figuring the other fighter would lead him to an airfield. It would have taken him to Debden, except that two miles short of the base, Pattison's engine quit, out of fuel. He picked out a field for landing but found it covered with anti-invasion steel poles, with heavy wire hawsers attached to catch German gliders. Pattison had just enough speed to hop over one wire and duck under the next to land wheels up. Pitchfork-armed farm workers who surrounded him needed convincing he was not a German. Some farm labourers were not the brightest, unable to tell an RAF roundel from a swastika. Pattison expected a tongue-lashing when he returned to the station but instead received a tremendous welcome. 'Great to see you old boy, we thought you had had it.'

On 14 September he was posted to 92 Squadron and the maelstrom that was Biggin Hill. A 109 got him nine days later. 'I am only slightly lame now,' he wrote from hospital to his anxious parents in March 1941, his earlier account of his downing apparently never received. 'Possibly the letter was sunk,' he said. Pattison would carry his limp for the rest of his life.

He told his parents again what had happened. He was hit from the sun and behind ('the Hun in the sun. I never saw the bloke') and struck by a 20 mm explosive shell just above the left buttock. It exited below his knee and the leg jerked back, tucking itself under the seat. 'I immediately undid my straps, oxygen tube and radio head phones to bale out. We were at 18,000 feet and I was going to roll upside down and shoot out.' But there was no fire and though the controls were sloppy he was over West Malling airfield in Kent, so decided to have a shot at landing:

> All went well. I came in low down on the motor, cut it [as he sailed over] the fence and dropped gently on the wheels. Unfortunately the plane started swinging to the right towards some trees. I pulled on full left rudder with my good foot but nothing happened so I grabbed the brakes — they were shot away too and as I was doing almost 75, I imagined there was going to be rather a mess and a big fire when I hit the trees. Luckily we ran into some sand bags around a gun post, knocking off a wheel en route and finishing up on our nose ... [The gunners fled their pit as the Spitfire rolled towards them but were back in an instant to pull Pattison from the cockpit. Then the doctor arrived with morphia.] ... The shell ... blew up inside so the surgeon had to carve me up fairly well to remove all the bits and pieces. Mincemeat. I was given morphia every night for a fortnight.

Pattison was in Preston Hall Hospital near Sevenoaks, Kent, for eight months, visited one day by the imperious MP Lady Astor, who pestered the patient, repeatedly asking him what she could get for him. Finally, desperate to shut her up, he said he'd love a New Zealand lamb chop. Lady Astor sent her chauffeur off to Sevenoaks. The man returned. 'I'm sorry,' said Lady Astor, 'he can't find a New Zealand lamb chop anywhere; I've bought you an English one and I hope that's okay.'

After Preston Hall, Pattison spent several months at an RAF officers'

DAY AFTER DAY

convalescent hospital at Torquay where he shared a room with friend Mick Shand, out of the Battle of Britain on 25 August when he force-landed on just his second sortie. Shrapnel severed a nerve just below Shand's shoulder and he didn't have the use of his right arm. The nerve took months to repair itself. The two of them used to go out at night for a beer in Torquay, Pattison on crutches. He remembered the first time it happened, 'I had one beer. I said to Mick, "I'm drunk, please take me back." After that I never needed a sleeping pill.' Pattison and Shand were to meet up again in 1942, on 485 Squadron.

GEOFF WELLUM — 'MANY SNAPPERS; KEEP A GOOD LOOKOUT'

Englishman Geoff Wellum joined 92 Squadron just before Dunkirk. He was eighteen years and nine months old, barely out of school, fresh from training truncated because of the onset of war and shortage of pilots. He had never seen a Spitfire close up and had flown just ninety-five hours solo. The fact that he had an 'above average' assessment saved him being sent straight back to an OTU.

On arrival, Wellum was questioned by 92 Squadron CO, Roger Bushell, a barrister in civilian life. He thought Bushell 'a pretty hefty chap and just plain ugly in a pleasant sort of way'. Bushell told the squadron adjutant later that he thought Wellum 'a cheeky young cocky little bugger' but just the same the adjutant thought the CO liked the cut of Wellum's jib.

Bushell, who was furious at the RAF sending him raw, under-trained pilots like Wellum, permitted the youngster to stay for on-the-job training. He was forbidden to fly operationally until after the squadron was posted to Wales. His experience there, with frequent patrolling and squadron exercises, probably saved his life when the squadron returned to Biggin Hill in early September. Now adequately trained, he played a full part in the Battle of Britain, surviving the fury of combat then and later. In 2001 he published *First Light,* his account of his early war years, to acclaim and bestseller status.

In it Wellum writes beautifully of the quiet no-words-wasted exchange between the ground controller (Sapper) and Brian Kingcome, the pilot then leading 92 Squadron — an exchange directing the squadron to the enemy in one action during the Battle of Britain. (Note that 92 Squadron's code name is Gannic, and an angel is an RAF term for 1000 feet of altitude, so angels one five refers to an altitude of 15,000 feet.) As the squadron clears the field on takeoff it begins:

Over the R/T:

R/T: Gannic leader, this is Sapper. One hundred and fifty plus approaching Dungeness angels twelve. Vector 120. Over.

R/T: Sapper, this is Gannic, message received and understood.

R/T: Gannic, bandits include many snappers. I say again, many snappers; keep a good lookout. Over.

R/T: Sapper, this is Gannic. OK, understood. I am steering 120 and climbing hard through angels seven. Over.

R/T: Thank you, Gannic leader.

Wellum: … This looks like being quite a day and quite a party. I swallow hard and find myself calm and excited … I glance at my altimeter … 9,250 feet … Turn on the oxygen …

R/T: Gannic, this is Sapper, you are very close now.

R/T: Sapper, this is Gannic. OK. Tally-ho! Tally-ho! I can see them.

They are at least angels one five and what's more there are hundreds of the sods.

R/T: Thank you, Gannic leader, good luck!

Wellum: … I look ahead into the far distance, the vast panorama of the sky. There it all is, the whole arena for bloody battle, and there they are, the enemy … These are the Huns attacking England, our small country, our island … We are on our own against this … Must be some other friendly squadrons about … at least I bloody well hope so … How the hell can ten of us cope with this lot …

R/T: Gannic from leader. OK boys, in we go. A good first burst and away. Watch for 109s.

Frank Gill and Bernie Brown

It's not every day an RAF fighter pilot in a car captures an Me 109 pilot, but on the evening of 30 September 1940 that's exactly what happened to New Zealander Frank Gill. Driving past Windsor Great Park, the vast green expanse adjacent to Windsor Castle, Gill, a flying officer at the time on 43 Squadron (Hurricane) watched an Me 109 crash-land, wheels up, close by. He jammed on the brakes, pulled off the road and raced across the fields to disarm the shaken but uninjured pilot and put him under arrest. He then put the German in his car, drove to the nearest RAF depot and handed over his prisoner. All in a day's work.

The Me 109 had tangled with fighters overhead and as it dived out of cloud its engine cut and it began to lose height quickly. The local newspaper's report said the aircraft tried to land in the Great Park on the Royal Agricultural Show ground but crashed into stout posts driven into the ground to prevent such landings. The fighter somersaulted, tips of both wings torn off. The pilot, who'd apparently opened the hood, was thrown clear on to the soft ground, groggy but alive — and a prisoner in the hands of Frank Gill.

The damaged 109, punctured by bullets beneath and behind the cockpit and duly inspected by the Princesses Elizabeth and Margaret, was dragged away for display in Windsor village as part of the local campaign to raise funds to buy Spitfires.

Gill, better known in later years as Minister of Police, and Defence, in the first Muldoon Government, and Ambassador to the United States before his death in 1982, was an SSC pilot. Sailing to England in mid-1939, he survived on 88 Squadron Battles in the Battle of France, then transferred to Fighter Command and 43 Squadron in September 1940.

His logbook and air force biography clearly state that he flew in the Battle of Britain with 43 Squadron and was awarded the Clasp by New Zealand authorities. There's not much firmer evidence than that, yet he is not listed among New Zealanders in *A Clasp for 'The Few'* by Ken Wynn or in other British Clasp rolls. One English book included him, simply describing him as 'British', but deleted his name from a later edition without explanation. The same is the case with Robert Strang, who flew at least two qualifying Battle of Britain ops with 66 Squadron and was later lost with 485 Squadron.

Gill was posted to bombers on 75 Squadron in February 1941 after a conversion course at a Wellington OTU. He was awarded a DSO, the citation gazetted in September 1941 noting in particular his gallant conduct with 75 Squadron on raids to Bremen and Berlin. Both times his Wellington was badly shot up, once by fire from a fighter, which his rear gunner shot down, the second by flak. Gill was lauded for 'consummate leadership, courage and determination'. He later

DAY AFTER DAY

flew in the Middle East, was involved in invasion planning and then commanded 490 RNZAF Sunderland Squadron in West Africa. He remained in the RNZAF postwar and was an air commodore when he retired in 1969 just as he went into politics, winning an Auckland seat for National.

Bernie Brown has always had an independent sort of mind, says what he thinks, looks after himself, and is underwhelmed by authority. When told by the air force after his 1938 application for an SSC in the RAF that he was to present himself for an interview in Wellington, he replied he couldn't attend because he'd be on holiday in the South Island. 'I wasn't going to give up my holiday just to go for an interview.' A meek reply came back: 'Please call in to the Defence Department on your way back to Stratford' [where Brown was working at the time as a postman].' Brown showed up with his suitcase at Defence at 10 a.m. on his way home, straight from the ferry. Still carrying his suitcase, he was taken to what he thought was a waiting room. Instead he opened the door to find four gold-braided officers.

> They did the old trick of trying to confuse me, one of them asking me a question, then another interrupting with another question before I could answer the first man. I was used to that, dealing with people complaining about the mail. I remembered each question and answered in turn. They weren't going to catch me that way. Eventually they gave up. So that was it. They said, 'thank you very much' and I said 'thank you', picked up my suitcase and walked to the station.

Brown had a medical, the first he'd ever had, and then received notification that he had been accepted. He was offered a choice: train at Wigram or in England. 'UK please. At least I would get a free trip out of it.' Brown was virtually alone in the world. He had a brother in Blenheim but his mother was dead and his father lived in Australia. When his brother learned he was going to join the RAF he said, 'What do you want to do that for? You've got a good job for life in the Post Office.' Knowing the pay scales and that he'd always be poor if he stayed with the Post Office, Brown was on the *Rangitane* when she sailed from Auckland on 23 September 1938.

Training and pilot selection were tough in the pre-war RAF. Brown was one of twenty on his first course. Four instructors, four trainees per instructor was the limit. 'They took us up and did aerobatics, put the planes upside down. Four would-be pilots were sick. They were out,' Brown says. He finished his training at Sealand — 'horrible place near Chester, steelworks just down the road' — and because he could type and do Morse code was posted to an Army Co-operation unit flying Lysanders. 'I didn't like that very much but still I had to put up with it. It was like spying; spotting and observing.'

Brown made one flight over the front lines during the Battle of France, watching what was going on, Morse keying information back to England. 'We had to keep away from the British army. They were very dangerous. To avoid Lewis machine-gun fire I never came down below 2000 feet.' He also made one abortive flight on an ancient Hector biplane from Hawkinge to dive bomb a German battery at Calais. Over the Channel he tested the two machine guns, firing through the propeller arc. As he pressed the button there was an enormous bang — a split pin on a gun muzzle attachment either failed or hadn't been fixed properly. Something flew off, punching through the main fuel tank, and petrol sprayed over Brown's face. He jettisoned his bombs and turned for home, enough gas left in the gravity tank to land on Hawkinge Golf

DAY AFTER DAY

Course, find out where he was and continue on to his field.

Brown volunteered for Fighter Command, converted to Spitfires in an afternoon with the instruction, not at all unusual at the height of the Battle of Britain: 'Here's the book of pilot notes, learn it and get up there and fly it.' He served briefly on 610 Squadron at Biggin Hill before it was sent on rest, and went north with it before a posting to 72 Squadron saw him back at Biggin Hill again. He remembers arriving to find an airman, list in hand, removing letters from mailboxes near the officers' mess. 'They won't be collecting their mail,' the man explained. Brown had come face to face with the realities of the air war raging over southeast England.

The New Zealander's stay with 72 was short. On 23 September 1940 on his second patrol an Me 109 shot him down.

They were above us and came down, guns firing; bullets, shells all over the place. Then there was a 109 below me. I was turning madly at the time. He must have pulled his nose up and let fly. A cannon shell came through the side of my aircraft, hit me in the left leg and exploded on the throttle box, took it away and the instruments in front. A helluva noise. I had no throttle, no control of the aeroplane so I thought, 'out you go'.

And did. Brown didn't know he'd been hit until he reached the ground, a marshy field near Eastchurch, an airfield on the Isle of Sheppey, Kent. When he tried to stand up he couldn't and discovered his leg was bloodied.

I looked up and saw a bloke from the Home Guard coming towards me. He got about ten yards away and stopped. Didn't say a word. Just stood back and covered me with his rifle. Fortunately an RAF truck came across the field. I'd been seen coming down. The blokes in the truck lifted me on and that Home Guard chap still didn't say a word. I was more frightened about him than anything else. That was the end of my shooting war.

Once recovered, Brown was able to fly again, but not Spitfires and Hurricanes. He instructed for a year in Rhodesia, then flew with Transport and Ferry Commands, delivering Wellingtons to Rabat, Morocco, with the latter. Postwar he flew with British European Airways for more than thirty years before returning to New Zealand and buying an orchard in the Bay of Plenty. In late 2010 and living in Tauranga, he was 92 and still forward-looking, having just built a new house the year before. When this book was finished he was one of four New Zealand Battle of Britain pilots still alive. The others: John Gard'ner, 92, also in Tauranga, night fighter pilot Alan Gawith, 94, in Nelson and Keith Lawrence, 91, who lives on the south coast of England.

Three New Zealand Battle of Britain pilots.

Above left: Bernie Brown in full flying kit. Lysander in background. He was wounded and shot down flying a Spitfire with 72 Squadron from Biggin Hill.
Bernie Brown

Above right: Jack Fleming, burned when he baled out of his blazing Hurricane, was an early member of the Guinea Pig Club. Mrs Joy Fleming

Left: Irving 'Black' Smith, a squadron leader with the DFC, stands on the wing of a Defiant night fighter talking to his flight sergeant gunner.
General Sir Rupert Smith

Left: Tony Dini, a standout fighter pilot in the Battle of France, alongside a Hawker Fury biplane at South Cerney, Gloucestershire, where he gained his wings. Just back from France, he died in a flying accident before the Battle of Britain. Mrs Janice Alford

Middle: A German inspects the remains of John Gillies' 92 Squadron Spitfire which force-landed in a field outside Calais on 23 May 1940. Gillies, English-born son of famed New Zealand pioneer plastic surgeon Sir Harold Gillies, settled in New Zealand postwar. Aircrew Remembrance Society, UK

Below: New Zealander Sir Keith Park, 11 Group commander, who directed the day-to-day action in the RAF's critical southeast sector in the Battle of Britain. This photograph shows Park's personal Hurricane OK1 (the O is on the other side of the roundel), which he flew throughout 1940. He signed the photograph, 'Keith and Friend, 15th September 1941'. Air Force Museum

From the farm to the Spitfire: Horry Copland fought a long struggle to be accepted for pilot training. He eventually achieved his ambition to fly Spitfires.

Above left: Copland with horse Silvie on his father's Southland farm.
Mrs Shona Scott

Above right: Success — a sergeant pilot in England. Mrs Shona Scott

Below: Setting off to clear bush with bulldozer, horse and trailers carrying fuel and supplies. Mrs Shona Scott

Dieppe aircrew.

Above left: Pilot Brian Wheeler, a New Zealander working in Argentina when the war broke out, joined the Royal Canadian Air Force. Here he stands in the cockpit of his 226 Squadron Boston, holding the squadron mascot, a white dog. He was killed in 1944. Mrs Susan Watts

Above right: Eddie Berry from Christchurch, CO of 3 Squadron, was shot down and killed flying a Hurricane at Dieppe. Berry Collection

Below: Aircrew photographed at Buckingham Palace investiture after Dieppe. New Zealand navigator Renton Rutherford (second from left) won the DFC. His pilot, Wing Commander Wilf Surplice (right), received the DSO. Renton Rutherford

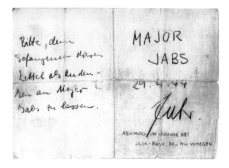

Top: Six 132 Squadron fighters, led by Geoffrey Page — shot down and burned in the Battle of Britain — made the first Spitfire penetration of Germany on 26 April 1944. Here, Page (second from left) and the other pilots on that operation study a map for press photographers. At right is Aucklander Bob Harden, killed four months later. JOHN CAULTON

Middle: Flying with the 132 towards Germany again three days later Hawke's Bay pilot John Caulton was shot down in Holland by Hans Joachim-Jabs. Germans examine the wreck of Caulton's fighter. JOHN CAULTON

Above: A slightly injured and patched-up Caulton talks to Jabs (left). JOHN CAULTON

Left: Jabs signed a small piece of paper for Caulton, a memento of the occasion. Caulton still has it. JOHN CAULTON

These two New Zealanders, flying rocket- and cannon-firing Typhoons of 198 Squadron from Dutch base Gilze-Rijen, died within three days of each other in December 1944.

Above left: Grave of Mate 'Timmy' Milich, a Northlander. He lies in Woudenburg, not far from Utrecht, Holland. ASSOCIATION OF 198 SQUADRON

Above right: Oscar 'Ossie' Oden. He was retained as a pilot for eighteen months in Canada after gaining his wings in August 1942 before being posted to England and Typhoons. This photograph shows him after a successful day's fishing in Canada. MRS AILSA CARMICHAEL

Below: A beaming Milich stands in front of a Typhoon wing. Note cannon poking from wing edge and rockets with 60-pound explosive heads slung on rails under the wing. AUSTRALIAN WAR MEMORIAL

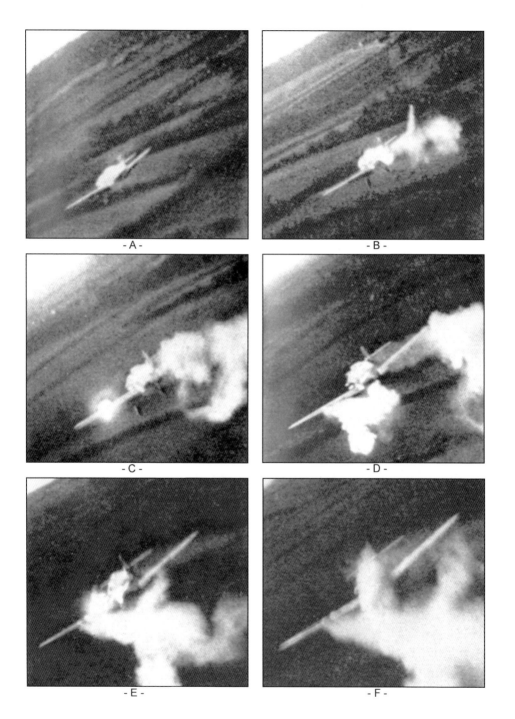

Hit just after takeoff by a hail of Typhoon cannon fire, a
Messerschmitt 109 goes down, engine and port wing flaming.
OFFICIAL HISTORY

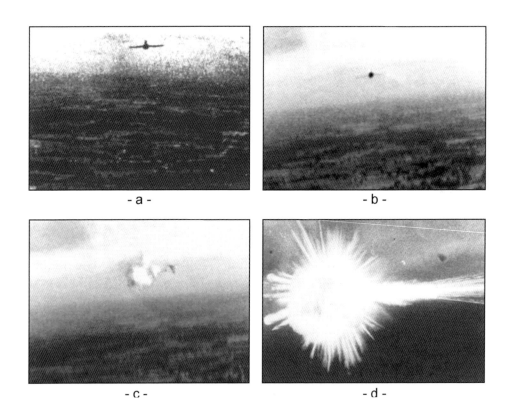

- a -   - b -   - c -   - d -

Above: A V1, chased by a fighter, explodes in a brilliant starburst. AIR FORCE MUSEUM

Below: Sergeant to air commodore. Highly decorated New Zealander Bill Crawford-Compton on the wing of a Spitfire. AIR FORCE MUSEUM

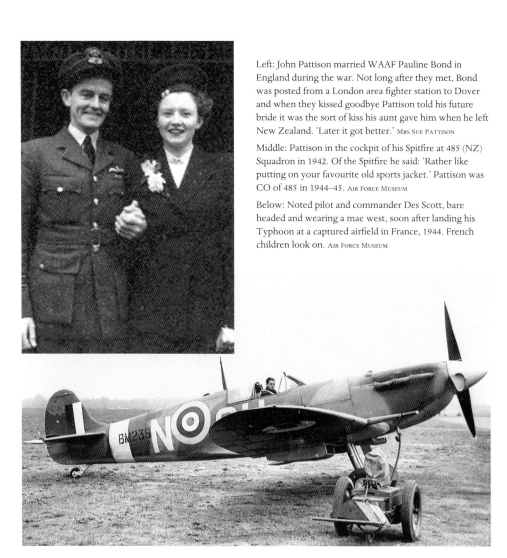

Left: John Pattison married WAAF Pauline Bond in England during the war. Not long after they met, Bond was posted from a London area fighter station to Dover and when they kissed goodbye Pattison told his future bride it was the sort of kiss his aunt gave him when he left New Zealand. 'Later it got better.' Mrs Sue Pattison

Middle: Pattison in the cockpit of his Spitfire at 485 (NZ) Squadron in 1942. Of the Spitfire he said: 'Rather like putting on your favourite old sports jacket.' Pattison was CO of 485 in 1944–45. Air Force Museum

Below: Noted pilot and commander Des Scott, bare headed and wearing a mae west, soon after landing his Typhoon at a captured airfield in France, 1944. French children look on. Air Force Museum

Above: Max Collett, who lives in Taradale, took this remarkable photograph of three 485 Squadron Spitfires ahead of him from his cockpit as they all flew in line astern. MAX COLLETT

Below: Byron Lumsden sits on the wing of his Typhoon. Note the bombs slung under each wing.
RICHARD LUMSDEN

A German FW 190 fighter goes down in 1942, victim of 485 Squadron pilot Tony Robson. Frame four of his gun-camera film shows the canopy flying off, five and six show the pilot baling out. Robson was shot down and taken prisoner in February 1943. AIR FORCE MUSEUM

Above left: Harvey Sweetman as a 486 Squadron flight commander in late 1942.
AIR FORCE MUSEUM

Above right: New Zealand High Commissioner Bill Jordan with some of 'his boys'. Left to right: Marty Hume, Garry Barnett, Jordan and Johnny Checketts.
AIR FORCE MUSEUM

Below: These four New Zealanders had five DSOs and nine DFCs between them at war's end. Left to right: Hawkeye Wells, Colin Gray, Al Deere and Bill Crawford-Compton. AIR FORCE MUSEUM

Above: Group Captain Jamie Jameson and his New Zealand squadron commanders at Volkel, Holland, in early 1945. Left to right: Evan Mackie (80 Squadron), Keith Thiele (3 Squadron), Jameson and Arthur Umbers (486 Squadron). AIR FORCE MUSEUM

Right: Standout pilot Bob Spurdle, commander of 80 Squadron in 1944, in his Tempest. AIR FORCE MUSEUM

Below: 486 Squadron pilot Ralph Evans taxis his Tempest to the runway at Volkel. A ground crewman sits on the starboard wing to direct him — pilots' forward views were restricted on the ground. AIR FORCE MUSEUM

On 1 January 1945 the Luftwaffe made an all-out attack on Allied airfields in northwest Europe. One target was Maldegem, Belgium, where 485 was based. The squadron's Spitfires line-up made tempting targets and the Germans destroyed most of them.

Above: Spitfire pyres. The fighters burn. MAX COLLETT

Below: After the attack. The remains of one Spitfire smoulder. AIR FORCE MUSEUM

Above left: Prince Philip (left) watches a 1953 air display in Germany with Jamie Jameson, who remained in the RAF postwar. JOHN JAMESON

Above right: New Zealander Corran Ashworth, killed flying a Typhoon over France in 1944 when his bombs exploded. This photograph was taken when he was in North Africa. VINCE ASHWORTH

Below: War booty in 1944. Jameson's passenger runabout, a captured German Ju 34 (two crew, six passengers), swastikas and crosses replaced by RAF insignia. Note Jameson's initials, PGJ, painted on the fuselage. JOHN JAMESON

It's all over. Max Collett in front of his tent in Germany on VE Day. Nicked street sign attached to tent pole. The 'chimney' leads from the stove inside. Note the canvas 'wash basin' in left foreground. MAX COLLETT

ROLL OF HONOUR: NEW ZEALAND PILOT DEATHS IN THE BATTLE OF BRITAIN

Sixteen New Zealand pilots died in the Battle of Britain (all RAF unless otherwise specified):

12 July

Flying Officer James Henry Leslie Allen, 25 (Napier), 151 Squadron (Hurricane). The squadron was on convoy escort off the Suffolk coast when it attacked three bombers. Allen's fighter was seen gliding down to the sea with a dead engine. Commemorated at Runnymede.

19 July

Pilot Officer John Richard Kemp, 25 (Wellington), 141 Squadron (Defiant). Bounced by Me 109s, shot down into the sea, while on patrol off Folkestone. Commemorated at Runnymede. See also next entry.

Pilot Officer Rudal Kidson, 26 (King Country), 141 Squadron (Defiant). Killed in the same action as Pilot Officer John Kemp. Commemorated at Runnymede.

22 July

Pilot Officer John Laurence Bickerdike, 21 (Christchurch), 85 Squadron (Hurricane). His aircraft spun off a half roll while approaching Debden after operations and crashed. Buried at nearby Wimbish.

11 August

Pilot Officer Donald Gordon Cobden, 26 (Christchurch), 74 Squadron (Spitfire). Shot down in combat while protecting a convoy. Died on his birthday. His body was later recovered and buried at Ostend, Belgium.

15 August

Pilot Officer Cecil Henry Hight, 22 (Stratford), 234 Squadron (Spitfire). Fatally injured in combat off the south coast. Baled out of his aircraft but did not open his parachute. His body fell in Bournemouth, where he is buried.

Squadron Leader Terence Gunion Lovell-Gregg, 27 (Picton), 87 Squadron (Hurricane). Shot down in the same general action as Cecil Hight. Crash-landed on fire among trees, thrown clear but dead when help arrived. Buried at Warmwell, Dorsetshire.

30 August

Pilot Officer John Sinclair Priestley, 27 (Wellington), RNZAF. 235 Squadron (Blenheim), Coastal Command but attached to Fighter Command. Died when his aircraft, practising circuits, crashed near his airfield, Bircham Newton, Norfolk. Buried at Great Bircham.

7 September

Flying Officer Kenneth Victor Wendel, 24 (Auckland). 504 Squadron (Hurricane). Bounced and shot down in flames over Kent. Badly burned and died in hospital later that day. Buried at Faversham, Kent.

20 September

Pilot Officer Howard Perry Hill, 20 (Blenheim), 92 Squadron (Spitfire). Killed by cannon fire when attacked by enemy fighters from above and behind north of Dungeness. Wrecked plane found in high trees miles away. Buried at Folkestone.

25 September

Pilot Officer Eric Orgias, 25 (Pohangina), 23 Squadron (Blenheim). Port engine failed shortly after takeoff from Middle Wallop, Hampshire, and crashed just south of the airfield. Buried at Over Wallop, Hampshire.

27 September

Flight Lieutenant James Alfred Paterson, 20 (East Chatton, Southland), MBE, 92 Squadron (Spitfire). Killed when his fighter was shot down in action over Kent. Buried at Orpington, Kent.

21 October

Pilot Officer Wycliff Stuart Williams, 20 (Invercargill), mid, 266 Squadron (Spitfire). Died when his fighter stalled and crashed following engine failure immediately after takeoff from Stradishall, Suffolk, where he had stopped to refuel after combat. Buried at Stradishall.

26 October

Sergeant Robert Holder, 23 (Hicks Bay), RNZAF, 151 Squadron (Hurricane). Crashed shortly after takeoff from a satellite field near RAF Digby, Lincolnshire, on a night training exercise. His aircraft lifted off just before that of Sgt Douglas Stanley (see below). Buried at Bidford-on-Avon, Warwickshire.

Flying Officer Geoffrey Mervyn Simpson, 21 (Christchurch), 229 Squadron (Hurricane). Killed after attacking a German float plane near Boulogne, France, and being in turn attacked by enemy fighters. Commemorated at Runnymede.

27 October

Sergeant Douglas Owen Stanley, 24 (Matamata), RNZAF, 151 Squadron (Hurricane). Died in hospital following a crash shortly after takeoff from a satellite field near RAF Digby, Lincolnshire, on a night training exercise the previous night in similar circumstances to Sergeant Robert Holder. Buried at Scopwick, Lincolnshire.

Chapter 8

HORRY COPLAND GOES TO WAR

The Royal New Zealand Air Force began to expand dramatically in 1940 and 1941 as thousands of young men, all volunteers, enlisted in this branch of the services. Many had fathers, uncles or older friends and acquaintances who had fought in the mud and trenches in World War I, and the stories of this bloodied generation left a deep impression. The air force offered an exciting, adventurous adrenaline-charged alternative for young men who might today be termed boy racers with brains. Even before the Battle of Britain, which only deepened the allure of the air war, many were inclined towards the air. Brought up on stories of the heroic deeds of pilots in the Royal Flying Corps and its successor, the Royal Air Force, they built and flew model aeroplanes, devoured Biggles and other air war literature and revelled in the between-wars development of aviation and pioneering New Zealand and trans-Tasman flights. Those who had enough money queued up for aeroplane joyrides and for them there was never much doubt about their choice in wartime. The air force. They all thought they were fireproof and had no notion that so many would not come home.

Horry Copland was breaking in land with a bulldozer on steep scrub-covered hills on his father's farm at Kelvin Grove, east of Gore, when the war broke out. He hated school, quit at 13, was poorly educated academically but already rich in life experiences. Labouring from dawn to dusk left little time for reading. He had, however, enjoyed the biography of famous fighter ace Mick Mannock — twice. When he socialised occasionally with other lads in the district, 'I would talk about what we would do if a war did start ... I had made up my mind that if I was the right age, fit and in a position to do so, I would try to become a fighter pilot.' In November 1939 he wrote his first letter to the air force, the start of a long struggle to achieve his aim.

Aucklander Allan Smith, on the other hand, simply breezed into the RNZAF. He was to command a Typhoon squadron and come out of the war with a double DFC. 'I had always wanted to fly ever since I saw Kingsford Smith land the *Southern Cross* on Takapuna Beach,' he wrote years later. He matriculated at fourteen, was a chartered accountant at seventeen and well on the way to a Bachelor of Commerce degree at Auckland University when war broke out. His father, severely wounded at Gallipoli, signed his papers as did his mother, although more reluctantly. Smith entered Levin on 23 March 1941 with 14 Course. When he reached England, after training here and in Canada, he asked to be a bomber pilot. The RAF said fighters.

Byron 'Lummy' Lumsden tried to join the RNZAF on 13 September 1939 at 16½, eighteen months under the minimum age. He had read *all* the books, admired 1930s pilots who flew over hometown Feilding, made model aeroplanes of balsa wood covered in fine silk, watched Kingsford Smith land at Milson and was shocked when Smithy told the crowd it was the worst bloody airfield he had ever landed on. 'I was horrified one of my heroes had sworn!' Lumsden wrote in a memoir of his wartime years. He was working at Ruakura Animal Research Station near Hamilton just after his 18th birthday when an aircrew selection panel came to town. He was interviewed on 17 March 1941 and his mother, a widow, gave permission for her son to enlist, a brave decision for a woman whose husband had suffered severely in the Great War. Lumsden presented himself at Levin on 4 May 1941, swearing on oath he would be 'faithful and bear true allegiance to our Sovereign Lord the King …'

The RNZAF set stringent age limits and tough education standards for pilots and navigators, although they eased them during the war as the number of volunteers thinned and authorities realised too many talented prospects were missing out. Education requirements were not set so high for air gunners and wireless operators and such 'trades' appealed to those who wanted to go to war quickly. The first batch of RNZAF gunners for attachment to the RAF sailed for Britain in February 1940 and the first handful of navigators, still under training, the following month. In May 1940 the initial draft of twenty-nine RNZAF-trained pilots for the RAF were dispatched. Soon, similar numbers of pilots were going each month and in October, as the Empire Air Training Scheme (EATS), also known in Canada as the British Commonwealth Air Training Plan — BCAPT), began, the first draft of wireless operator/air gunners (WOp/Ags) shipped out to Vancouver for attachment to the Royal Canadian Air Force (RCAF). As they finished their training they sailed on to England for advanced or refresher training before posting to squadrons. In February 1941, the first group of fifty-two pilots left New Zealand for training in Canada.

The numbers of fully trained RNZAF pilots going direct to Britain to join the RAF or via Canada for immediate trans-shipment across the Atlantic swelled dramatically in 1941 and 1942, as did the numbers of pilots and other aircrew shipping to Canada under EATS for training. On 29 April the *Awatea* sailed from Auckland for Vancouver with 367 aircrew aboard and thee months later the *Dominion Monarch* left Auckland with another 398, bound for Liverpool via Halifax. Remarkably, in 223 sailings with New Zealand aircrew passengers in World War II, only three ships were lost and only three RNZAF personnel, all navigators, were lost. Many aircrew had unpleasant, dangerous trips across the North Atlantic, especially in winter, on lone dashes on fast ships, or in convoy, but all made it safely to Britain. Some travelled in reasonable style, others crammed into filthy overcrowded ships with appalling food.

Errol Martyn's tables in *For Your Tomorrow,* Volume 3, tally 3130 RNZAF-trained aircrew for attachment to the RAF between February 1940 and October 1944 and another 7891 RNZAF personnel for Canada between October 1940 and July 1944. Additionally 1080 New Zealanders chosen for Fleet Air Arm training in Britain left between November 1939 and June 1945, while 634 RNZAF-trained ground crew sailed to Britain for attachment to the RAF in roughly the same period.

A handful of RNZAF pilots and other crew arrived in England to take part in the latter stages of the Battle of Britain, but they only began to arrive in numbers direct from New Zealand after its conclusion, and in 1941 and 1942 began flooding in.

Newcomers in late 1940 and early 1941 arrived to find RAF Fighter Command in a state of transition and expansion. The big battle against the Luftwaffe over southeast England had been won. Many thought Hitler might try a second attempt to destroy the RAF and invade in the summer of 1941, not knowing that by then Hitler had turned his mind to the Soviet Union and Britain was safe from invasion. The onset of autumn after the Battle of Britain and then the severe winter of 1940–41 put a severe crimp in flying strategies. Germany's fighters mainly stayed home, though its bombers ranged far and wide at night, on bombing missions against British cities and docks. London was hammered from 7 September 1940 until 10 May 1941 with countless raids in what became known as the Blitz. Night fighters, some squadrons now equipped with the new radar-armed Beaufighters, gradually took an increasing toll of Luftwaffe bombers and their crews. But the sustained assault by night on Britain's cities only ended in May when Nazi bomber squadrons were ordered east for the June 1941 attack on the Russians.

The winter and early months of 1941 gave the RAF a breather, offering it the opportunity to reorganize, rebuild units battered in the struggles of 1940 and to form new squadrons with the rising flow of Spitfires and Hurricanes from the factories. The air defence system was expanded and radar coverage extended. Many squadrons were involved in long patrols and covering convoys, and in the new year RAF fighters began tentative sweeps over the coast of occupied Europe, looking for enemy aircraft.

The more offensively minded Sholto Douglas and Trafford Leigh-Mallory, who'd taken over from Dowding and Park, wanted to challenge the Germans on their home turf. Sweeps were the outcome, where squadrons, and later wings, flashed across the Channel searching for ground targets and enemy fighters. The Luftwaffe often didn't play ball, staying clear of the RAF unless they were in an advantageous situation, preferring to pick off stragglers and the unwary and set ambushes.

Bob Spurdle, an increasingly confident pilot, flew his debut sweep in the first days of March 1941, unusually well rewarded with two Messerschmitt 109s, one over the French coast between Cap Gris Nez

DAY AFTER DAY

and Boulogne and the second on his way back to Manston. He climbed beneath the first, pouring fire into the 109's belly. 'There was a flash and burst of flame,' he wrote. He damaged another and fled. Flying home he spotted a 109 stalking a lone Spitfire southeast of Ramsgate.

> The Spitfire was soon trailing glycol and smoke. The Jerry turned away from his victim back towards France. He hadn't seen me and, opening fire, I closed to point-blank range almost head-on. Clouds of black smoke! Flames! The Hun fell down out of the sky like a flaming torch.

The wounded Spitfire made it back for a forced landing on a beach at Ramsgate, the pilot nonchalantly walking away through the mined sand, ignoring shouting soldiers. Many pilots, Spurdle among them despite his success, hated sweeps because losses frequently outnumbered successes, especially from late 1941, when the new Focke-Wulf 190s, outpacing the Spitfire marks then flying, began to appear.

In 1941 the RAF also began to fly what became known as Circus operations — missions mounted by combined teams of bombers and accompanying fighters, the latter a few squadrons strong early on, with many more later. In the early stages half a dozen or so light bombers capable of only small bomb loads were used. More and heavier bombers took part in Circuses later but lighter aircraft were still being employed at later dates. Poorly performed Venturas, American aircraft, flown by 487 Squadron were massacred by FW 190s over Amsterdam on 3 May 1943 when close-escort fighters failed to materialize. The bombers were left unprotected and suffered horrific losses.

This period also saw the start of hit-and-run raids by German fighters on south coast towns and cities. Me 109s thrashed across the Channel at low level, indiscriminately dropping the couple of bombs they carried and spraying machine-gun and cannon fire before hightailing it back to their bases. They were often too quick for standing patrol Spitfires, who were frequently not in the right place at the right time. It would take the arrival of the Typhoons with their superior speed in 1942 to really catch the raiders, inflict growing losses and largely put an end to the practice.

On a summer day in 1942, Horry Copland, the Southland farmer, began to write about his battle to become a fighter pilot and his life in the RAF as he sat in the cockpit of his Spitfire *Canterbury* (paid for by public subscription in Kent), on the grass strip at Merston airfield, West Sussex. He was with 131 Squadron, part of the Tangmere Wing charged with combating the south coast hit-and-run tactics of the Luftwaffe, and flying sweeps over France. He wrote in a notebook while sitting at readiness in his fighter, which could be off the ground in two minutes if the squadron received word of raiders.

It had been a long hard journey to Merston for the young man from Kelvin Grove. In 1939 he had written his first letter to the air force, and was greatly distressed by the reply. He needed matriculation. Horry didn't have it, having only spent a few months at high school. But he was determined, saying, 'I would not be beaten as easily as that. I would think of something.'

He considered an expensive private course in maths and told the ministry. Back came the answer. 'If you try hard you may be able to pass as an air gunner but there is no chance of becoming a pilot.'

One day he found a notice in the Gore *Ensign* about aircrew night classes at Gore High School. 'I thought I would go for a while and then let [the air force] know I was attending and how I was getting on

Day after Day

and see if they would give me a chance.' He wrote once more, telling them he was doing night courses and asking, 'How much would I have to know to become a pilot and would I get petrol [already rationed] to take me into Gore?' Back came the answers: Do the 21-assignment course (by correspondence), send it to Wellington for marking and then sit an examination. He would need 70 per cent to be a pilot, 50 per cent for an air gunner. No petrol.

Copland rode a horse to and from Gore to learn Morse code — eight miles each way. While he struggled with his papers, he set up a tent, hacking more land out of scrub, bulldozing, fixing the engine and using his own forge to repair damaged implements. On Sundays he worked on algebra, trigonometry, mechanics and arithmetic, his answer papers soiled by dirt- and oil-stained hands. His supervisor in Wellington told him, 'Not neat enough.'

He explained his difficulties, enclosing a photograph of himself working at his table in the open; tractor, plough and tent in the background. This time he received an encouraging answer: 'Quite good, keep it up!' He finished his last assignment and went home to help with lambing and shearing. In November, 1940, he sat the exam in Gore and passed with 77 per cent — honours. This time the air force said: 'You will be notified later when to report to Ground Training School to begin training as a pilot. You will need over 80 per cent in your exams there to pass and be selected as a pilot.'

Copland's vaccinations had a quick and adverse reaction. He wobbled up the road in Gore, where he met two girls he knew. They giggled as, unsteady on his feet, he lay down on a bench. 'A rumour reached my ears that I was drunk in the main street of Gore.' On 19 January 1941 Copland entered camp at Levin, where for six weeks he and the other hopefuls square bashed and studied. The results board showed Copland 88 per cent, 90th of 200 — triumph.

He flew for the first time at Taieri's Elementary Flying Training School on 3 March and on the 21st he soloed. He had totalled forty-one hours by the time his course finished and he began final leave. He sailed on the *Awatea* on 29 April for Vancouver — one of 104 trainee pilots, almost half of whom would be killed. Among those on the same draft were Evan Mackie, destined to become the highest-scoring RNZAF fighter pilot of the war, and George Jameson, top-scoring New Zealand night-fighter pilot. Copland would not become an ace but he would fly Spitfires and he would play a full role in the air war, like thousands of other aircrew. And because he was careful, and maybe lucky, he survived. Copland watched as far ahead as he could from the bow as the *Awatea* surged into the Pacific and mused, 'There lies my future, an absolute blank.'

The man from Kelvin Grove and close friends Alan Edwards, 20 (Dunedin), and Mick Maskill, 20, an itinerant South Islander, flew Harvards at Moose Jaw, Saskatchewan, in sweltering summertime temperatures that reached 110°F in the shade. The station had double runways and planes flew twenty-four hours a day. The three mates emerged with their wings on 8 August 1941, in the top third of their class. They were now sergeant pilots.

A year later Edwards would be dead. On his 105th op, the day before Dieppe, his 129 Squadron Spitfire was seen to ditch and break apart off Cherbourg after an engagement with enemy fighters. His body was picked up nine days later by a destroyer in the Channel and buried at Felixstowe, Suffolk. Maskill survived the war with a DFC, spending almost two years with 485 Squadron and late in the war becoming CO of 91 Squadron.

Their ship arrived in the Clyde on 15 September after a horror trip across the Atlantic via Iceland. Next morning they disembarked at Greenock without breakfast and with nothing to eat until midday, as the train headed for the reception centre at Bournemouth on the south coast. Pies and lettuce. At Bournemouth Copland caught up briefly with Jack Roy, who'd been at those night classes in Gore. 'Poor Jack,' Copland wrote the following year. 'He was only 20 or 21 years of age … He was a fine lad and keen on flying … he deserved to live if anyone did … when my farewell party was held at Waimumu, Jack and Pat Cooney, who is also missing, were on leave and both came to it.' Roy was killed the night of 25–26 June 1942, one of twelve New Zealanders lost over Bremen in the third 1000-bomber raid. Cooney had died three months earlier, the Wellington he was piloting brought down over Belgium. He was twenty-two.

Copland, Maskill and Edwards were among forty New Zealanders posted from Bournemouth to an OTU, at Heston, London. 'We found out they had Spitfires there so we had got what we wanted.' At a London station on the way Copland saw his first Spitfire overhead. 'Would I ever be able to fly one … I felt scared stiff.' On 10 October 1941 he did it. 'I got my parachute and helmet … then I strolled out to the aircraft … I could not believe that the time had come when I was to fly one. I put my parachute on and found my hands were shaking and was glad nobody was standing close to see it.' Soon he was turning into the wind and slowly opening the throttle. 'Before I knew it I was airborne.' Copland flew around for thirty minutes at 250 mph, careful not to lose sight of the airfield.

About to make his first touch-down, he was warned to come in with extreme caution — a plane had just pranged. 'I must land this aircraft without mishap,' Copland said to himself.

Wheels down, how is my height? Flaps down, fine pitch, rich mixture in case I have to make another circuit. Control the rate of descent with the engine, set the trim. That great nose certainly blocks my view. Keep well away from the crash. A look above to see if anyone is landing on top of me. Keep the motor on until I am sure I am almost touched down. Throttle closed, ease back on control column, sinking touch down, a bit of a bump and I was running up the aerodrome landed — flaps up. Then I taxied in feeling very happy with life. Switched off.

Copland signed off at the dispersal office and wrote in his logbook, *First pilot — Self. Aircraft — Spitfire.* 'I had made it but it was hard to believe ... I was now a Spitfire pilot.' On 19 November he was posted to 131 Squadron on Spitfires, ten months to the day after arriving at Levin. Later in the war as the pressure for aircrew eased, the process would take up to twice as long.

While at Heston, Copland met and admired Squadron Leader Michael Pedley, a six-year RAF veteran converting to Spitfires. Copland was expert at rolling his own cigarettes. Pedley was 'very taken by my hand-made cigarettes and often during lectures he got me to roll one for him'. Copland didn't dream then that Pedley was to be his CO at 131 Squadron and that he would fly with him, often as his No. 2, for almost a year. He described Pedley as a 'perfect' squadron leader and as fair a person as he ever met. The two men had a reunion in Southland years later. Pedley won the DSO and DFC during the war, an OBE later and retired in 1957 as a group captain.

Two- and occasionally four-aircraft 'Rhubarbs' were flown from December 1940. This was RAF code for an operation where a section of fighters or fighter-bombers crossed the Channel to harass the enemy, taking advantage of low cloud and poor visibility. They would drop down below cloud level and search for targets of opportunity — railway locomotives and rolling stock, aircraft on the ground or enemy troops and vehicles.

Poor weather was a must for such operations because murky conditions gave the attacking fighters some security — somewhere to hide if they ran into trouble. Weather conditions in England might seem perfect for a Rhubarb but be clear over the French coast, in which case the RAF fighters would turn tail. On these freelance sorties over enemy territory, pilots attacked any target that took their fancy — gasometers were popular because the results could be dazzling explosions. Railway engines and wagons were often blasted and of course Rhubarb pilots sought out low-flying or parked-up German aircraft, airfield buildings, troops and vehicles.

Though many pilots disliked Rhubarbs and their low-flying perils, others revelled in the challenge. They might be on stand-down when someone would bounce into the mess with, 'Who'll come on a Rhubarb with me?' There would be shouts of dismay but in the end someone would usually volunteer. Horry Copland thrived on them.

Operations were planned carefully, particular areas targeted, courses and landmarks plotted. In his memoir, Copland chose not to write much about his ops and combat, preferring to write more about the countryside and farming and his leave-visits to friends and relations. But he did record details of one of his Rhubarbs, an action he called 'the most exciting thing I have ever done'.

He and his No. 2 took off from Merston one July day in 1942 with the cloud base at fifty feet, maintained R/T silence as they whipped across the Channel barely above the waves, navigating abruptly around a British convoy that appeared out of the mist and sent up streams of shells. 'You just cannot come at a convoy even in a Spitfire as they think you are the enemy carrying torpedoes.' Approaching the French coast the weather was clearer, ceiling 500 feet to 1000 feet.

> I am looking for a landmark. I see the harbour, it is to the left. I alter course and in a short time we are crossing coast into a large town. Something is wrong! The targets are different. I open fire on a power station and railway trucks. Looking right I see three trains in the station … to get these engines I must go through the town, turn and come back, but this is forbidden in a Rhubarb. It seems too much of a golden opportunity to miss. As I turn at house-top level at 300 mph and come in from the side, the air is filled with what is like a red hail storm [flak]. The engines blow up, one, two, three.

Back at Merston, Copland discovered his revolver and knife had affected the compass and manoeuvring around the convoy had not helped. Instead of the planned target, Copland and his partner had mistakenly attacked Dieppe, a month before the air and sea assault, and thus of great interest to Intelligence. Flak had damaged his rear spar, almost blowing off the tail.

The events were unrelated but the following day Pedley called him in and asked, 'Sergeant Copland, will you accept a commission?'

'Yes, sir, I will,' the New Zealander replied, astonished.

The Royal Air Force history *The Fight at Odds* (Denis Richards) says that between 20 December 1940 and 3 June 1941, 104 Rhubarbs resulted in only eighteen engagements with German fighters. 'In the course of these we claimed seven enemy aircraft for the loss of eight of our own pilots.' Eleven Circuses in the same period cost twenty-five pilots, while only sixteen enemy were claimed. On the plus side for the RAF was the damage done on the ground.

Rhubarbs were eventually banned, results simply not worth the loss of skilled pilots, but sweeps and Circuses continued, increased after June 1941 when Hitler's forces began their onslaught on the Soviet Union. It was then necessary to up the stakes, to keep heavy pressure on German Luftwaffe forces facing the Channel, in order to deter them moving fighter units east to bolster the Nazi forces attacking the Russians. The more German fighters that could be kept in the west the better.

Chapter 9

ASR — AIRCREW SAVIOURS

The RAF fought the Battle of Britain over home soil but from 1941 it was the Germans who operated close to their bases in occupied France, Belgium and Holland as the RAF increasingly took the battle to the other side of the Channel. German pilots fleeing England in the summer of 1940 feared the Channel. Now it was the RAF's turn.

British pilots baling out over occupied territory faced the prospect of capture and long imprisonment unless they were lucky enough to evade the Germans. Most of those who succeeded did so with the aid of brave people in occupied Europe, who risked severe consequences for helping RAF flyers on the ground.

Pilots of crippled aircraft and those with engine problems now also confronted the perils of the English Channel. Baling out over the sea was a daunting prospect, especially in winter. Even in summer the Channel waters were never warm. Ditching was even more dangerous and was usually attempted only if an aircraft was too low to permit a pilot to parachute. Putting a Spitfire or Hurricane down on the sea was a high-risk operation. Normally, most aircraft sank like stones in seconds. Pilots thrown forward by deceleration forces, knocked cold, heads smashing into gunsights or other parts of the cockpit, had little chance of escaping.

One such death was that of brilliant Irish pilot Paddy Finucane, DSO, DFC and two bars, with thirty-two enemy aircraft to his credit when he perished. Coming out over the French coast at low level on 15 July his radiator was hit by fire from a single German machine gun on the ground. Far too low to bale out after his engine quit, he plunged into the Channel. Fellow pilots that day remember his last R/T words, 'This is it chaps.' He was never seen again. Two months short of his 22nd birthday, he was the youngest wing commander in the RAF.

For those who survived bale outs or ditchings, rescue was problematical in the early stages of the war, when air-sea rescue was rudimentary. Chances of being picked up improved dramatically as the conflict wore on, but early on there was no properly organized system for finding and rescuing aircrew down in the seas around Britain. Pilots who survived coastal or Channel bale outs or ditchings in the Battle of Britain relied on lifejackets to keep them alive until rescue — if they were lucky. And quick rescue was paramount. Men swimming in the Channel, with or without a lifejacket, did not last long and one-man dinghies attached to the parachute packs on which pilots sat were yet to come.

On 23 April 1941 about 6.30 a.m. Alan Kelly, 23, a Dunedin school teacher before enlistment, was flying a 247 Squadron Hurricane returning from a two-plane shipping patrol over Falmouth, Cornwall. Formatting closely on his leader, they went down to get under cloud cover. When the leader emerged in clear sky Kelly was no longer with him. Someone ashore reported a Spitfire landing in the sea about half a mile from the coast off St Agnes Head on Cornwall's west coast. The RAF theorised Kelly might have run out of main-tank fuel and not realised this was the cause of subsequent engine failure, or force-landed while changing to his reserve tanks, while distracted. An RAF accident report records that searching aircraft spotted him three times but *For Your Tomorrow* says, 'Sadly, rescue efforts were delayed through a series of errors [one false report said he had swum ashore] and he was dead when picked up after midday.' He may well have lived had he been in a dinghy. The RAF report stressed the need for the urgent issue of single-seat dinghies to pilots on convoy duties. Such dinghies later carried a sail.

Keith Park took a hand in improving the rescue odds in July 1940 by borrowing Lysanders, acting as spotters, to work closely with high-speed launches and other craft. This move was vital — about 200 pilots lost their lives in the sea around Britain during the Battle of Britain.

Another New Zealander played a key role in advancing air-sea rescue. Russell 'Digger' Aitken, who was born in Outram in 1913, arrived in England in 1935 to seek an SSC. Working during the Battle of Britain as an instructor at Gosport, on the west side of Portsmouth, he saw many aircraft on both sides shot down and, the *Official History* discloses, conceived the idea of using amphibians to pick up pilots.

Says Alan Mitchell in *New Zealanders in the Air War*: 'He scrounged a Walrus from the Fleet Air Arm and took up what he regarded as a strategic position off the Isle of Wight. Here he waited patiently for air battles to develop.'

The Germans had the same idea and a Heinkel 59 would float not far from Aitken's Walrus. Mitchell quotes Aitken as saying that when battle casualties were seen drifting down, 'like a couple of ducks, waddling and flapping' they would both take off and set out on their missions. In his brief period of pioneering ASR, Aitken and his crew picked up thirty-five men from both sides, alive and dead.

His work soon led to the establishment of permanent ASR squadrons equipped with Walruses and Lysanders. One Walrus squadron alone rescued more than 600 aircrew. The ugly little Walruses pulled off some amazing and heart-warming rescues over the years.

Aitken himself knew what it was like to be rescued. While serving with the Fleet Air Arm he was washed off the quarter-deck of HMS *Ark Royal,* spending half an hour in a cold sea without a lifejacket before being picked up by a destroyer's boat.

The Air Sea Rescue service was formed officially in February 1941. Walruses, Lysanders, RAF high speed launches (HSLs), naval craft, coastal life-saving units, fishing trawlers, other elements and better communications were welded together into a highly effective rescue system by war's end. Squadrons made enormous efforts to find their downed pilots and as the war went on the RAF and ASR developed a range of life-saving craft, some engined-powered, which they dropped to single pilots and bomber crews to aid survival. Despite best efforts, however, many pilots endured harrowing times before rescue.

John Pattison's Spitfire was one of four lost by 485 Squadron on 26 April 1942, the only time other than 22 August 1943 that losses reached such a level. Pattison parachuted into the Channel, Travis Goodlet was taken prisoner and Jack Liken died of injuries after he was picked up from the water near England. Lloyd 'Mac' Ralph got his badly damaged fighter home but it was such a wreck it was written off. Enemy fighters in strength waded into the squadron, which was acting as high cover to Hurribombers (Hurricanes carrying 250- or 500-pound bombs) raiding Calais, inflicting heavy losses. Goodlet was blown out of his Spitfire when it exploded and floated down to be grabbed by German troops.

Liken, 28 (Oamaru), was hit by enemy fire and wounded. He nursed his critically damaged fighter across the Channel but was forced to bale out near the coast. He was soon plucked from the water but died in hospital that night.

In his interview with Alison Parr in 2006, three years before his death, Pattison remembered 485 Squadron was working with a new radar system that afternoon. '[Control] said they could tell the height and position of German fighters. We were at 20,000 feet over France and they reported thirty plus Focke-Wulfs 10,000 feet below us. A wonderful position to dive down and attack … they were 10,000 feet above us.'

The 190s screamed down and let fly and in a moment had shot down three Spitfires and left Ralph's badly damaged. Pattison's machine was hit in the coolant system and soon the glycol began to burn, white smoke filling the cockpit. He pushed button D to give a Mayday and received an acknowledgment from England. Then he glided as far as he could towards home, gave a final call, saying, 'It looks bloody cold down there', and baled out at 2000 feet.

Once in his dinghy, Pattison had trouble staying in it because of the rough seas. After a while a powerfully engined rescue boat approached, presumably in response to his Mayday, but it stopped short of him, picked up another pilot — certainly Liken because Pattison says it was someone from 485 Squadron — and turned away towards the coast.

It was now getting dark and very cold but Pattison was lucky. A lone low-flying Spitfire passed over him then climbed, obviously having seen him. Eventually he spotted a pair of boats heading his way.

One of them found me and came alongside. They dropped a rope ladder but even though I had only been in the water an hour and forty minutes, I was so cold I couldn't climb up it. They had to haul me on board and then the skipper poured me a large mug full of neat rum. I put it to my nose and said, 'I'm sorry, I'm seasick and can't drink it.' 'Bad luck chum,' he said and down it went. So then we went back to Dover.

When Pattison gave his Mayday it was heard by his future wife, Pauline Bond, working at the time in the plotting room at the sector station at Kenley where 485 Squadron was based. They began their courtship there, and Pattison said that when Pauline was posted to Dover they kissed goodbye. 'I said, "That's the sort of kiss my aunt gave me when I left New Zealand." Later it got better.'

On 26 April 1942 the name of young pilot officer Evan 'Rosie' Mackie appeared on 485 Squadron's honours board for the second time. Mackie's probable was the only success that day to balance the squadron's heavy losses. A month earlier he had his first success, a half share of an Me 109, a fighter downed jointly with Bill Crawford-Compton. When he left the squadron in January 1943 for North Africa with the half and the probable to his name, it's likely no one imagined he would end the war as the top-scoring RNZAF pilot with twenty-three enemy aircraft credited to him and a chestful of decorations.

Johnny Checketts, eventually a wing commander, was still a lowly pilot officer on 485 Squadron when he was shot down into the Channel on 4 May 1942. The squadron, on a fighter sweep, was bounced by enemy fighters, first by one small group and then by more, in the Boulogne area. Checketts and David Russell, 25 (Auckland), parachuted and both landed in the sea alive. Luck then played its hand. Checketts was picked up from his dinghy by a naval launch in about an hour. Russell, however, was not found until several hours later and died from exposure later that night.

ASR — AIRCREW SAVIOURS

Their Spitfires had taken off from Kenley at 7.05 p.m. so the sky was darkening as the search began, the men's position radioed by their comrades. Checketts struggled into his dinghy with great difficulty. According to Vincent Orange's book on Checketts, *The Road to Biggin Hill,* the pilot then 'felt blissfully at ease — until he realised that the dinghy was half full of icy water and that he had never been so cold, so frightened or so tired in all his life'. Orange adds that now it was 9 p.m. and Checketts knew that unless he was rescued before dark he had little prospect of seeing another dawn. Spotting what seemed to be a buoy with a mast, he tried to paddle towards it, but already weakening, he failed to make much progress. A few minutes later a Lysander flew overhead and dropped a smoke float almost on top of him. Orange says the mast Checketts had thought was attached to a buoy began to approach and turned out to be part of a 'lovely little vessel', HM *Motor Launch No. 139.* The crew plied him with rum, rubbed him down with a rough towel and rolled him in a blanket with three hot-water bottles and gave him a slice of brown bread and Marmite. The launch pulled into Dover at midnight and in the morning Checketts was flown back to Kenley. The next time he was shot down Checketts would take much longer to make it back to his unit.

Johnnie Johnson called Jim Sheddan 'a prickly pear', while Johnny Iremonger wrote that he 'enjoyed off-duty life' to the full. Ill-discipline, drinking episodes and sheer cussedness spelled trouble for Sheddan in his early years. Eventually he smartened up and with Des Scott's understanding prospered. By war's end he was the CO of 486 Squadron, a maverick made good.

Sheddan's Typhoon was hit by flak coming out of France on 3 October 1943, and his engine failed. He could either jump or ditch

DAY AFTER DAY

and perhaps surprisingly chose the latter option. He jettisoned the hood, tightened his straps and turned off the switches. 'Nothing is more disastrous than the engine giving a feeble splutter as you are about to touch down,' he wrote in his 1993 book *Tempest Pilot*. Sheddan levelled off a foot above the flat calm sea and maintained backward pressure on the control column, retaining lift as his speed dropped. The tail made first contact and the Typhoon planed along. 'A piece of cake,' Sheddan thought as he loosened his straps, getting ready to leave in a hurry. But as the water reached the leading edge of the Typhoon's thick wing — bang! From seventy to eighty miles per hour to zero. 'It was like hitting a concrete wall,' he wrote. 'With no straps ... I was pitched head first on to the gun sight and for me the lights went out.' His scalp split open to the bone, deep gashes above and below his lips cut through to the gums. He regained consciousness quickly, scrambled out of the cockpit and popped to the surface. 'A moment of panic and I would have had my time.'

In his dinghy, at that stage unaware he had rocket flares, he spent an uncomfortable, cold afternoon. While 486 Squadron had radioed his position, the squadron was sent out to pinpoint a downed Boston crew and 197 Squadron dispatched to look for Sheddan. It was a mistake. Sheddan could see the searching Typhoons but they were too far away. At dusk as the wind rose two Spitfires almost took off his head, they were so low. Sheddan crouched in the bottom of the water-filled dinghy to avoid them. They didn't see him. That night he froze in a rough sea, doused by waves that defeated the dinghy cape. Almost as soon as it was light 486 Squadron, led by Scott and determined to find their man if he were still alive, took off from Tangmere. They did and to make certain they'd seen him, Sheddan fired off a rocket. But as 486 Squadron drifted further away so as not to alert watchers on the

French coast to what was going on, they lost sight of the dinghy and feared Sheddan might now be dead or passed out from exhaustion, because he was no longer firing rockets.

When a Walrus arrived on the scene Scott was unable to give him Sheddan's precise position so the rescue plane circled towards the French coast and spotted the dinghy. The Walrus landed and the crew, with great difficulty in the big, short sea now running, snagged Sheddan's lifejacket and dragged him aboard. As the aircraft started its surging run for takeoff a large wave tore off the port float and swept it away. The Walrus lost flying speed. No way could it get back in the air. Minus the float and thus port wing low, the Walrus crewman and Sheddan crawled out on to the starboard wing tip, hands curled around the leading edge, toes hooked over the trailing edge — as human counterweights. For an hour they stayed there, frozen to the bone in danger of being ripped into the sea while the skipper taxied towards England. Eventually an ASR boat rescued them all. 'Those Air Sea Rescue boys were the real heroes of World War II,' Sheddan wrote — with just cause. He died in December 2010.

On 13 April 1944 New Zealander Peter Donkin splashed into the Channel, parachute folding down beside him, soon after 11 a.m. as his No. 2, Australian pilot Frank Normoyle, circled and watched Donkin safely clamber into his dinghy and wave, before heading for England. Donkin was rescued by a British minesweeper off England's southeast coast at 7.30 p.m. on 19 April; given up for lost, he had survived six days and five nights.

At the time Donkin was a group captain, commanding 35 (Reconnaissance) Wing, set up as the invasion loomed to provide reconnaissance photographs and intelligence for the many units of 84 Group. Basically it comprised Mustang Squadrons 2 and 268, and

DAY AFTER DAY

Spitfire Squadron 4, and operated from England until 15 August 1944, when it flew to Europe.

Donkin and Normoyle, a 268 Squadron pilot, had taken off from Gatwick at 10.30 a.m. to take oblique photos of the Belgian coast at Ostend. The intelligence officer, Squadron Leader Laurence Irving, wrote later that he 'deplored Pete's appetite for action' (group captains were not expected or encouraged to fly but some did and workaday pilots applauded such action), and when he learned Donkin was missing was appalled by the prospect of his loss for 'I [knew] of the wing's dependence on his wise and stern control of its activities.' He also thought that if captured Donkin might be liable to tough interrogation by Germans, who would suspect such a high-ranking officer might have information about the coming invasion.

In calm, overcast weather with visibility down to 1500 yards, Donkin turned his Mustang over and dived steeply for his target. At 500 feet the two planes swept past Ostend through heavy flak. Climbing away, Donkin called the Australian to close. He was streaming glycol and could see it trailing away in his mirror, telling the Aussie he would have to take to his chute. Donkin transmitted a Mayday, turned the Mustang on its back and fell out. He made a rough landing about fifteen miles off Ostend, slightly injuring a hand and thigh but, more importantly, losing the dinghy's smoke flares.

Intensive search and rescue operations began immediately, squadron after squadron searching unsuccessfully. That night Irving broke the news to Donkin's pregnant wife. Fog hampered the search the next day and as the third day ended hope for Donkin ebbed. So many pilots had clambered safely into dinghies and had never been seen again.

At 3.30 a.m. on 20 April Irving was woken with the news that Donkin had been rescued. He found his New Zealand friend in a Dover hospital sitting up in bed eating breakfast. 'He looked like a famished eagle, his beak-like and sun-scorched nose projecting from his pale and emaciated face below a pair of dark sockets from which his eyes blazed fiercely.' Swollen feet were his only major problem.

Donkin was sustained by his fierce determination to survive, self-discipline and patience. Four of the dozen concentrated chocolate and condensed milk tablets in his rations were still in reserve when he was found. Heavy rain one day had temporarily slaked his thirst. His worst moment was when he fell out of his dinghy. He managed to get back in but realised it would be fatal to fall out a second time. At one stage wind and tide carried him towards the French coast, then changed and moved him closer to England.

Donkin was quoted in one news report saying that not the least of his trials was the habit of Marauders (Allied light bombers) testing their guns as they flew out on ops. 'The bullets often peppered around too near to be healthy. Sometimes planes passed so close that they stirred my hair, but they never saw me.'

Donkin returned to duty at the head 35 Wing in May 1944 until his posting in the August to a staff job. He was an exceptional leader who deserves to be better remembered in New Zealand.

Chapter 10

485 AND 486 SQUADRONS BEGIN TO FLY

Fighter combat tailed off after the end of the Battle of Britain, on 31 October 1940, and casualties declined. The only Fighter Command New Zealander killed in the November to December period, and that accidentally, was Hurricane pilot Jack Courtis, 26 (Invercargill). He received his wings in New Zealand and arrived in Britain in late August. He joined 111 Squadron in Scotland a month later and earned his Battle of Britain Clasp flying patrols and escorting convoys in the north. He died three weeks before Christmas, his Hurricane smashing into a hill in bad weather, on a ferry flight from Drem to Montrose.

Despite this lull in fighter pilot losses, New Zealanders continued to die in the air war. Twenty of them in Bomber and Coastal Commands were lost in the same period in late 1940, most on operations. It was a pattern set to continue — 268 New Zealanders died serving in Fighter Command in World War II and another forty-seven in Second Tactical Air Force (2TAF). Coastal Command deaths reached 272, while 1851 died serving with Bomber Command. One of the reasons for the frightening toll in Bomber Command was the fact that when a bomber went down it was normally carrying between five and seven aircrew. The chances of death were far greater in bombers than in fighters. No wonder the fighter boys looked with awe and compassion on aircrew in Bomber Command.

New Zealand pilots and other aircrew poured into Britain in 1941 and 1942, spreading to every part of the country and to every RAF command. Normally most aircrew went straight to south coast reception centres, billeted in seaside hotels, flats and guest houses and given a few days' leave. Fighter pilots were then usually posted to an Advanced Flying Unit (AFU) for a brief refresher course and to familiarize themselves with their new environment — poor weather, industrial haze, balloon barrages etc. Next was an OTU for conversion to the types of aircraft they were to fly — Hurricanes or Spitfires in the early days and Mustangs, Typhoons and Tempests later — and combat training. Postings to squadrons followed. Almost all of them were sergeants or pilot officers; progress to higher ranks depended on performance, sometimes luck and casualties. Growing numbers were transferred to Malta, the Middle East and Egypt as the war situation in those areas developed. Some went further afield to India and Burma, particularly later in the war.

Making it to theatres edging the Mediterranean became a difficult and lengthy process. The RAF Official History notes that until the Germans overran France in June 1940 and Italy entered the war, the RAF staged aircraft through southern France, French North Africa, Malta and the Western Desert to Egypt, or had them carried by ships through the Mediterranean. Once Italy joined the Axis everything changed. The Italian air force began attacking shipping and the Vichy French control of French possessions on the southern side of the Mediterranean meant staging became almost impossible, except for long-range aircraft flying direct to Malta or Cairo via Gibraltar. The major solution was the 4000-mile cross-Africa delivery based on the route developed by Imperial Airways in 1936 for a weekly service from Lagos to Cairo across Nigeria and French Equatorial Africa to Khartoum in Sudan, then north to Egypt.

The RAF chose Takoradi on the coast of what is now Ghana as the western terminus and began urgently developing facilities. Cargo ships and carriers started delivering crated aircraft and fighters, which only needed their wings attached before they were ready to fly. On 19 September 1940 the first six Hurricanes, guided by a shepherding Blenheim, took off from Takoradi. Five surviving fighters — one was wrecked — and the Blenheim reached Cairo seven days later. Until the Germans were defeated in North Africa in 1943, thousands of aircraft were delivered through Takoradi. It was a roundabout journey and aircraft needed overhauling in Cairo, but it was effective.

Malta was a special case. When the Italians began bombing the island in June 1940 Malta's defences amounted to four Gladiators. Soon only the famous threesome, *Faith, Hope* and *Charity* were left. Four Hurricanes were added late that month after just such a staged journey, but more were desperately needed. On 12 August a dozen were flown off the carrier HMS *Argus* and reached Malta safely. A repeat operation on 16 November ended in disaster.

Powerful Italian naval units were at sea and on the hunt. Aware of the threat, the navy launched the Hurricanes between 400 and 450 miles west of Malta, further away than planned. The first flight of six fighters and a Skua, acting in a navigating role, encountered strengthening headwinds and two of the Hurricanes ran out of fuel, ditching short of Malta. One pilot was rescued. The second flight of six

Hurricanes, their fuel exhausted, went into the sea one by one. None of the pilots were found. Their accompanying Skua crash-landed in Sicily, its tanks dry and its crew captured.

One of the six second-flight pilots was New Zealander Pat Horton, 20 (Wellington). He had flown and survived the Battle of Britain with 234 Squadron only to lose his life in a tragic cockup, what one admiral called a 'frightful failure'. In the case of Horton it was a particular waste of a talented and promising fighter pilot. He had volunteered for the Middle East and was posted to 261 Squadron at Luqa on Malta, and promoted to flying officer on 7 November, about the time he embarked on *Argus*.

One young New Zealand pilot reached the Mediterranean by an extraordinary route. Gerry Westenra, great-uncle of singer Hayley Westenra, was at the beginning of a trip in Kenya when the war began and signed on with a training flight of the Kenya Auxiliary Air Unit. By February 1940 he was in the RAF, undergoing pilot training in Iraq. Westenra flew Gladiators with 112 Squadron in the ill-fated Greek campaign with great success, and Hurricanes in Crete. His was among the last one or two serviceable Hurricanes in Crete when he escaped to Egypt with nothing but his toothbrush. He continued to fly with distinction in Egypt and Libya on 112 Squadron Tomahawks and Kittyhawks (he is thought to have played a leading role in the painting of the famous 'sharks' teeth' on the squadron's fighters), with 601 Squadron (Spitfire) further west in North Africa and led 93 Squadron (Spitfire) in Italy from September 1943 to February 1944. Eventually posted back to England, he commanded 65 Squadron (Mustang) in England and France from March to July 1944; altogether Westenra flew more than 350 sorties.

Two New Zealand squadrons that would play a prominent role in

Fighter Command and 2TAF operations formed in England in the second and third years of the war. First was 485 Squadron in March 1941, followed a year later by 486 Squadron.

The other New Zealand squadrons — 487, 488, 489 and 490 — are outside the scope of this book: 487 Squadron operated Venturas and Mosquitoes as bombers; 488 Squadron was equipped with Beaufighters, flying as night intruders, and later with Mosquito night fighters; 489 Squadron flew Hampdens then Beaufighters on anti-submarine and anti-shipping attacks; 490 Squadron, based in West Africa, performed anti-submarine, convoy escort and ASR flights with Catalinas and Sunderlands.

The RNZAF, far distant from the European air war, couldn't possibly fully man (especially with ground crew) and run these squadrons. Even though they officially carried RNZAF titles, they became squadrons within the RAF, with a New Zealand identity — a follow-on from 75 Squadron, which began life in April 1940 with Wellington bombers bought by New Zealand and intended for New Zealand use. They were gifted to the RAF when war broke out.

The first 488 Squadron was an exception. It was formed entirely of New Zealand personnel at Rongotai in September 1941 and shipped to Singapore, where it received its aircraft and was always known as 488 Squadron RNZAF. After the galling British defeat in the Far East in early 1942 the remnants returned to New Zealand, where the squadron disbanded, to be reborn in England as a New Zealand squadron.

New Zealanders always comprised a fair percentage of the aircrew on the 485–490 squadrons, particularly 485 Squadron and 486 Squadron, but not exclusively so. Britons, Australians, Canadians and others served with them and many felt a mix of nationalities was best. Some New Zealanders 'broke their necks' to get on to a New

Zealand squadron; others had no desire to serve with their fellow countrymen, reckoning they didn't travel 12,000 miles to Britain to fly with other New Zealanders. Sometimes New Zealanders had a say in their postings, mostly not, although smart New Zealand COs could wangle New Zealanders they wanted from other squadrons. The RAF was cognisant of nationalities and often strove to place New Zealanders in 'New Zealand' squadrons, especially when 485 Squadron and 486 Squadron formed.

On 1 March 1941, 485 Squadron began life at RAF Driffield in Yorkshire, a famous bomber base taken over briefly by Fighter Command. The bombers returned in April and the squadron moved to nearby Leconfield, just north of Hull, for three months.

The squadron had ten COs from its founding until August 1945, when it was disbanded. All were New Zealanders, with the exception of Scot John Niven.

The first was Marcus Knight. Reading between the lines in some squadron members' comments he was not the most popular CO, described by one writer as distant. However, he accomplished the task of forming the squadron and knocked it into shape. It flew its first operation, patrolling a convoy off the Yorkshire coast on 12 April, and Knight, fittingly, scored the squadron's first success, downing a Ju 88 on 2 June 1941 when the squadron trapped the German on a convoy patrol. Knight came from a well-to-do farming family in New Zealand but worked his way to England in 1935 to join the RAF. He instructed during the Battle of Britain year then flew Hurricanes with 257 and 310 (Czech) Squadrons, before being posted to 485 Squadron. He left the squadron in November 1941 and later served in North Africa and the Middle East. He retired from the RAF in 1958 with the rank of group captain.

Knight was followed, in order, by Hawkeye Wells, Reg Grant, Reg Baker, Johnny Checketts, Marty Hume, John Niven, Johnny Pattison, Keith Macdonald and Stan Browne — great fighter pilots who each led the squadron with distinction. Wells and Checketts, both with a high tally of German fighters, are perhaps the most familiar today. The New Zealand Official History says in one place Fighter Command credited 485 Squadron with the destruction of fifty-eight enemy aircraft but in another says the squadron destroyed sixty-three in combat with another 25 probables. Paul Sortehaug and Phil Listemann, in their compact history of the squadron, list seventy-two confirmed and twenty-five probables. Thirty-nine pilots were killed and another thirteen became POWs. Nine of the twenty originals were among the dead, killed at various times of the war, and nine New Zealanders are listed as original ground crew.

The founding twenty pilots of 485 Squadron, all New Zealanders, were quite a mix. Both flight commanders, Frankie Brinsden and John Martin, had flown in the Battle of Britain, and so had three others. Wells, already with three German aircraft to his credit at 41 Squadron, took over as a flight commander when Martin was posted, and was promoted to command 485 Squadron when Knight left. He was to prove outstandingly successful as a fighter pilot and leader. One or two of the rank and file had prior experience on RAF squadrons, but about half were sergeants, and recent arrivals from New Zealand. Two of the non-commissioned men were to make indelible marks as the war wore on.

Harvey Sweetman, who left New Zealand in October 1940, later flew Typhoons and Tempests with 486 Squadron and was given command of historic 3 Squadron in September 1944.

Bill Crawford-Compton had an enormously successful war and

career, rising from the ranks at 603 Squadron and then 485 Squadron, to become an air vice-marshal in the RAF postwar. He shot down twenty-one enemy aircraft to put him among the top-scoring New Zealanders and, arguably, was the most highly decorated with the DSO and bar, DFC and bar and a clutch of foreign medals. Not bad for a boy from Invercargill who gave up a lowly job in a shop and left New Zealand on a ketch in 1939, hoping to get to England to join the RAF. He did, but only after the boat was wrecked off New Guinea, the crew living on an island among primitive tribesmen for six weeks before finally making it to civilisation. Taken on as a crewman aboard a tramp steamer, he eventually reached England three days after the war began. He enlisted as a lowly ground crew aircraftman, was chosen for pilot training, and served briefly on 603 Squadron before being posted to 485 Squadron. He had five enemy planes confirmed in his first year on the squadron, the same as Wells. A flight commander, he was groomed to replace Wells as CO but broke an arm and missed his chance.

Others of the twenty did well after their time at 485 Squadron, including Jim Porteous who won a DFC in the Middle East and commanded 122 Squadron (Mustang) late in the war. High-scoring Buck Collyns, Johnny Houlton, Evan Mackie, Jack Rae and Gray Stenborg all flew at various times with the squadron.

Unlike 485 Squadron with its New Zealand leader, 486 Squadron, when it was formed on 7 March 1942 at Kirton-in-Lindsey, Lincolnshire, was under the command of Bob Roberts, a Londoner and pre-war RAF. He'd flown in France and over Dunkirk but missed the Battle of Britain, grounded for medical reasons. New Zealanders made up the rest of the squadron. Flight commanders were Harvey Sweetman, posted over from 485 Squadron after a year with the Spitfires and still only 20, and

Johnny Clouston, ex 258 Squadron, where he had served under his CO brother Wilf, 403 (Canadian) Squadron and 111 Squadron.

Another twenty-four pilots made up the roster. Among them were men whose names would become familiar to droves of newspaper readers in New Zealand as the exploits of 485 Squadron and 486 Squadron were recorded by Alan Mitchell, New Zealand Press Association correspondent in London.

The roll call of 486 Squadron COs and flight commanders reads like the pages of a New Zealand wartime Who's Who. Roberts was followed as squadron leader by the notable Des Scott, one of New Zealand's air war greats, Ian Waddy, Arthur 'Spike' Umbers, Keith 'Hyphen' Taylor-Cannon, Warren Schrader and Jim Sheddan. Englishman Johnny Iremonger, an interloper as it were but a good bloke, served for a year as CO between Waddy and Umbers. Leading 486 Squadron proved to be a risky job late in the war. Waddy was shot down and captured in 1944 and in 1945 Umbers and his replacement, Taylor-Cannon, were killed in quick succession.

Sweetman flew two separate operational tours as a flight commander before his appointment as CO of 3 Squadron, Clouston went on to become a squadron leader as did Allan Smith, leader of a flight in 1943–44. Waddy, Umbers and Taylor-Cannon were flight commanders before they took charge of the squadron. DFCs were sprinkled on the squadron like confetti and Scott was made DSO in August 1943 for his leadership of the squadron.

Over its three years of existence 486 Squadron claimed eighty-one and a half enemy aircraft destroyed in the air, the half credited as the squadron's first. Sweetman shot down a Dornier 217 on the night of 23–24 July 1942; it was clearly his but a Canadian Spitfire pilot also put in a claim and the aircraft was eventually recorded as a shared, the half always standing out like a sore thumb. Twenty-eight pilots died while flying with the squadron.

For three months 486 Squadron flew Hurricanes, before switching to Typhoons at Wittering, just west of Peterborough, where it was posted after a brief stay at Kirton. The squadron was re-equipped with deadly and faster Tempests in January 1944, with which it operated until war's end. When the squadron arrived at Wittering, commanded then by the already legendary Basil Embry, it found itself sharing the field with the Mosquitoes of 151 Squadron, with whom New Zealander 'Black' Smith had already made his name. Also there was Jamie Jameson, wing commander flying with Spitfire squadrons.

The squadron worked first with a flight of Havocs and Bostons based at other fields and equipped with the Turbinlite searchlight. The Havocs searched the night skies for German raiders with still primitive radar and if they found one, closed and snapped on the powerful searchlight located on the nose of the aircraft. The idea was that accompanying Hurricanes would then be able to see the enemy aircraft and shoot it down. The plan had its supporters but never really worked, and in January 1943 it was finally abandoned.

In June 486 Squadron was put to work with Turbinlite-equipped aircraft, their Hurricanes painted black. The squadron never managed to score a German bomber while working with the Turbinlites and ironically Sweetman got his 'half' when he used his own eyes to spot and attack the Dornier on a lone, local patrol just after midnight.

The New Zealanders received their first Typhoons in the last days of July 1942 and gradually converted to the new monster fighter with its thick wings, enormous three-bladed propeller, huge twenty-four cylinder Napier Sabre engine and distinctive deep-chin radiator. The Typhoon, affectionately known as the Tiffy, was a flop as a high-altitude interceptor with a slow climb and poor performance above 20,000 feet. But its high speed at low level made it ideal to counter the Luftwaffe's FW 190, which was too fast for the range of Spitfires then in service. It found its true role as a ground-attack fighter before and after D-Day 1944 and reigned supreme. It did enormous damage to the German army's tanks and artillery and German foot soldiers hated and feared its rockets, bombs and four 20 mm cannon.

The Typhoon had the most difficult birth of any RAF fighter. It came off the drawing board of the brilliant Sydney Camm, as the successor to his Hurricane. The prototype first flew on 24 February 1940, bad timing because the war was about to start in earnest and in the dark days that followed no one was much interested in a new fighter while the aircraft industry strained to produce Hurricanes and Spitfires. Production Typhoons began to reach squadrons at last in September 1941, with 56 Squadron the first to get them. Problems apparent at the test stage worsened as the aircraft were worked hard by squadron pilots. Engine failures were common and, worse, tails began dropping off. Test pilots and squadron pilots died. One was New Zealander James Jones, a 23-year-old sergeant on 56 Squadron. He was flying formation practice on 18 August 1942 from RAF Snailwell, Cambridgeshire, when the rear fuselage failed and broke away. He never had a chance. His was the third such death in a relatively short time and more followed. Jones had flown Typhoons for forty-three hours when he was killed, leaving a wife and a daughter in Auckland.

On 16 October 486 Squadron's first loss from engine defects occurred when Dave Clark, 23 (Dunedin), crashed in flames in a field near Battle, inland from Hastings on the south coast. He was returning from a routine standing patrol when he reported his engine on fire, apparently caused by excessive wear in a cylinder sleeve. The sleeve problem was to cause many such fires and deaths before it was fixed. Continuing crashes, the poor performance at height and other faults, such as carbon monoxide leaking into cockpits, led critics to suggest the scrapping of the Typhoon. But the RAF needed a fighter with high speed at low levels able to outpace the FW 190, and the makers and squadrons persevered until gradually the problems were overcome. By the end of 1942 the worst seemed to be over.

On 29 October 1942, 486 Squadron flew its Typhoons to Tangmere, inland between Brighton and Southampton, after a couple of intermediate moves in the previous month. There it would stay until January 1944, building a fine reputation.

And there, on 1 April 1943, it welcomed its second CO — Des Scott, a man who commanded great respect as a fighter pilot and leader. He arrived in England as a sergeant, climbed the ranks incredibly quickly and ended the war a group captain, having commanded a wing of four Typhoon squadrons in Europe in the climactic stages of the war. He won the DSO, the DFC and bar and decorations from France, Belgium and Holland. Born in Geraldine in 1918 and educated in Christchurch, he signed on with the RNZAF in March 1940, at the age of twenty-one.

A photograph in his book *One More Hour* shows him and seven of his course at Wigram, lined up in front of an ungainly Fairey Gordon. Scott, smiling, clutches one of the propeller blades. Two of the eight were retained as staff pilots. Of the other six, four were killed and the fifth, close friend Spud Murphy, was taken prisoner. Scott was the only one standing, as it were, at war's end — pretty much an average death toll for those who enlisted early.

First to go, Daniel 'Mun' Walker, 21 (Christchurch), fell in the far north of Scotland in February 1941, his Wellington crashing at an OTU.

265

Dick Bullen of Blenheim, old for a newcomer fighter pilot at 29, died on 23 June 1941, the first 485 Squadron pilot killed on air operations. He was shot down into the Channel by an Me 109; his body was never found. John Wallace, 21, who'd worked on his father's farm at Walton in the Waikato prior to enlistment, perished at the controls of a Wellington, shot down with his crew near Hamburg on his twenty-third operation in the August. Last to die was Ernest 'Nipper' Joyce, 24, (Hamilton), a squadron leader when he was killed over northern France during an armed reconnaissance in his 122 Squadron Mustang in June 1944. At his death he had nine German aircraft to his credit and had flown a Hurricane off an aircraft carrier to Malta a year earlier, before commanding 73 Squadron — the second New Zealander after Derek Ward — in North Africa for six months. He was on his 267th op when killed. Scott's book has another photo of eight pilots on 3 Squadron's B flight in the Orkney Islands. Seven of them were dead by the end of the war.

Scott and the group from Wigram arrived in Scotland in late November 1940, in time for the brutal British winter. He was sent to Sutton Bridge in Lincolnshire, an airfield he hated — 'cold, low and wet' countryside with amenities to match. The pilots slept, twenty in each awful wooden hut, wrapped in greatcoats to keep warm. But here he learned to fly Hurricanes with the usual before-first-flight warning: 'Good luck Scott. She's all yours. Break it and I'll break your ruddy fingers.' Scott didn't break it and called the Hurricane 'the nicest and most versatile aircraft I ever had the pleasure to fly.' He says he never understood the accident rate on squadrons 'for if any aircraft was free of vices it was the Hurricane'.

At Sutton Bridge he watched the steady stream of pilots flying machines beyond their capabilities, crashes, and sometimes the deaths of tyro pilots, screaming as they burned, trapped in the cockpits of mangled Hurricanes. One pilot, unnerved by the death of a friend, 'was arrested trying to bite into the wing of a Hurricane and was later committed to a mental asylum'.

Scott and Joyce, successful at Sutton Bridge, were posted on 1 February 1941 to 3 Squadron, resting after the Battle of Britain at Skeabrae, an airfield then under construction near Scapa Flow in the Orkney Islands. 'Thus began five years of my life as a pilot in the wartime RAF. An age when the excitement, the fear and dread, the sheer swift clamour of it all burned into the memory, so that much of life since has been a slow-moving backwater by comparison.'

Gale-driven snow piled up at Skeabrae and it was much the same at frigid Castletown, just back on the mainland at the far north of Scotland, where the squadron moved a week later. One afternoon, sitting ready in his Hurricane, Scott watched a 3 Squadron plane and its Norwegian pilot crash to earth not fifty yards away, the pilot killed instantly. Scott and another pilot dashed to the crash site and helped lift out the shattered remains — 'his uniform looked like a bag full of blood and bones.' Scott and the other pilot were severely reprimanded for leaving their cockpits without permission, but the telling off never stopped Scott making similar attempts to rescue pilots. In May 1944 he was awarded an OBE for pulling a pilot out of a blazing, crashed Spitfire at Hawkinge, where he was then station commander and a wing commander. Despite the flames and exploding ammunition, Scott, burned on his face and hands, dragged the pilot out of his cockpit, firemen playing foam on both of them. The young man later died but the citation lauded Scott for his 'great gallantry'.

He was also a straight speaker. After the squadron flew south to Martlesham Heath on the flank of 11 Group it began to take part in

DAY AFTER DAY

fighter sweeps, Roadsteads (escorting bombers or fighter-bombers against shipping), Circuses and night patrols. One day Scott and 3 Squadron accompanied Blenheims attacking a ship off the French coast. He returned to forward base Manston, re-armed and refuelled and made a second attack, as ordered, with Beauforts. He was incensed to arrive home to find some of the squadron hadn't made the second trip. Scott tore in to the flight commander 'and I think it was only his conscience that saved me from being matted for insubordination'.

Scott flew everything going at 3 Squadron — night intruder patrols over occupied France and Holland, attacks on German ships and flak vessels in the Channel, convoy patrols, sweeps, Circuses — he even did a stint at nights with Turbinlite aircraft.

He was commissioned at 3 Squadron, skipped flying officer, made flight lieutenant and then appointed squadron leader and posted in August 1942 to a staff job at Bentley Priory, headquarters of Fighter Command, for six months. He left 3 Squadron with four German aircraft and several probables to his credit and the ribbons of a DFC and bar on his chest.

Chapter 11

DIEPPE

The seaborne landing at Dieppe on the French coast on 19 August 1942 was a failure, a first-class disaster. Some call it an unnecessary adventure. Others argue it was a necessary learning prelude to the successful invasion of Europe almost two years later, when better tactics, better planning, heavy pre-landing bombing, surprise and, above all, control of the skies ensured success in Normandy. Luftwaffe fighters and bombers swarmed into the air over Dieppe; on D-Day they were virtually absent over the beaches, successfully neutralised.

More than 3600 Canadian and British troops, the great majority Canadian, were killed, wounded or taken prisoner. The navy lost a destroyer and many landing craft, suffering more than 500 casualties. In one day the RAF lost more than 100 aircraft to the Germans' forty-eight, with sixty RAF aircrew killed and another twenty ending up as POWs. Others were plucked from the sea after baling out.

The Dieppe raid was to have been launched on 4 July but the weather turned sour and the landing was postponed. Operation Jubilee eventually occurred two weeks later. The Germans seemed to know what was planned and the defences at Dieppe were stiffened and ready. Any element of surprise vanished when landing-craft escorts ran into German naval units. Tanks supporting attacking troops bogged down on the pebble and shingle beach or ran into heavy anti-tank fire. Commandos reached one battery of heavy guns and knocked them out but attempts to neutralize other batteries failed. RAF fighters armed with cannons were foiled by heavy concrete surrounding the big guns and well dug-in and protected lighter ordnance. Paratroopers might have done the job, but their participation was cancelled and Canadian troops were mown down on the beaches or on the outskirts of the town itself. The raid began at 4.15 a.m. — the order to withdraw was given at 11 a.m.

The RAF pulled together its greatest concentration of aircraft to date to cover the ground troops and the navy — seventy-four squadrons, sixty-six of them fighters. When the Luftwaffe responded, the tangle of aircraft over Dieppe developed into one of the great air battles of the war. The RAF largely kept German aircraft away from the men on the beaches and ships but the Spitfires, Hurricanes and the few squadrons of Typhoons lacked the firepower to destroy the enemy guns that butchered the Canadians. Light bombers used to attack the gun sites made little impact, although they laid smoke screens brilliantly.

The RAF gave its all, and many lives at Dieppe, squadrons and men flying four times, pausing only long enough at English south coast airfields to refuel and rearm. The light-bomber Bostons of 88 Squadron operated no fewer than five times. RAF casualties included three New Zealanders — Hurricane pilots Squadron Leader Eddie Berry and Pilot Officer James Barton, and Boston wireless operator-air gunner Pilot Officer Laurence Waters. Another two were taken prisoner — Wing Commander Mindy Blake and Mustang pilot, Flight Lieutenant Arnold Christensen.

New Zealanders served on most of the Dieppe-bound squadrons packed on to airfields in the south — many of them had flown to the fields nearest France in the two or three days before from bases further afield, to give them the shortest possible flight and the longest possible time in action. Tangmere was crowded with seven Spitfire and Hurricane units; Ford had six squadrons, four of them Hudsons.

Dieppe is a small town midway between Boulogne and Le Havre, its port formed by the Arques River cutting through high steep cliffs to reach the sea. Major gun batteries sited on the cliff tops flanking the port and town and machine guns dug into the cliffs poured devastating fire onto the landing craft and assault troops.

Bostons and Blenheims were first off in pre-dawn darkness not long after four o'clock, briefed to lay smoke to shield the attackers and bomb the big guns. Screened by Spitfires of 65 and 11 Squadrons, the two-engined bombers, thirty-two of them, went in to open the attack as landing craft chugged towards the beaches and destroyers moved in to pound shore defences. Heavier naval units had been ruled out. Leading ten Bostons of 226 Squadron tasked with laying smoke to shroud the guns was Wing Commander Wilf Surplice, his navigator 33-year-old New Zealander Renton Rutherford. As their phosphorus bombs burst on the ground, great clouds of smoke poured out. Some of the aircraft laid their own thick smoke — as Surplice turned his aircraft away from the shore, an early-on-the-job FW 190 winged towards them. Gunner Len Longhurst got in first and the fighter turned away, engine trailing heavy smoke.

Surplice was made DSO for his work, while Longhurst was awarded the DFC, as was Rutherford, his citation saying he'd displayed 'courage and skill' on a vital and dangerous mission. Rutherford, who was born in Edinburgh, arrived in New Zealand aged eighteen, after attending an agricultural college. He managed a sheep and cattle farm in Poverty Bay, then joined State Advances as a farm appraiser.

New Zealander Graham Magill piloted another 226 Squadron Boston, which was hit by Royal Navy 20 mm rounds, forcing him to jettison his smoke bombs as close as possible to his targeted gun battery. Norman Franks in *The Greatest Air Battle* noted that Magill's Boston carried a crest featuring a kiwi, kangaroo and Welsh dragon on a boomerang 'ensuring a return ticket, they hoped!' Magill flew with an Australian navigator and a Welsh gunner, and their good-luck crest got them home.

New Zealander Ken Sutton, acting squadron leader with 605 Squadron, was also among the first over Dieppe, leading another Boston in to unleash bombs on key batteries at 4.59 a.m. according to Franks. Alan Baxter, yet another New Zealander on Bostons, navigated 88 Squadron's CO Des Griffiths' aircraft and five others on a bombing run to a battery after an urgent order for action at 6.45 a.m. Franks notes that most of the 190s trying to attack the Bostons were held at bay by escorting Spitfires.

The bombers had a job getting out safely, nosing down to sea level to afford some protection from deadly German fighters. Fortunately their combined firepower and tactics got them out of a tight spot. Baxter also got the DFC at Dieppe, the citation calling his navigational ability 'matchless'. Unusually, Baxter gave away navigation after two tours and became a bomber pilot. He flew Lancasters on a full tour late in the war with 75 Squadron. Postwar he was Labour MP for Raglan 1946–49 and died in 1976, at 64.

Magill, born in Cambridge in 1915 and educated at Te Aroha, learned to fly in 1935 at the Auckland Aero Club. The following year he made his own way to England, where he was accepted for an SSC. In 1940 and 1941 he flew the ugly-looking, double-canopied single-engined Vickers Wellesley, bombing Italian forces in Ethiopia and Eritrea. He emerged from East Africa with a DFC and was later awarded a bar. After Dieppe he was posted as CO of 180 Squadron, a Mitchell light bomber squadron, then saw out the war on staff duties. He stayed in the RAF postwar, retiring in 1968 as Air Vice-Marshal Graham Magill, CB, CBE, DFC*, mid. He died in 1998.

Late in the morning four fresh 226 Squadron crews, including New Zealand pilots Brian Wheeler and Wilf Gellatly, flew to Dieppe to lay smoke on the still-active German batteries as landing craft moved in to evacuate troops. Franks notes another two crews trailed smoke over the beach at low level. The six aircraft flew through a curtain of German flak and naval AA as the navy fired at increasing numbers of 190s overhead. Wheeler noted in his logbook, 'Heavy light flak [from the Germans] and heavy opposition from our own navy!!' Wheeler's aircraft escaped unharmed but Gellatly's Boston suffered; Waters, 21 (Blenheim), on only his first op, was killed and the navigator wounded. Gellatly crash-landed, wheels up, at Gatwick. Ten years later Waters' much younger brother Cyril died when the 75 Squadron Mosquito he was piloting crashed at RNZAF base Woodbourne, the day after an Air Force Day display. His father saw the crash.

Gellatly went to 487 Squadron post-Dieppe and then commanded an ASR squadron. He remained with the peacetime RAF and later became chief test pilot for Fairey Aviation-Westland Helicopters.

Wheeler was a wing commander and CO of 88 Squadron when he perished with his crew on 15 February 1944, while attacking a V1 site at Cherbourg. Post-226 Squadron he'd flown with 487 Squadron Mosquitoes. Although Wheeler was very much a New Zealander, he was in the RCAF. His parents had a Romney stud farm between Marton and Hunterville and in May 1939 Wheeler, an only son, accompanied a flock of sheep his father sold to an Argentinian breeder. Wheeler stayed on to manage the buyer's farm and was still in Argentina when war broke out, travelling to Canada to enlist a year later. By Dieppe he already had a DFC for bringing a badly damaged Boston home from Le Havre in April 1942 and for a masthead attack on a ship off the Dutch coast in September the year before. That day, his Blenheim, hit in one engine, twice struck the sea as it staggered away. Wheeler and Rutherford were good friends and when Wheeler married WAAF Connie Taylor, on 3 June 1943, Rutherford was best man. The Wheelers' only child, a daughter called Susan, was born three months after Wheeler was killed. Mother and child visited New Zealand in 1946 and returned in 1949 for good.

Magill led the last smoke-laying operation of the day at Dieppe, his four 226 Squadron aircraft flying low to trail smoke to obscure the aim of German gunners firing shells at naval units still in range. The Bostons were escorted by the Spitfires of New Zealander Bob Yule's 66 Squadron, which was bounced by 190s on the way home and lost two of its planes. Magill landed safely at Manston at 4.30 p.m.

All morning and early afternoon the sky above Dieppe was a tangled maze of RAF and Luftwaffe fighters. Many pilots had seen nothing like it since the Battle of Britain. The RAF planes were outnumbered, most of them outpaced by the swift FW 190s, which made diving attacks from high levels.

The Hornchurch Wing of 81, 122, 154 and 340 Squadrons were among the earliest fighter units over Dieppe about 5.30 a.m., relieving the Spitfires of 65 and 111 Squadrons, which had accompanied the Bostons. Two of the Hornchurch Spitfire units were led by New Zealanders — John Kilian (122 Squadron) and Don Carlson (154

Squadron). Kilian, a South Islander, was a pre-war pilot in the RNZAF — when he arrived in England in October 1941 he wore 'RNZAF' on his shoulder flashes, not 'New Zealand'. He flew as a flight lieutenant with 485 Squadron, commanded 122 Squadron from March to November 1942 and in July 1943 was posted as CO of 504 Squadron.

Kilian returned to New Zealand and flew four tours in the Pacific, commanding 19 and 14 Squadrons. The French rewarded him with a Croix de Guerre for his participation at Dieppe but, puzzlingly, his service in the RNZAF and RAF was never recognised with an award. He shot down two aircraft, one in Europe and one in the Pacific, and with eight others shared the destruction of a bomber trying to get at the troops at Dieppe.

Carlson, an SSC pilot in the first draft of eighteen, which left New Zealand in July 1937, had been working on his father's farm at Okoroire in the Waikato. He flew first with 616 Squadron then 245 Squadron and 74 Squadron before joining 154 Squadron, flying Spitfires, as CO six months before Dieppe. He was with 245 Squadron in Northern Ireland during most of the Battle of Britain but didn't fly because he had been injured in an accident. He commanded 154 Squadron for fourteen months and was awarded the DFC six months into his term. The citation called him a 'skilful and energetic squadron commander' who had destroyed at least three enemy aircraft. Carlson later flew in the Middle East and ended the war a wing commander.

Because they were members of the Hornchurch Wing, Kilian's and Carlson's squadrons operated closely together on patrols, each making four on the day. On the second trip, Kilian's unit, himself included, overwhelmed a Dornier, while Carlson and eight of his squadron blew a Dornier to pieces on their second patrol.

DAY AFTER DAY

A 12 Group wing formed at West Malling for the Dieppe operation was led by Jamie Jameson, now Wing Commander Jameson. He had been leading the Wittering Wing when he was called into the operation to form the Dieppe Wing. His squadrons, 485 which he personally led, 411 (Canadian) and 610, commanded by Johnnie Johnson, arrived over Dieppe on one flight to be met by hordes of FW 190s and a few Me 109s.

According to Jameson:

My section was attacked at least twenty times in as many minutes. Our situation was rather critical as we had to maintain position over or near the ships and beaches to protect them from air attack … I shot one FW 190 down in flames and had several squirts at others. I found the best way to attack the German fighters was from astern and slightly below, shooting into the soft underbelly of the aircraft. The fuel tank was in a vulnerable position and when hit nearly always resulted in a flamer.

Jameson led four wing patrols that day, flying with 485 Squadron, one of whose pilots, Colin Chrystall, downed a FW 190, their only victory that day. New Zealander Chrystall, a newcomer, had made his first operational patrol only the previous month. His is an extraordinary story. Twice turned down for an SSC in New Zealand, he sailed to England in April 1938, joined the RAF as a trainee wireless operator, completed his exams and then went to a Blenheim squadron, where he did a gunnery course. Fully qualified as a WOp/Ag and flying, Chrystall still wasn't satisfied and applied to become a pilot. 'Some time in the future,' he was told. He manned the radio and guns during Dunkirk patrols and then joined 235 Squadron, also on Blenheims, flying myriad operations throughout the Battle of Britain. Finally he began pilot training, and once completed, joined 485 Squadron. He wrote a brief, succinct combat report after his Dieppe success, no mean feat against the 190 while 485 Squadron was still flying the slower Spitfire VBs. What's more he hit the 190 fatally at 500 yards, a long-distance burst that somehow hit home.

> When flying as Red 4 ... I broke away to attack a FW 190, attacking from 1/4 astern at about 500 yards with a two to three-second burst. I broke sharply to port then turned back and saw E/A going down and pilot bale out. I claim this E/A as destroyed.

Chrystall was posted to the Middle East in late 1942, but was flying 243 Squadron Spitfires in Italy in June 1944, where he was hit by ground fire. He force-landed and evaded capture but while trekking to the coast trod on a mine and had part of his right leg blown off. He was taken prisoner and shipped to Germany, but was quickly repatriated. In January 1945 he was awarded the DFC, but died tragically in 1961, killed by a cave-in while working in a drag-lined trench on his Foxton farm.

At Merston, the Tangmere satellite, CO Michael Pedley briefed 131 Squadron pilots about Dieppe on 18 August and then told them, 'Go to bed early and get a good sleep.' Horry Copland, one of the twelve pilots chosen to fly, was wakened at 3.15 a.m., splashed water on his face, threw on clothes and rode a bike to dispersal where he donned flying kit and mae west. He made sure he had his good luck sprig of white heather and escape money in case he was shot down, and to his amazement sat down to breakfast of fried eggs sent over from

DAY AFTER DAY

the kitchens. Such was not routine on 131 Squadron.

After a brief and false early scramble to combat raiders, 131 Squadron was called into action about 8.30 a.m., roaring off the field in formation. The Spitfires could expect to have thirty minutes over Dieppe after the eighty-mile flight. They flew low over the Channel with the Spitfires of 130 Squadron and the inexperienced 309 (US) Squadron in Spitfires above them. While still a long way from Dieppe, Copland could see smoke.

> The convoy, anchored a few miles from shore, was enveloped in smoke as if the ships were on fire. Some were, hit by big guns during the landing, but the greater part were still undamaged … The other squadrons we were relieving soon left but before they did there were more aircraft twisting and turning in a smaller area than I had ever seen.

Suffering heavy losses in severe combat, 131 Squadron's cover raced for home, short of fuel, a situation 131 Squadron also faced when they spotted 190s diving to attack the convoy and moved to cut them off. 'How we got through that last half hour will remain a miracle. We all had bullet holes but all survived. Then the relief arrived as we headed for the nearest aerodrome with low revs and weakened mixture [to conserve fuel].' Copland's engine stopped as he taxied in.

Refuelled and rearmed, 131 Squadron took off again for Copland's best action bout of the war. As they reached Dieppe only a few 190s were about but then Copland spotted swarms of the fighters coming, protecting bombers — Dornier 217s.

> This was the one time I left my CO's tail. I reported on the R/T. 'Red 1, Red 2 going into attack' and he gave me the OK. I closed on a Dornier

at right angles, laid off three widths of sight and gave a burst. There were explosions near the tail. Needed a little more deflection — another burst and the engines burst into flames. I turned to another coming around behind. I used the remainder of my ammo before I left him with smoke pouring out of his engine and losing height as he crossed the French coast.

Alone after the combat, attacked by 190s and out of ammunition, Copland dived to sea level, fighting for his life as again and again he evaded the German fighters. Eventually he broke clear, joined three other Spitfires and flew home. 'I knew I had photos on my camera gun of two German bombers shot down.'

Copland's fourth sortie for the day, his last for a total of six hours forty minutes in the air, was also the last made by his 'faithful' Spitfire *Canterbury*. In deteriorating weather at 7 p.m. the squadron was ordered away from patrolling home-bound convoy remnants to intercept a couple of bomber-raiders headed for England. One section attacked a Dornier 217, Pedley and Copland the other, a Ju 88. The New Zealander lost his boss in cloud but dived through it and hoped the 88 would emerge. It did.

I was able to come up underneath and set his engines on fire but as I broke I received a burst from the rear gunner ... [Smoke poured from his engine, the heat gauge rose dangerously high, the oil gauge flickered, pressure fell. The engine ran until the coast was in sight.] ... and then, just as a horse would run until it died, the engine stopped.

But it had kept going long enough to allow him to glide over the cliffs to crash-land on farmland among 'obstacles, ditches and fences'. When

DAY AFTER DAY

he clambered out, his right knee stiff and sore, he found the kiwi he'd painted on the plane covered in mud, the fighter wrecked and the gun camera crushed, the film proving he had nailed his Germans destroyed. A farmer took him to his home for a large whisky, before he returned in heavy rain to guard what remained of *Canterbury* until the authorities arrived.

Back at Merston the sergeant pilots lined up ten more whiskies and told him to drink them before supper — egg and chips as a special favour for being shot down and surviving. 'This was the end of a perfect day and the most exciting I have ever spent in my life.'

A couple of days later he was promoted flight sergeant and when his commission came through, he went to London to get his new uniform with its single ring. Told he was to become an instructor, Copland completed his training course and was posted to Tealing, Dundee, where he stayed until August 1943, when he joined 485 Squadron at Biggin Hill, before he came home.

Always a farmer at heart, he used to bicycle around the English countryside and was known to hop off his bike and over the fence to help fix binders and reapers, and to lend a hand to get crops in. As has been said before, you can take a boy out of the country ...

Hurricane pilot Jimmy Barton (21), a motor mechanic in Christchurch when he enlisted in 1940, died in the early stages of Dieppe when his 245 Squadron fighter was shot down by flak while attacking the beach guns at low altitude. The squadron lost three aircraft and pilots in quick succession as the planes ran in against murderous flak, through smoke and the half dark of dawn which made it difficult to distinguish targets. As part of operation Jubilee, 245 Squadron and 3 Squadron, led by Berry, were flying from Shoreham, Kent. They had lifted off at 4.40 a.m., to be joined overhead by 43 Squadron, from another field. Married to a WAAF telephone operator just ten days earlier, Barton had been with the squadron one day short of a year when he was killed. His body was never found and he is one of the thousands commemorated at Runnymede. The ferocity of the gunfire opposing 245 Squadron was underlined by the damage sustained by the entire squadron. *For Your Tomorrow* notes that of the eight Hurricanes which returned to England, only one remained serviceable. Berry survived his two strafing runs but one of his pilots was shot down.

Byron Lumsden of Feilding flew with 3 Squadron through that flak and called it 'exciting'. He had joined 3 Squadron on 25 May 1942, one year and twenty-four days since enlisting. He was aged nineteen years and two months, and here he was at Hunsdon, north of London, in 11 Group with the third squadron formed in World War I and the first equipped with aeroplanes (1 and 2 Squadrons operated balloons). His early fascination with aircraft and flying had led to this, one of the most famous squadrons in the RAF. 'It was a great thrill to belong to such an old squadron with such a distinguished history.' Berry had taken over as CO the month before Lumsden joined.

In his memoir which he wrote not long before his death in 2008, Lumsden tells a wonderful yarn about himself and Air Chief Marshal Lord Portal, head of Bomber Command in 1940 and Chief of the Air Staff 1940–45. Lumsden remembered a high-powered 1950 function in London, where he was then working. Portal was the guest of honour, not quite sixty at the time. At a latish stage in the evening Lumsden was invited to meet Portal.

> The gin had flowed freely and I was at something of a loss for something to say to his Lordship. So the best I could do was tell him I'd been on

DAY AFTER DAY

3 Squadron … and asked him facetiously how he had become Marshal of the RAF without serving on 3 Squadron. He replied, 'My dear fellow, I was a flight commander on 3 Squadron in 1915.' I was then able to introduce him to my friends as my old squadron mate Portal. He took it in good heart, bless him.

Next morning Lumsden was thanked by a brigadier for looking after Portal. The brigadier 'did, however, say that he felt the only jarring note was when I called across the very large room to him saying, "For Christ's sake get another sherry for Lord Portal".'

Lumsden says 3 Squadron was often called the Kiwi Squadron because so many of the pilots were New Zealanders — fifteen out of the twenty-four at the time Lumsden joined, with Des Scott a flight lieutenant. Lumsden was worked hard by experienced pilots at 3 Squadron, learning the tricks and not doing his first operational flight until 11 June — a convoy patrol off Orfordness. For the next few weeks he did more of those and night-fighter flights as the squadron prepared hard for what turned out to be Dieppe. Of 19 August, he wrote:

Just as we approached the coast we could see the convoys of landing craft lining up for their run-in so we started our run as instructed at the left hand end and turned over the end of the breakwater … Since photos were taken in the July the Germans had installed multiple anti-aircraft cannon on the end of the pier. They had also moved up a weight of flak guns right along the beach. It was like flying through a firework display with various coloured tracers coming up round the aircraft. Most exciting … At 7.50 a.m. we went back again and strafed gun posts at the western end of the town. Not so much flak this time … once again no marks on [my] aircraft … at 11.15 a.m. we did a fighter sweep to the north from Boulogne down to Dieppe … no aircraft came to bother us.

Lumsden and the others did their last patrol of the day at 1.45 p.m., taking off from Shoreham. As usual, the squadron was headed by Berry, but this was to be his last operation, his Hurricane shot down by a 190 and crashing in flames onto the cliffs. Lumsden described the attack, strafing heavy coastal guns in concrete emplacements with machine guns, as pointless. 'I was flying No. 3 in the second group of four aircraft and was immediately behind Berry when he was attacked by an FW 190 which came over the top of me and set [Berry's] aircraft on fire.' Hopefully, Lumsden unleashed a six-second burst at 400 yards, opening to more than 600 yards as the German swung away at high speed. 'No pieces flew off him so no claim. Pity.' For years Lumsden tried to find out the name of the German pilot who'd killed Berry to ask if he'd taken any hits. He said he finally learned the man's name in 2004 — Egon Mayer, one of Germany's best fighter pilots who had 102 Allied aircraft to his credit, all in the west, when he was shot down and killed in March 1944 by American Thunderbolts.

Berry, Christchurch educated, joined the RNZAF in 1937 as a wireless operator, but was selected for an SSC two years later and arrived in England five days before the war began. He was posted to 3 Squadron in September 1940 and rose from junior pilot officer to command the unit. His body was washed ashore at Boulogne after Dieppe and he was buried, appropriately, at Dieppe Canadian War Cemetery.

But 245 and 3 were not the only Hurricane squadrons to suffer casualties trying to silence Dieppe's guns — 174 Squadron lost five 'Hurribombers' that day, with three pilots dead, one on each of their three sorties, and two captured. One of the dead was the newly appointed CO, Frenchman Emile Fayole, who disappeared into the Channel on the way home from the squadron's first strike. The squadron took off from Ford at 4.40 a.m. to bomb a four-gun battery behind the town.

Among the pilots was Sergeant James Wetere, who was to survive the war as a flight lieutenant with the DFC. He was one of a handful of Maori in Fighter Command/2TAF. Born at Hoe-o-Tainui in the Piako district, he joined the RNZAF in November 1940 and trained in New Zealand. He flew thirty-eight ops with 174 Squadron and then at least forty-eight with 184 Squadron in Europe in the last year of the war. Along with 245, 174 and 175 Squadrons, 184 Squadron formed 121 Wing with four Typhoon squadrons. Wetere was awarded his DFC in September 1945. On 174 Squadron's second sortie of the day, which had them over Dieppe at 11 a.m., they were escorted by the Spitfires of Yule's 66 Squadron.

Mindy Blake, a gifted pilot and leader, had ten Germans to his credit when he was shot down at Dieppe. He had flown to Thorney Island on the south coast with 130 Squadron the day before Dieppe and was flying as No. 2 to its CO, Peter Simpson. He took out an FW 190, knocking it down as it tried to attack ships off Dieppe, but was then engaged by others flying nearby. Head-on fire blasted through his canopy, filling an eye with Perspex. Unable to see, he somehow managed to make it out as his plane plummeted into the sea. His chute opened just before he hit the water. Blake had been rescued once before after paddling hours following a ditching, but this time wind and tides were against him and the Germans picked him up from the sea on the afternoon of 20 August — the most senior RAF officer captured in Operation Jubilee.

Arnold Christensen was doubly unfortunate — shot down at Dieppe on his first operational flight and then executed in 1944 by the Gestapo after the Great Escape. He was a reporter on a Hastings newspaper when he enlisted in the RNZAF in June 1914, and still only eighteen. Trained and commissioned in Canada, he joined 26 Squadron just six days before Dieppe after converting to Mustangs. It seems remarkable in hindsight that such an inexperienced young pilot, barely twenty, was thrown into action before he'd even got to know his squadron mates, and clearly a tribute to his abilities. He took off from Gatwick at 8 a.m. on 19 August with one other pilot on a tactical reconnaissance (Tac/R) flight with an Army Co-operation Command squadron charged with flying around and beyond the battle zone in pairs during the day, checking German airfields and roads and watching for German reinforcements moving towards Dieppe. Christensen was brought down and made POW, as was the man with whom he flew, and was among those who escaped from Stalag Luft III, Sagan, Poland, on the night of 24–25 March 1944. Recaptured at Flensburg, near the German-Danish border, he was murdered in a field near Kiel on 29 March. Several of his killers were hanged postwar.

The Mustang Christensen flew at Dieppe was a Mark I, the first operational model of this famous World War II fighter in RAF service. Designed in the United States for the RAF, it was powered by an American engine. Later marks, fitted with a British Rolls-Royce Merlin engine married to the American airframe, turned an ordinary aircraft into magic. A Cinderella story.

As always, Tac/R was a dangerous occupation at Dieppe, at low level the aircraft vulnerable to both flak and fighters. Christensen's 26 Squadron lost no fewer than five pilots on 19 August — three killed and two captured. Between them three other Tac/R squadrons at Gatwick lost two dead, one captured. Yet another ditched, with the pilot saved.

Wing Commander Peter Donkin, a New Zealander and then CO of 239 Squadron, one of the Gatwick Mustang squadrons, is quoted by Franks as describing the recce planning as inept. Donkin was particularly critical of how the Mustangs were routed in and out over Dieppe when they should have crossed in and out away from the town. As it was, the Mustangs were soft targets for German fighters. 'This business of not getting anywhere near fighter battles was found always a good idea later in 1943–44 when recce was working in France. We rarely got intercepted even as far in as near Paris,' Donkin said.

Donkin, born in Invercargill in 1913, had an outstanding career in the RAF. After early schooling at Waihi School, Winchester, he was sent to England by his parents at the age of ten to be educated. His father died in a motor accident in Picton in 1925 and his mother then moved to England. Donkin entered Cranwell as a flight cadet in 1931, when he was 18, and was posted to 16 Squadron after graduation. In 1939–40 he commanded 225 Squadron and 4 Squadron, flying Lysanders on convoy patrols and ASR. He was appointed CO of 239 Squadron in September 1940 and from then spent most of the war on photo-reconnaissance intelligence, later commanding 33 and 35 Wings. He was forced down in the Channel in April 1944 and spent a remarkable six days in his dinghy before rescue. Donkin remained in the RAF postwar and when he retired in the late 1960s after commanding RAF Hong Kong, he was an air commodore with a CBE and DSO.

Chapter 12

Evaders

Thirteen New Zealanders serving on 485 Squadron became POWs, with Vic Goodwin the first on 7 August 1941, and Mac Sutherland and Jack Rae the last, two years later. Six others who came down in enemy territory evaded capture by the Germans and made it back to England.

Goodwin, twenty-six at the time, baled out over St Omer, his Spitfire in flames on a Circus operation. He was being treated for burns in St Omer hospital at the same time as Douglas Bader, the brilliant legless fighter pilot. Bader was downed over France in circumstances which are still not entirely clear. Another much more seriously wounded pilot, Bill Russell, 21 (Gore), of 485 Squadron, was in the same room as Bader. Russell was shot down five days after Goodwin, during a low-level attack at Bethune. Although he's not named, Russell features in *Reach for the Sky*, Paul Brickhill's book about Bader. The night the Englishman made his famous 'knotted-sheets' escape from a window of the hospital's first floor his first 'rope' of bed linen was too short. How to lengthen it? Pinch the sheet from under a comatose form in a bed — 'New boy, came in while you were out [meeting German ace Adolph Galland],' another prisoner told Bader. 'Sergeant pilot. Shot down yesterday. They've just taken his arm off. He's still under the dope.'

The patient was Russell, and the room reeked of ether as Bader clomped over to Russell's bed on his tin legs. Brickhill describes how Bader gently worked the sheet from under Russell and said: 'This is frightful, but I've just got to.' Said the other prisoner: 'He won't mind. I'll tell him when he wakes up.' His rope of sheets now long enough, and with Russell's bed moved to the window to act as an anchor, Bader made it down and out of the hospital grounds, but not much further, before his recapture.

Russell's story has a sad ending. Incarcerated in Stalag VIIIB (Lamsdorf) when his left arm healed, he was medically repatriated to Britain in October 1943 and treated in hospital until March 1944, when one-armed and unfit to fly operationally, he could have called it quits. Bravely he persevered, overcame official doubts and, with an artificial limb, flew on 631 Squadron, which at the time was supplying planes for Anti-Aircraft Co-operation flights with gunnery ranges in Wales. His plane suffered engine failure on 28 February 1945 and Russell died when it dived into a river. Investigators considered his handicap might have caused loss of control in the emergency.

In Stalag Luft III (Sagan) POW camp Bader made a nuisance of himself to the Germans — and to many fellow RAF prisoners. According to 92 Squadron pilot John Gillies' memoir Wing Commander 'Wings' Day's policy of outward politeness to the German authorities meant fewer sudden searches and less interruption to the prisoners' underground work — escaping, tunnelling, creation of false papers, civilian clothing work, getting information from new prisoners and coding of letters. Bader's continued baiting of the Germans had the opposite effect. 'Luckily for the very limited war effort that POWs could manage, Bader's influence was short-lived,' Gillies wrote. The Germans removed Bader to Colditz Castle where inveterate escapers and other troublemakers were held. Gillies said most of the prisoners were delighted to see the back of him. 'However much one admired Bader for his wonderful achievements as a fighter pilot, his actions in the air force POW camps were indeed shameful.'

Malcolm Sutherland, 24 (Port Chalmers), and Aucklander Jack Rae, 24, were among four 485 Squadron pilots who went down while escorting bombers over France on 22 August 1943, one of the squadron's worst two days of the war. The other pilots were Fraser Clark and Les 'Chalky' White. A large flock of FW 190s intercepted the Spitfires and a battle royal followed. Sutherland was shot down, badly wounded and captured, while Rae got a 190 before his engine seized. Clark, 20 (Wanganui), was shot down and killed on his sixty-eighth op, most of them with 485 Squadron, the rest earlier with 41 Squadron. White, a big Southland farmer, also got a 190 before force-landing, but unlike Rae he evaded capture in an epic journey through France into Spain and freedom.

Rae's war effectively ended that day over France but when he got back to New Zealand it was as a flight lieutenant with a double DFC, credited with eleven enemy aircraft and a bunch of probables. He joined 485 Squadron in mid-July 1941, a sergeant pilot fresh from New Zealand, and flew with the squadron until the following April, scoring twice. Posted to Malta, he flew a Spitfire to the island from the carrier USS *Wasp* on 20 April. He established a fine reputation in Malta with at least four victories and numerous probables.

In his book *Kiwi Spitfire Ace,* Rae recounts the misfortunes on Malta of an unnamed and inexperienced New Zealand pilot shot down twice in quick succession, once by Maltese flak, and once by a Stuka rear gunner. Both times the young pilot baled out. Up again for a third time he was badly hit by an Me 109, but this time he didn't jump. His tail was obviously in tatters as watching pilots on the ground willed him to jump.

> But no, he came on making a slow skidding highly unstable turn. Then unbelievably he put his wheels down and headed for our aerodrome, losing height rapidly. He tried to turn into the wind but had no control, went sideways over our flight-path and crashed into the rocky bank on the other side.

The billowing smoke and dust convinced everyone he was dead. But from under the smouldering wreckage the pilot yelled, 'Get me out of here.' Amazingly he had survived, but with injuries that ended his flying. Asked why he didn't jump, the youngster said he was sick of baling out. When his rescuers found his parachute it was full of holes from cannon fire and shrapnel, and would never have supported him.

Back in England by August 1942, Rae spent eight months instructing, a few days with 118 Squadron and then in May 1943 he rejoined 485 Squadron. In the short three months before he was captured, Rae, now with a wealth of experience behind him, accounted for five German planes, three Me 109s and two FW 190s, including a pair of 109s five days before his last flight.

On 22 August 485 Squadron flew escort to American Marauders bombing an airfield at Beaumont-le-Roger, southwest of Rouen. As the Marauders and Spitfires approached the target, 485 Squadron was confronted by thirty-plus 190s. Wheeling to face them, another group of Focke-Wulfs barrelled in from the left. Rae says the enemy seemed as confused as the New Zealand pilots and one 190 crossed right in front of him. 'I fired at point-blank range and the 190 exploded with pieces of aircraft flying everywhere.' Rae dived away, intending to clear the immediate scrap and then climb again. As he came out of his dive and opened the throttle, 'the engine gave an ominous belch and coughed out masses of smoke'. Oil temperature raced off the clock and the glycol temperature registered very high, with Rae later blaming pieces of the German aircraft thudding into his coolant system.

Rae chose not to bale out, but gliding as far as the Channel was impossible so he looked for an isolated field. He was jumped by two Me 109s, escaping only with some quick, deft manoeuvres. Unfortunately these turned the prop over, causing hot oil to pour over the fuselage and into the cockpit. Hardly able to see, Rae crash-landed safely in a far-from-isolated spot — a field bounded by woods and a military camp. Despite trying his best to escape he was soon picked up by a group of German soldiers. About to be driven away, an officer appeared by the car, saluted and asked in halting English:

'Do you know Auckland?'

'Yes, do you?' Rae replied.

'No, good day,' the officer answered, saluted and walked away. Rae figured the man had seen his New Zealand shoulder flashes. But how had he heard of Auckland?

White, hit in the glycol tank, also accounted for a 190 before his engine seized. He crash-landed in the same general area as Rae and was also quickly captured, held in a small building with just one dim-witted guard. The German was no match for the burly White who knocked him out, hid in a rainwater-barrel just outside and later made a clean getaway. Unable to speak French and relying on wits, audacity and incredible luck, White travelled the length of France without help from any escape line. Eventually he crossed the Pyrenees into Spain, was taken to Gibraltar and by October 1943 was home and back to 485 Squadron and a job as flight commander. His adventure was told by Errol Brathwaite in *Pilot on the Run*.

Amazingly, Garry Barnett and Stan Browne, shot down the same day over France, independently followed more or less the same route to freedom, the first two 485 Squadron pilots to evade capture. Barnett learned to fly at the Wellington Aero Club pre-war and joined up in November 1939 but didn't get overseas until December 1941, held back as an instructor. He had been with the squadron less than a month when he was shot down over France on the last day of May 1942, while on a fighter sweep.

Barnett, on his ninth operation, had seen enemy aircraft several times but had neither fired his guns in anger nor been a target. He didn't fire this time either, but ended up on the ground, caught by an FW 190 he didn't see until after he was hit. Approaching the coast between Dieppe and the Somme Estuary at 20,000 feet, the radio warned the squadron the enemy was coming at them in large numbers and a couple of minutes later they were told the Germans were engaging the Polish Wing, their high cover.

In the late 1980s Barnett transcribed parts of his wartime diary for his family telling what happened that day: 'The first indication we got [of the German attack] was one of the Poles spinning through us in flames.' Bill Wells then told his men he had seen the Huns above and a few seconds later gave the order for the squadron to break. Barnett followed his Yellow section leader Reg 'Baldy' Baker as the Spitfires fell away out of formation. He suddenly felt dull thuds in front of him and immediately an FW 190 passed within 50 yards.

There was not the slightest doubt that he had hit my plane, and badly, in the engine. By this time there were Spitfires and FWs everywhere and there was only one thing to do and that was to get the hell out of it. Although we were at 20,000 feet and only about 10 miles inland there was no hope of my getting back to England and, as I did not fancy … the sea, I decided to land in France.

The fighter's engine failed and the whole aircraft vibrated so badly Barnett could hardly read the instrument panel and the radio was gone. The plane still responded perfectly to the controls and there was no fire. He dived for welcoming clouds at 12,000 feet and after getting through them decided to keep the aeroplane to within a couple of thousand feet of ground.

I headed inland and saw that no enemy fighters were following me down. At about 3000 feet I opened the hood and prepared to bale out. This proved to be a bit difficult at first because the hood kept shutting and caught between the parachute and the harness. I was struggling … when at about 1500 feet the engine fell out and immediately there was an uncanny silence. The sound of cannons firing above me was quite audible. The plane almost stood still and it was the simplest thing to merely step out and that's what I did. I must have been a little lower than I thought because after pulling the ripcord I had no recollection whatever of the parachute opening and of my falling with it. It seemed to be almost instantaneous between my jumping and landing in a tree. I was in no way hurt although smothered in oil which must have come from the broken pipelines as I was getting out of the plane … I did not see the aircraft after baling out.

Barnett climbed down the tree after cutting the chute's shrouds, which

DAY AFTER DAY

were hopelessly entangled in the tree's canopy. Peasants working in nearby fields took absolutely no notice and Barnett started walking. It was the beginning of an evasion saga that was to last until the Royal Navy landed him in England four months later.

On his first night in France, Barnett knocked on the doors of two houses in an isolated village but received little help, walked some more and then slept under a hedge for a couple of hours about dawn. He pointed himself towards Spain with his tiny compass but then made a decision that went against escape lecture rules.

> We had been told ... to keep to the fields, avoid all contact with human beings and head south. The little walking I had done up to date decided me that I would be a very old man before I arrived at the Spanish frontier, so I there and then decided to take to the main road and try to get to places that way. [He found the main route to Abbeville.] ... The roads were clearly marked, all the signs being intact and it was easy to locate myself on my escape map.

Barnett's boldness paid off — just. A cyclist stopped, recognised who he might be and told him to get off the road because the Germans were searching for him. The young man told him his family would help. They did, twice coming to where he hid, providing food and giving directions to their house to which he was to go after dark. But Barnett couldn't find the dwelling and in desperation marched up to the biggest and best-looking house in the neighbourhood and knocked on the door. He was lucky. He chanced on Allied sympathisers who put him into 'a beautiful big double bed with clean sheets'. Next morning, fed, dressed in a peasant's jacket and beret and taken to the local railway station, he simply bought a ticket for Paris and later in the day sat on the bank of the Seine eating the bread, cheese and boiled eggs he'd been given. Barnett's luck held as he rode the underground to the outskirts of Paris and met a young woman who took him to her parents' home. He was put on a train to Bordeaux, a city within striking distance of Spain. He reached there safely just three days after being shot down. He figured that if he now bought a ticket to Toulouse in unoccupied France (Vichy France) he might be nabbed by Germans monitoring the demarcation line, and chose to walk the thirty miles to the border. This he did, even stopping one hot afternoon, parched and dying for a beer, in what he described as a country pub. The bar was empty save for the girl behind the counter. She was friendly, he told her his story and they soon began drinking good wine. 'We had a most enjoyable afternoon, and I left there about 5.30 p.m., feeling very pleased with life and full of the beauty of France.' Close to the demarcation line, Barnett received more help and slipped over into Vichy France in the darkness with the aid of a guide. Then it turned to custard. At the railway station where he finally bought a ticket for Toulouse he failed to notice a plain clothes gendarme checking identity papers on the platform. When he couldn't produce any he was detained — on 6 June 1942 — his 24th birthday.

His freedom over, Barnett was transferred from the local lockup to Fort de la Revere, a former mountain-top fortress halfway between Nice and Monte Carlo, overlooking the Mediterranean. A week after he arrived, Stan Browne was brought into the camp.

On the night of 23 September Barnett and four other British airmen, among them New Zealand bomber crewman Pat Hickton, who was credited with the escape idea, broke out of the fort. They got into the camp kitchen through a tunnel lined with barbed wire, filed through iron bars, dropped by rope into the moat surrounding the fort, and crawled into a sewer via a drain. Hacking through more bars at the end of the sewer, they emerged on a hillside and scarpered to nearby Monte Carlo, where they linked up with the Resistance. Four days later the escapers rode a train to Marseilles and were hidden for three weeks before going by train again to Perpignan. A few nights later they were being spirited out of France, after they waded out to a 30-foot fishing boat.

On the fourth night at sea a Royal Navy destroyer appeared out of the gloom and took them aboard. The navy landed the five airmen in Gibraltar, from where another navy warship took them home to freedom, and on 7 October they docked at Greenock, Scotland. Barnett then rejoined the squadron. He wrote: 'The feeling of being chased and of outwitting the enemy was exhilarating in the extreme.' He later flew with 167 Squadron (Spitfire), commanded in succession 234 Squadron (Spitfire), 501 Squadron (Spitfire/Tempest) and 274 Squadron (Tempest) and was awarded a DFC.

Browne, like Barnett, was close to getting out of France when he was captured entering Vichy France and also taken to Fort de la Revere. He broke out two weeks after Barnett, but linked up with his fellow New Zealander on the beach near Perpignan and arrived back in England on the same ship as Barnett, before also rejoining the squadron. He was twenty-two when he first flew as a sergeant with them in December 1941, and had been a medical student in Dunedin before enlisting. Back for only two months after his French escapade, he was posted to the Mediterranean theatre, serving with 93 Squadron (Spitfire) in North Africa and Malta during the Tunisian campaign and the invasion of Sicily, and was credited with five and a half enemy aircraft. Browne, DFC and bar, later returned to 485 Squadron, where he was the last CO before its disbandment.

The other New Zealanders from the squadron who evaded capture after coming down over France were Terry Kearins, 21 (Palmerston North), Johnny Checketts and Jim Mortimer, 27 (Auckland). Kearins was shot down in flames on 15 July 1943, by four FW 190s on a bomber escort sortie over France. He avoided German patrols and found sanctuary with a French farm family who tended his badly burned legs and nursed him back to health at grave risk to themselves. He was passed through various Resistance groups and taken back to England on a fishing boat from Brest, rejoining the squadron in December.

Checketts' evasion story is told in detail in his biography. CO of 485 Squadron at the time, on 6 September 1943 he parachuted down over France, burned and punctured by shrapnel. Like Kearins, he was treated and helped by the Resistance, returning to England by fishing boat.

Mortimer spent the longest time of all the evaders on French soil. He had flown in Malta and accounted for three enemy aircraft before September 1943, when he was posted to 485 Squadron. Early the following month he was shot down over the Somme Estuary when the squadron scrapped with FW 190s while escorting Marauders. In this action Maori pilot Bert Wipiti, 21 (New Plymouth), was killed moments after sharing in the destruction of a 190. He had earlier flown Buffaloes in Singapore, credited with three enemy aircraft. Awarded the DFM, he is remembered on the panels at Runnymede. Mortimer was credited with a probable and damaged another before falling victim to return fire. He ditched in the estuary, struggled out of his sinking Spitfire and made it into his dinghy. At dawn next day his little craft was swept into the estuary and washed ashore. Eventually he made contact with the Resistance and was sheltered for almost a year before he made it back to England.

Chapter 13

THE YEARS BETWEEN

Allan Smith did his early flying in New Zealand and once the course was finished, half the group completed their wings training at home while the other half, Smith among them, sailed to Canada on the *Dominion Monarch*, to complete theirs. Smith topped his class at Dunnville, the Ontario airfield where many New Zealanders trained, and on 11 November 1941 was commissioned as a pilot officer. He and nine other pilots sailed to Britain on an old banana boat in a convoy shredded by submarines. Tankers were torpedoed on either side of their ship. 'I think we were saved by the fact we were so small we weren't worth wasting a torpedo on. We wore our life jackets day and night though we wouldn't have lasted long in the cold water,' Smith wrote in 2001. Eventually the convoy scattered and Smith's boat sailed on alone, so far north that the sea spray froze as it came in over the side, and the topsides carried thick ice.

At 56 OTU, Sutton Bridge, Smith learned to fly Hurricanes and was reunited with close mate Vaughan Fittall, whom he'd first met in Levin on induction and had trained with in Canada. The New Zealanders had dribbled from Canada to England on different ships. Smith and Fittall were to become lifelong friends, best man at each other's weddings in England. At Tangmere both met WAAFs who became their wives. In March 1942 the New Zealanders at Sutton Bridge were posted to 486 Squadron, at Kirton-in-Lindsey, as foundation members. The squadron flew Hurricanes at first but Typhoons began arriving in July. Before Smith made his first flight in one of the 'monsters' he listened to pilots who had flown them, studied the pilots' handbook at length and sat in the cockpit for some time checking out the controls and instruments. He started up and taxied out.

> Once I had lined up I took a deep breath and opened the throttle. I had never experienced power like it and the 'brute' took off without too much help from me. I flew around for a while to get the feel of the aircraft and then came back for a series of circuits ... it was not too long before I decided that I was going to like this aircraft.

After brief moves from their base at Wittering to North Weald and West Malling, 486 Squadron settled at Tangmere in late October 1942, staying there until the end of January 1944. With their fast Typhoons, 486 Squadron's job was to combat the south coast hit-and-run raiders. Until March 1943 the New Zealanders patrolled in pairs, once or twice a day, up and down the Channel, on sectors parallel to the English coast. The planes stayed at ground and sea level from takeoff, using the R/T only in emergencies. The squadron's first victory was scored by Aucklanders Gordon Thomas and Artie Sames on 17 October, when they shot an FW 190 into the sea. Thomas, 25, was killed the following April in an accident at the Sutton Bridge gunnery school, while flying a Spitfire.

Patrolling for raiders was routine and often unrewarding, though results improved once low-level detection radar was installed at some south coast points. After a long period of fruitless patrols, 486 Squadron shot down seven enemy planes between mid-December and the end of the month. Despite the nature of the work, Smith remembered benefits:

> We flew about 50 feet above the water about ten to twenty miles out to sea where we would be picked up on the radar by 'Blackgang' on the Isle of Wight. We flew as low as we could so that we would not be picked up by the German radar, which was much further away, with the No. 2 flying line abreast so that we could cover each other's tail ... most of my patrols were with Frank Murphy as my No. 2. With the constant flying together we reached a stage where we were almost able to read other's thoughts. We flew backwards and forwards on the patrol line using lean mixture and low revs to conserve fuel so that we would have maximum reserves in the event of combat. We developed skills at flying low above the water, bad-weather flying and an uncanny ability to hit the right landfall when returning to base. Each section leader developed leadership qualities and learnt to make decisions in emergencies. These skills were to stand us in good stead later.

Fittall admired the skill of the Blackgang radar operators and controllers, even though one day they directed him to something that wasn't an enemy raider. Vectored to a contact just south of the Isle of Wight, Fittall heard Blackgang repeating, 'You must be able to see them, you are so close.' Fittall remembers getting worried, and nearly screwing his head off in case they were behind him. Neither he nor his No. 1 could see anything. What was showing on the Blackgang radar screens was a large flock of seagulls fishing, enough to create a decent blip.

In late February 1943 Smith and Murphy gunned down a pair of bandits heading towards England. Radar controllers cleverly positioned them behind the Me 109s, which finally spotted the Typhoons and swung for home. The New Zealanders shared one and then Smith closed on the other and gave it several bursts from behind.

> There were strikes all over the aircraft, pieces started to come off and it burst into flames. I moved off to avoid the debris and as the 109 lost airspeed I finished up about twenty feet to the left of it. At this stage the pilot turned and looked at me — it was my first face-to-face meeting with a German and I will remember that until the day I die. I pulled away and shortly after that he hit the sea ... I felt no elation, rather a fear that God would strike me from the sky for taking a human life.

Many pilots on both sides saw their opposites close up during the war when they flew alongside aircraft they had fatally damaged. Des Scott, who took command of 486 Squadron on 1 April 1943, was appalled by his actions when he shot down an Me 109 early in his new posting. He and three other 486 Squadron pilots intercepted two enemy fighters between the Cherbourg Peninsula and Le Havre. A burst from Scott shattered one, pieces of it flying off in all directions, including the canopy. The German's propeller windmilled and black and white smoke came from his exhausts. In *Typhoon Pilot* Scott described what happened as his victim began a slow shallow dive towards the sea:

> I throttled back in formation with him. He was trying to climb out of his cockpit and I could see quite clearly the terrified expression on his young round face. You do things when your blood is up and your heart is pounding that you would not do under normal circumstances.

I followed him down ... Still clinging to the side of his cockpit, he pulled himself on to the starboard wing when only about 100 feet above the water. For reasons which I have never been able to analyse, I pressed the firing button again, and he and his aircraft hit the sea almost simultaneously in a fountain of spray, framed only by the pattern of my own cannon fire ... I buried my head in the cockpit and was suddenly overcome with a feeling of deep remorse ... why had I fired that last burst? ... It had not been necessary ... why could I not have kept my bloody fingers out of his final moment? ... The passing years have not erased the magnitude of this brief encounter. I often see him looking back at me — and well may he ask 'Who won?'

Historic 1 Squadron exchanged their Hurricanes for Typhoons at the same time as 486 Squadron (July 1942) and also went hunting raiders — on the northeast coast, not normally the scene of much action. One of the squadron's early successes, in September, was scored by Invercargill pilot Des Perrin. Flying from Acklington, Northumberland, he and a fellow pilot intercepted a pair of Me 110s. Perrin went after one, his mate the other, and both fighter-bombers fell into the sea. This was Perrin's only success in a two and a half-year stint on 1 Squadron before he transferred to 198 Squadron and was killed in France. He had already survived one brush with death in September 1941, two months after joining 1 Squadron. Fresh from training in New Zealand and Canada, he had collided with another Hurricane on ops over the Isle of Wight. While Perrin baled out safely, the other pilot was killed.

The Typhoon squadrons running the south coast patrols weren't the only ones to lose pilots. Flying a Spitfire with 91 Squadron, Irvin Downer, 22 (Christchurch), died when he was shot into the sea by an enemy fighter on 29 December 1942 during a two-plane standing patrol between Dungeness and Beachy Head. Commissioned just two months earlier, Downer had survived a bale out after engine problems and a crash-landing following combat a year earlier. His fellow pilot, New Zealander Bill Mart, 23 (Wellington), searched unsuccessfully for him and Downer is another remembered at Runnymede. He had married in England and left his widow and a daughter. The month before his death he had tasted success, intercepting and shooting down one of two German fighters about to attack a convoy.

Tired of endless Channel patrols hunting sneak raiders in late 1942 and early 1943, things changed for the pilots of 486 Squadron when CO Bob Roberts was posted and replaced by Des Scott, fresh from his six months' staff work at Fighter Command headquarters. He wanted to go on the offensive, and soon showed what he and 486 Squadron could do as hit-and-run raids tailed off; German losses against the destructive Typhoons were mounting and the Luftwaffe began to find the results not worth the candle. Smith wrote of Scott:

> He was a very strong character and took hold of 486 Squadron by the scruff of its neck and changed it from a good average squadron to a first class fighting machine, of which I was very proud to be a member. He had an effect on me that was to last me for the rest of my life because through flying with him I learnt to believe in myself. I must also say he was rude, arrogant and egotistical and these characteristics made him unpopular with people who did not fly with him, particularly those who got in his way. However, the pilots who flew with him would follow him anywhere and achieved standards that they never dreamed they were capable of.

Smith, an excellent pilot and leader, was later appointed CO of 197 Squadron (Typhoon). He was hit by flak and force-landed to be captured on the last day of 1944.

Bee Beamont who commanded the Tempest Wing comprising 3, 56 and 486 Squadrons in 1944 remembered how good the New Zealanders were, though he couldn't quite fathom them. He said in his book *My Part of the Sky:*

> I could never make out the New Zealanders. They flew better than any of the other squadrons [3 and 56], even better formations than my old 609, though I would never admit that to them. I was happy flying with them and they, I think, with me but there it ended; perhaps they could not forget their old New Zealand CO, wing leader and idol Scotty, to my disadvantage. [Remembering a sweep the wing flew after D-Day, he added:] We were not pressed for time so I began a leisurely circuit after takeoff and looking back watched the aircraft as, pair by pair, they sped off down the runway and, once airborne, curved left to cut off the corner and join formation. Johnny Iremonger's 486 NZ Sqn was formed up and drawing into position on my right before 3 had even settled down around me. Those New Zealanders were good, but it would not do to tell them so too often.

Beamont was shot down and captured in October 1944, while on a ground attack mission over Germany.

In July 1942, 486 Squadron lost its first pilot when Aucklander Ian Irvine (26) died after crashing during an Army Co-operation exercise. He had done just five ops with the squadron but had earlier 100 with

152, a Spitfire squadron, and won a DFM. Four more were killed in the last three months of the year and in 1943 another seven died.

Meanwhile, 485 Squadron lost five pilots, four of them New Zealanders, in the July–December 1942 period. Two of the New Zealanders were killed on successive days, involved in Rhubarbs over Belgium and Holland, showing just how dangerous such operations were. Norman Langlands, 21 (Tirau), died on 2 August and Ron Vessey, from Ashburton, the following day. Vessey, two days short of his 20th birthday had been on his first squadron, and for barely a month.

Remembering the ceaseless roll of deaths, Fittall wrote that when he read his wartime diaries years later he was amazed how casual some of the entries seemed. 'X crashed in the sea and did not surface. Wrote a couple of letters and went to the pictures.' He reflected:

> Obviously this was a defence mechanism that I didn't know I had developed, and I suppose if you couldn't do this, you could not have continued. I must also have been able to divide my life into separate compartments, and switch from one to the other at will. Violent action, rest and sleep, eating and drinking, entertainment, and romance!

One of 485 Squadron's big operations of the year was its participation on 12 February in the RAF's fruitless attack on the battle cruisers *Scharnhorst* and *Gneisenau*. The big ships, accompanied by the heavy cruiser *Prinz Eugen*, embarrassed Britain with their breakout from Brest and through the Channel to their home ports in northern Germany. They sailed from Brest under cover of darkness and in filthy daylight weather were not spotted until they were in the Straits of Dover. The British navy and air force response was disorganized, ineffective and

DAY AFTER DAY

too late. At 6 p.m. the three ships and a large number of smaller escorts vanished into the blackness of night.

The British lost thirty-seven aircraft without result in their afternoon attacks on the ships, though the gallant aircrews of the Fleet Air Arm Swordfish, who pressed home their torpedo attacks in the face of massacring fire, were lauded, their leader Eugene Esmonde awarded a posthumous Victoria Cross. However, 485 Squadron was one unit to come out of the action with its reputation not only intact, but enhanced. Newspapers splashed a photograph of their pilots over their pages; London's *Express* under the heading 'These men did a grand job for Britain'.

The squadron was detailed to escort torpedo bombers but in the murky weather couldn't find the other aircraft and flew on alone to the target. One section led by Bill Crawford-Compton encountered Me 109s off the Belgian coast and promptly shot two down. Harvey Sweetman and Dave Clouston (Wellington) shared one and Crawford-Compton got the other. The squadron's other two sections reached the battle cruisers and saw them through breaks in the cloud. Wells took one section down one side of the high-speed German line, leaving a motor torpedo boat (E-boat) badly damaged. Garry Francis' section went down the other lane and tangled with fighters. *New Zealanders with the Royal Air Force* says Francis drove an FW 190 down with smoke pouring from its engine, Reg Grant got a 109 and Jack Rae blew off the hood and shattered the tail of another before he was forced to break away. A good day for 485 Squadron in tough conditions.

One Fighter Command New Zealander was lost on 12 February — Ivan Stone, 25 (Wellington). He was a newcomer, flying with 118 Squadron (Spitfire) and on just his seventh op. He and another 118 pilot battled enemy fighters after losing the rest of their squadron in

306

bad weather off Ostend. The other pilot got home safely but Stone was never seen again and is commemorated at Runnymede.

Grant, made a pilot officer on 12 February, arrived as a sergeant at 485 Squadron in October 1941 with a good reputation, a DFM, and eighty-four ops with 145 Squadron (Spitfire) behind him. He was destined for much higher things. He was commissioned in November and promoted to squadron leader and appointed CO of 485 Squadron on 6 May 1942, succeeding Wells.

The Grant family was enveloped in tragedy. Reg's brother Bill, older by nine years, joined the RAF on an SSC in 1929 and flew in India before returning to Britain. He was in Northern Ireland when taken ill and died in February 1932, in an RAF hospital.

Reg and his remaining brother Ian, younger by almost eighteen months, enlisted on the same day in November 1939 and trained together at Bell Block and Woodbourne, but Reg suffered injuries in a training crash and was on sick leave for several months. Ian left New Zealand earlier than his brother and reached England in time for the last month of the Battle of Britain, flying convoy patrols with 151 Squadron to earn his Battle Clasp. Later he worked as a staff pilot with a bombing and gunnery school, flew briefly with 501 Squadron (Spitfire) and joined 485 Squadron as a flying officer in November 1942 under his now CO brother, Reg.

The two Grants took off with the squadron from Westhampnett, Sussex, on 13 February 1943 on Rodeo 168, a fighter-only offensive sweep over northern France that went badly wrong. The squadron dived on enemy fighters but were bounced in turn by a bigger group of Germans coming out of the sun. One attacker latched on to Ian's Spitfire from behind. His brother tried four times to warn him of the danger, his messages apparently unheard, and Ian was shot down and

DAY AFTER DAY

killed. Reg avenged his brother's death, immediately destroying the German, but it was a pyrrhic victory. Ian, then aged 27, was on his 22nd op.

Two other 485 Squadron Spitfires were shot down in the fierce fighting. Revell Steed, 23 (Gisborne), died and Tony 'Slim' Robson, 26, was captured after crash-landing near Boulogne, the engine of his fighter hit and damaged. Gisborne-born Robson had joined the squadron as a sergeant in October 1941 and was awarded a DFM before he was commissioned. He was a flying officer when he was brought down over France, with his the only DFM among the squadron's many decorations.

Reg Grant's almost year-long command of the squadron ended in March 1943. He then did a lecture tour in the United States and from November commanded 65 Squadron (Spitfire / Mustang) for a short period before promotion to command 122 Wing on 21 February 1944, part of 83 Group in 2TAF. He was dead a week later, killed not in action but in an accident. He took off from Gravesend in a Mustang of 65, one of the wing squadrons, to participate in a Noball, the name given to raids on V1 sites. At 2500 feet he reported engine trouble, turning back for the field, but between 1000 and 1500 feet rolled and abandoned his fighter at about 400 feet. He didn't pull his ripcord and was killed when he hit the ground. *For Your Tomorrow* says investigators concluded oil thrown out of the engine may have obscured his windscreen, and that before baling out he might have been overcome by fumes. After Jack Rae returned to New Zealand from POW camp he married Vera Grant, the three Grant brothers' sister, and their parents' only surviving child.

A development in late 1942 marked a new phase in the RAF's war against Germany — the first penetration of German air space

308

by British fighters. Bombers had long been dumping their loads on German targets, but on 21 October the appearance over the Fatherland of fighters from England stunned the enemy.

Wing Commander Alan Anderson led four Allison-engined Mark 1 Mustangs of 268 Squadron, an Army Co-operation unit, on a Rhubarb over Holland and northwest Germany to the Dortmund-Ems Canal, a regular Bomber Command goal. The other Mustangs were flown by a flight lieutenant and two New Zealanders, Flying Officer William Hawkins, Wellington, and Pilot Officer Owen Chapman, Timaru.

The four Mustangs flew from their Snailwell, Cambridgeshire base, refuelled at Coltishall and lifted off again at 10 a.m. to cross the North Sea to Holland in murky weather, with gale force winds. They followed the Dutch Frisian Islands from Texel to the end of Terschelling and then turned south to cross over the coast to the Dutch mainland and on to Winschoten, near the Dutch-German border, before flying into Germany and heading for the Dortmund-Ems Canal. As they entered the Nazi homeland they opened fire on a range of targets — a line of camp huts they left blazing, a gasometer and factory, canal barges, a small ship in a lock. Homeward bound, the Mustangs attacked canal shipping in Holland and along the Dutch coast, then turned for England. All landed safely.

Australian Colin Ford, 268 Squadron historian, says: 'This mission caused a great deal of consternation to the German High Command, as the presence of single-engined RAF fighters operating from the UK over Germany meant that a new level of threat had to be considered and defences put in place.'

Proudly, Chapman wrote and underlined in his logbook: 'Shot up camp, barges, factory, 2 ships. FIRST FIGHTERS TO FLY TO GERMANY'. After reaching England in 1942 he spent his entire

DAY AFTER DAY

operational career with 268 Squadron — two tours and a total of 109 ops with a six-month spell of instructing in between. He commanded a flight on his second tour and was rewarded with a DFC. On 15 January 1945 he was posted for repatriation and an enormous shindig followed that night. 'Mitch' Mitchell, an Englishman who migrated here postwar and still lives in New Zealand, told Ford:

> The party of farewell that evening was memorable. I do have vague (and I mean very vague) memories of the mess party we had on 15th January to farewell Chappie ... It was one hell of a 'do' and we were all nearly paralytic by the time we staggered off to bed in the early hours.

Hawkins, who flew with Chapman on that historic op into Germany, was killed eleven months later. He had flown with 613 Squadron (Mustang) before his attachment to 268 Squadron, with which he flew thirty-six ops before returning to 613 Squadron, also based at Snailwell. He died on 27 September 1943 on a Jim Crow, a shipping reconnaissance sortie, off the Dutch coast. Homebound after attacking E-boats off Terschelling, he and another Mustang were intercepted by two enemy fighters, Hawkins was shot into the sea and died the day after the squadron was told he'd been awarded the DFC. He is commemorated at Runnymede.

Three days before Hawkins' death, one of New Zealand's top fighter pilots of the war, one whose name, sadly, is hardly recognised here today, was killed in combat over France. Gray Stenborg, only child of Auckland couple Gunnar and Ruby Stenborg, was shot down while on a Ramrod, escorting bombers raiding Beauvais, inland from Dieppe. *For Your Tomorrow* says it's believed to have been his Spitfire seen going down streaming glycol after an engagement with a large number of fighters near the target area. At the time of his death, still only twenty-one, Stenborg was credited with fourteen victories. Remarkably all his successes were against FW 190s and Me 109s. Just as remarkably, his first four were 190s, all downed within the space of five days in late April 1942, when he was flying the slower Spitfire VB over France with 111 Squadron. He had joined Treble One in January 1942 after just three ops with 485 Squadron, to which he had first been posted after arriving in England.

Despite those early successes, Stenborg really made his name in Malta on 185 Squadron, where he won a DFC and claimed another seven enemy fighters, all 109s. Amazingly his victims included two pairs, on 5 and 9 July. When he got back to England at the end of August Stenborg told Alan Mitchell about his last Malta flight, a scary one on 19 August. He tangled with a group of 109s and shot one down just before another finished his Spitfire.

A great hunk flew off my starboard wing. I heard explosions, the plane shook everywhere and black smoke poured into the cockpit. I began diving out of control at 27,000 feet. I tried to get the hood off but it would not budge. I tried all ways while the Spitfire fell 14,000 feet at over 400 mph ... it was a horrible feeling. I expected the plane to blow up at any moment but fortunately the hood came off and I suddenly found myself thrown out. I had seen a German pilot open a parachute at that speed and the harness ripped off by the force of sheer speed, so I waited for a while before pulling the rip-cord to slow up.

Stenborg landed in the sea five miles from shore, struggled for five minutes to get free of his parachute and climb into his dinghy. He was picked up promptly but said that last sortie 'shook me to the teeth'.

Day after Day

Back in England, in May 1943 he was posted to 91 Squadron, now flying Spitfire XIIs, after instructing for six months. It took him a while to make an impression again but he had a 'hot' month in the final few weeks of his life, shooting down three fighters including one the day he died. With an all-up tally of 188, Stenborg had flown 120 ops with 91 Squadron.

Ray Hesselyn, Stenborg and Jack Rae (see Chapter 12, Evaders) were New Zealand's best at Malta. Strangely all were shot down in quick succession over France in 1943 — Rae on 22 August, Stenborg on 24 September and Hesselyn on 3 October. By coincidence Hesselyn was downed in combat with German fighters while escorting Marauders over a Beauvais airfield, the same area where Stenborg died.

Dunedin-born Ray 'Hess' Hesselyn made his name at Malta and is linked indelibly with the 'brave little island' which won the George Cross. He went there as a sergeant, after brief service with 234 Squadron following his arrival in England. He flew a Spitfire to Malta, one of the first groups of such fighters on the island, from the carrier HMS *Eagle* on 7 March 1942, at the height of the combined German-Italian aerial assault. He left on 26 July with twelve enemy aircraft to his name, a big reputation, a commission and a double DFM, the only man in the RNZAF so awarded in World War II. The twelve included seven 109s, three Stukas and two Ju 88s. He had a slow start but was deadly in April and May when he scored ten of his victims, two in one day on 13 May.

His citation for the DFM, awarded on 22 May 1942, noted his skill, gallantry and 'outstanding determination' in pressing home attacks. The citation for the bar, bestowed an astonishingly short seven days later, said that although fighting at great odds Hesselyn 'never hesitates in his efforts to destroy the enemy'.

After he returned to England Hesselyn and his friend, Australian ace Paul Brennan, collaborated with a journalist to write *Spitfires Over Malta*, a wildly successful book about their time there. Brennan, repatriated to Australia in April 1943, died in a flying accident in Queensland two months later.

Hesselyn instructed in England during his six months' rest, served briefly on a couple of squadrons and was then posted to 222 Squadron on 1 July 1943, flying sixty-nine ops with them before he was shot down. In that time he boosted his victory tally to eighteen. His final flight ended when he was attacked by an FW 190, after sending a 109 down. Cannon shells thudded into his cockpit and the plane burst into flames. He fought a desperate struggle to get the hood off; by the time he did some of his clothing was afire and his face and hands burned. He was captured the moment he landed in a field near Beauvais about 5 p.m. and the Germans treated him in hospital before he ended up in a POW camp. He made one escape but was at large for only a day, enough to earn himself fourteen days in the cells on bread and water. Hesselyn was awarded an MBE in December 1945 for his work as personnel officer, and then intelligence officer, at Stalag Luft I, Barth, on the Baltic Sea coast. Said the citation: 'This officer contributed very considerably to the well-being of British and American prisoners of war by his unstinting work on their behalf.'

Hesselyn had a scary start in the RNZAF, surviving a crash on 24 April 1941, near the end of his training, at Lake Grassmere landing ground. Piloting a Vincent, he crashed during an attempted landing, an inquiry finding an 'error of judgment'. He was rescued, slightly injured, from his petrol-soaked aircraft by a ground crewman who risked his life to get Hesselyn out of the aircraft, winning himself an air board commendation. Hesselyn's postwar life in the RAF ended sadly. He commanded a Meteor squadron briefly in 1951 but a growing problem with alcohol blighted his career and he died in an RAF hospital on 14 November 1963, at just forty-two.

Another New Zealander killed in June 1943, whose name is not well known today but should be, is Vince Pheloung. In January 1943 he was appointed CO of 56 Squadron, one of Fighter Command's best units and in September 1941 the first to be equipped with Typhoons. It was later to fly Tempests alongside 486 Squadron in the assault on the flying bombs over England, and later on the Continent. Pheloung, born in 1914 in Christchurch, where he was raised, was a veteran pilot at 56 when he was appointed, but not greatly experienced on ops. He travelled to England on his own accord in March 1937, aiming to join the RAF. He succeeded in gaining an SSC and earned his pilot's wings in July 1938, but it was more than four years before he finally got on to ops. He spent that time at various units, probably as a staff pilot, sometimes the fate of even top-class pilots. He broke the cycle in September 1942, posted to 485 Squadron where he flew five ops before moving on to 181 Squadron (Typhoon) after just six weeks with his fellow New Zealanders. His stay there was also short, before his posting to 56 Squadron, although he was probably already being groomed for higher things.

Pheloung died on 20 June after leading the squadron for six months from Matlask, a base near the north Norfolk coast, its job attacking enemy shipping, usually over Dutch coastal waters. This was where 56 Squadron was operating on 20 June when Pheloung led it down to attack a pair of minesweepers and two armed trawlers. *For Your Tomorrow* records that immediately afterwards Pheloung's Typhoon was seen streaming white smoke. He radioed that his engine temperature had climbed so high he was baling out, climbing to 1200 feet and sending a Mayday. His No. 2 flew protection, watching for enemy aircraft. When he looked at the stricken Typhoon again it was in a steep diving turn at 600 feet, just before it plunged into the sea. No parachute was seen. Pheloung's body was later recovered by a German minesweeper and buried in Dunkirk.

The curtain of flak put up by shipping under attack, often boosted by coastal artillery if ships were close to land, and especially around harbours, cost the lives of countless Allied flyers. The deadly combination of combined shipping and coastal flak killed New Zealander Gerry Rawson on 24 October 1943. Flying a Typhoon with 183 Squadron from the Warmwell airfield, west of Bournemouth, he died attacking the German cargo ship *Munsterland* in Cherbourg Harbour.

The *Munsterland*, a blockade runner, had reached Bordeaux from Japan in May 1942, where she remained until well into 1943 before scuttling along the French coast to Brest and then Cherbourg. On the night of 22–23 October the Royal Navy cruiser *Charybdis*, accompanied by six destroyers, tried to intercept the *Munsterland*, which was thought to be heading along the coast. The poorly planned and executed operation ended in disaster when German torpedo boats clashed with the British force, sinking the cruiser and one destroyer, with the loss of 426 sailors on the *Charybdis*.

On the afternoon of 24 October the RAF made a major effort to sink the *Munsterland*, launching three separate strikes against her at Cherbourg. At 3 p.m. twenty-two Mitchells bombed the target from 12,000 feet, followed soon after by a low-level attack by Whirl-winds, each carrying two 250-pounders escorted by a squadron of Typhoons that blazed away at the ship. Two of the Whirlibombers were shot down. At 6 p.m. eight bomb-carrying Typhoons of 183

Squadron attacked at mast height. Three of them were destroyed by murderous flak, including those of Rawson and the squadron CO. The New Zealander's body was never found and he is remembered at Runnymede. Sometime later the *Munsterland* was badly damaged by fire from heavy coastal guns at Dover and driven ashore west of Cap Blanc Nez, France, to become a total wreck.

Several years ago French and Dutch researchers Mickael Simon and Rob Philips began checking the graves of several unidentified airmen in Cherbourg Cemetery. They felt one of these, marked with the date 24 October 1943, might be the resting place of Rawson, but eventually came to the conclusion it was not. Rawson, 25 when he was killed, was born and raised in New Plymouth, and he was a student teacher in Auckland when he enlisted in November 1940. In England he flew Spitfires with 603 Squadron and Hurricanes with 486 Squadron before being posted to the Middle East. He never got there. Bound for Malta on the fleet carrier HMS *Furious*, on 17 August 1942 he was hit and injured by debris when a Spitfire crashed off the side of the ship near him on takeoff. Rawson was returned to England and spent ten days in hospital, then in January 1943 joined 183 Squadron.

Gerry Westenra, posted to England in early 1944 after his long service in Greece, Crete, North Africa, and Sicily where he commanded a Spitfire squadron, was appointed CO of 65 Squadron, flying Mustang IIIs (the Rolls-Royce-powered versions) in March on long-range escort for bombers and other duties. On 17 May he took part in one of the most celebrated Ranger operations of the war, Ranger the RAF codename for deep penetration patrols into enemy territory targeting aircraft and transport.

This one was to Aalborg, near the northern tip of Denmark. The distance had already been tried out and found viable. Eight Mustangs led by Wing Commander Robin Johnston, a South African, were chosen for the attack — five from 65 Squadron and two from 122 Squadron. These squadrons, plus 19 Squadron, formed 122 Wing, which Jamie Jameson would command in Normandy from late June until the arrival of the Tempests three months later.

The Aalborg participants from 65 Squadron included three New Zealanders — Westenra and his squadron's two flight lieutenants, Buck Collyns and Richard 'Dicky' Barrett. The Mustangs flew from their south coast base of Funtingdon to Coltishall in Norfolk to refuel before lifting off a few minutes after 9 a.m. for the 330-mile trip across the North Sea. The fighters flew at low level before reaching the Danish coast, then flew north for another 100 miles to Aalborg. German radar either didn't pick them up or marked them as friendly. Over Aalborg at precisely midday, the group split into two, Johnston and the New Zealanders to the north side of the town, the others to the south.

In a matter of minutes the ground was thick with blazing German wrecks. The RAF pilots destroyed bombers and training aircraft in the air and flying boats at their moorings, none alert to the danger of unexpected enemy. Some of them then tangled with fighters that were about to land and shot back up to meet the invaders. Four Ju 88s were downed, Westenra and Collyns getting one apiece and shares in others. The final tally claimed was nine enemy aircraft before the Mustangs turned away and headed for home. The attackers paid a price — Barrett was killed, in combat with a fighter, but may have shot down one German, and perhaps even two, before his loss, and a 65 Squadron flight sergeant, Roland Williams, force-landed after material flying off a German lodged in his air scoop. He was lucky, snatched up by the Danish underground and quickly returned to England. Barrett,

DAY AFTER DAY

24 (Wellington), an experienced pilot on his 156th op when he died, crashed in shallow water. His body was recovered and he was buried a week after the action in Frederikshavn, alongside German airmen killed in the fighting.

A month after Aalborg, Collyns transferred to 19 Squadron, where one week later he was hit by flak on a fighter-bomber op over the beachhead, but baled out safely into Allied-held territory. On 9 August, now operating from France, 19 Squadron shot down four FW 190s in an engagement over Chartres, Collyns claiming one and another shared. Ten days later he scored an Me 109 probable near Dreux, but then his luck ran out.

The next day a seventeen-strong group of Mustangs from 19 and 65 Squadrons, again led by Johnston, fought a fierce battle with 190s over Rouvres, Cobber Kain's old 73 Squadron base, northeast of Paris. Collyns shot down one German but was then bounced and shot down in turn. *For Your Tomorrow* says his Mustang crashed near a railway crossing, his body thrown twenty metres from the wreckage. It adds that he was buried in Rouvres two days later 'in the presence of the whole village, such an abundance of flowers being present that it was said the Germans protested'. Collyns, 31, was later reinterred at Villeneuve-St Georges, about 20 km from Paris. At the time of his death Collyns was credited with five victories and two others shared.

A few days after Westenra was posted away, another New Zealander who had flown under him on 65 Squadron lost his life. Corran 'Ash' Ashworth, a younger brother of noted bomber pilot Artie Ashworth, had his baptism of fire over Dieppe with 253 Squadron before sailing with the squadron to North Africa for almost a year. Back in England he instructed, then on 10 June 1944 he joined 65 Squadron. He had flown twenty-four ops on the Mustangs when he was killed on 3 August,

318

dive bombing barges on the Seine being used to ferry withdrawing Germans across the river, twenty miles south of Rouen.

Ashworth, the last of twelve to dive from 12,000 feet, was at the bomb-release height of about 4000 when his aircraft blew up in a violent explosion. The remains of the fighter plunged into the river in a ball of flame, destroyed not by flak but the premature explosion of the two 1000 pound bombs it carried, one under each wing. His body was never found and Ashworth is remembered at Runnymede. Fellow 65 Squadron member Tony Jonsson, the only Icelandic pilot in the RAF, wrote later that seven or eight 122 Wing pilots were killed this way — it was considered technically impossible but nevertheless happened. The 'mysterious phenomenon' ceased when the wing reverted to 500 pounders. 'It was bad enough having to fly through concentrated flak without the added risk of our own bombs killing us in some inexplicable way.'

Three weeks before the war ended, noted New Zealand pilot Ron Bary was killed in similar circumstances over Italy — by 500 pound bombs. Bary, commanding 244 Wing, was diving on a close ground support operation on 12 April 1945 when one of the bombs on his Spitfire exploded at the 4000–5000 feet level. There was no flak in the area and *For Your Tomorrow* says it was assumed one on the bombs exploded prematurely, either while still attached to the aircraft or immediately on release. The aircraft disintegrated in the blast. Another pilot on the wing had suffered a similar fate twenty-four hours earlier.

All through 1943 and 1944, RAF fighters and fighter bombers — with new squadrons added to their strength — battered the Germans in France, Belgium and Holland, even ranging into Germany itself. New marks of Spitfires first regained — then exceeded — the performance of the FW 190, with fighters escorting greater numbers of bigger and better bombers. The first Mustangs had reached into Germany in late 1942; in the spring of 1944, Spitfires with long-range drop tanks began to intrude into German airspace.

On 26 April, 132 Squadron, led by Geoffrey Page, made the first Spitfire penetration into Germany on a Ranger. An Englishman, Page was badly burned and disfigured when he was shot down in a Hurricane in the Battle of Britain, and was one of the founders of the famed Guinea Pig Club. By 1943 he had endured more than 40 plastic surgery operations before returning to operational flying.

At mid-afternoon on 29 April 1944, eight 132 Spitfires were over Holland heading for Germany again when they spotted an enemy aircraft approaching to land at Deelen, just north of Arnhem. New Zealander John Caulton, flying low with Page, found himself head-on to the enemy aircraft and opened fire. Caulton couldn't have found a worse target. The heavily armed Me 110 was piloted by Hans-Joachim Jabs, a leading German night-fighter ace who would have fifty victories to his credit by war's end. When Jabs realised the Spitfires were approaching him he turned his nose cannon on to Caulton. Shells exploded on the Spitfire, tearing open the leading edge of one wing, smashing holes in the radiator and oil tank and ripping out the bottom of its long-range fuel tank. Some of Caulton's fire hit home as Page wisely turned to come in behind Jabs.

Caulton headed for home with no hope of getting back. The fighter's engine soon seized and, too low to bale out, Caulton did a wheels-up landing in a field — almost on top of a small group of German troops. The Spitfire hit hard, gouging its way across the field, before it was finally halted by a small earth bank. Caulton suffered an injury to his right knee and a gashed head. Jabs had been damaged in the encounter, but managed to shoot down another Spitfire, killing its pilot, before he force-landed at Deelen, sprinting to safety from his wrecked aircraft. Page wrote in his combat report: 'I fired short bursts until E/A crashed into a dispersal at west end of runway. E/A broke up.'

Feeling sorry for himself, Caulton was taken to a hut by his captors. There he was bandaged, treated well and soon found himself talking to a group of German officers — including Jabs who'd arrived to meet his victim. Jabs put out his hand and asked, 'You were flying the Spitfire?' Caulton admitted he was. Jabs replied simply, 'I was the other pilot.' He didn't let on his own aircraft had been forced down.

'Jabs wanted to know when the invasion would take place,' Caulton remembers. 'I told him Churchill hadn't told me yet. I also told the officers they couldn't possibly win the war and cheekily suggested they give up on the spot.' They didn't take up his offer. Before he left, Jabs dated and signed a piece of paper carrying a message saying: 'Please let the prisoner keep this souvenir.' Caulton folded the paper in four, put it into a pocket and looked after it carefully. He still has it. He was then driven away to begin his long journey to the POW camp.

Twenty-six years later, Caulton discovered Jabs survived the war, and was living in Germany. The two men exchanged letters and Caulton visited Jabs, who had established an agricultural machinery firm, with New Zealand one of its export markets.

On the other side of the world, Caulton bought a small ice-cream company in Hastings, his place of birth, and introduced New Zealanders to real fruit in their ice-creams. He then built it into one of the country's most successful ice-cream companies — Rush Munro's. Jabs died in 2003, while Caulton lives in retirement in Havelock North, at the age of 90.

Caulton didn't fly with 132 Squadron on the afternoon it made the first Spitfire intrusion into Germany in the Aachen-Cologne area, but one New Zealander who did was Bob Harden. An Aucklander born one week before Christmas 1921, he was posted to 132 Squadron in August 1943 and had flown 145 ops with the squadron and been commissioned before 15 August 1944, when he was lost. He took off with the squadron just before 8 a.m. from B19, Lingevres, in Normandy, on an armed reconnaissance over Falaise. After reporting he had been hit by flak, Harden's aircraft was last seen at a very low level, streaming glycol. When the area was liberated soon after, his fighter was found crashed in a field at Ouville. Extensive searches failed to find any sign of his body and he is commemorated on the Runnymede Memorial. Did someone find his body, bury it and never notify authorities? Or did he share the fate of some Allied flyers, who survived the landing only to be picked up and executed? An enduring mystery that will never be solved.

Chapter 14

DIVERS

Almost every book and feature article about the V1s, the flying bombs that rained down on southeast England in the summer of 1944, has the same story about a Londoner that's pretty much identical except for the persona and home address. Here's the one from *Diver! Diver! Diver!* by Brian Cull and Bruce Lander. A typical Londoner was asked how he managed to remain so calm during flying bomb raids:

> I see it like this. It must take the Germans a lot of trouble to make the bloody things, and then they have to get them into those pits and up into the air, and it is quite a long way from France to London, and if they do get to London, they have still got to find Hackney. And even then, it isn't everyone who can find 37, Bulstrode Road, and even if they do it's ten-to-one I'm in the pub!

It illustrated English stoicism and humour perfectly. London had endured the Blitz of 1940–41 and now it endured a different kind of attack. More than 6000 people were killed and thousands more injured by the V1s as they crashed down mainly on London and the southeast counties, their explosive warheads demolishing homes, factories, schools, hospitals and countless other buildings. Many more dug large holes in open fields. In mid-July newspapers reported that up to two million people had quit London, tired after five years of war and now this, the last straw. It had been a cold, wet summer and a prevailing impression was of V1s scuttling along in and out of heavy clouds. The smell of powdered brick dust and plaster filled the air, while broken glass from numberless smashed windows crunched underfoot.

Hitler's almost-last throw against Britain (only the V2 ballistic missiles — rockets which could not be stopped — were yet to test London) was a vain attempt to alter the course of the war. The V1s, though they caused enormous loss of life and damage, were defeated by the skill of RAF fighter pilots, anti-aircraft gunners, barrage balloons and eventually by the Allied land armies overrunning the launch pads in France's Pas de Calais area.

The first V1s were targeted against England the night of 12–13 June. Their start-up had been repeatedly delayed and when the campaign finally began only a fifth of the fifty-five planned launch sites were ready. Instead of the planned enormous salvo of the new terror weapons only ten lifted off. Four immediately failed, arcing down to earth and exploding. Another two fell harmlessly into the Channel. That left four. One impacted in a potato field near Gravesend about 4.15 a.m. while another crashed five miles from West Malling airfield. One crashed in the back garden of a house near Borough Green in Kent, smashing two rows of glasshouses and the other landed in Bethnal Green, where it damaged a bridge and railway track and killed six people, including a young woman and her baby. Three nights later bombs started to fall on London in earnest and forty-six people died.

While most people called the V1s doodle bugs, buzz bombs, dingbats or flying bombs, pilots knew them as divers. In essence they were crudely guided winged missiles with explosive heads, weighing close to a ton. They had short stubby wings in the centre, a tailplane and rudder and were powered by a pulse-jet engine mounted above the rear of the 'aircraft' and burned low-grade aviation fuel. Their flight limit was about 150 miles and they flew more or less straight and level at an average speed of about 400 mph, normally at about 2000 feet. However, speed and altitude varied considerably. On reaching the planned target area an automatic system cut off the fuel, the engine quit and the missile began heading down.

Anti-diver pilots found the V1s easier to pick up at night because of their long bright trail of exhaust flames, but the distance from the target when attacking was harder to gauge in the dark. In daylight hours range was easier but the divers were less visible from above as they flew over the countryside.

They were noisy, and sounded like a motorbike without a silencer, while some people thought they were like a poorly maintained steam train going uphill. Everyone knew when to take cover — when the engine quit and the missile was overhead. If the engine kept going it meant the V1 was going further and someone else was the target.

Cull quotes an American serviceman on leave in London when a V1 ended its racket almost overhead as he emerged from lunch in the Rainbow Club.

The V1 passed overhead about 200 feet up and crashed with an ear-splitting roar about three blocks away. Almost immediately the traffic, pedestrian and vehicular, that had come to a standstill, was back to normal. A little old woman scurried away from a wall where she had sheltered muttering to herself, 'Bloody nuisance, these buzz bombs.'

Some V1s acted strangely. One, damaged by gunfire, flew over RAF Brenzett very low, wobbled, then lifted and climbed away west. Next it turned east and orbited the field twice, before disappearing over a nearby hill and crashing. Air and ground crew threw themselves flat three times.

The V1s' arrival was not unexpected. British intelligence had kept track of their development and Bomber Command had unleashed huge loads of explosives on launch sites and warhead storage dumps for months, at the cost of many aircrew. Fighter-bombers with rockets and cannon joined in the attack. Basil Collier in *The Battle of the V-Weapons 1944–45* notes that more than sixty of the later type of German launch ramps, easier to build and harder to detect than the so-called ski-ramp sites the Germans abandoned, had been built by early June, but Allied bombing had not been concentrated enough to destroy them and post-D-Day commitments meant the bombing slackened off.

The anti-V1 campaign in England was organized and run by Air Vice-Marshal Roderic Hill, who moved hundreds of AA guns to the south coast, giving fighters a clear but narrow area in which to chase flying bombs that somehow managed to negotiate the storm of coastal artillery fire before they reached the barrage balloon and gun defences around London. Collier also says the combined guns/balloons and fighter onslaught 'eventually proved highly effective but the system took time and experimentation'. The introduction of newly developed proximity fuses in AA shells made ground fire more effective and shifting the guns to the south coast meant shrapnel and unexploded shells fell harmlessly in the sea. The V1s were also attacked over the Channel, day and night.

New Zealander Jack Stafford of 486 Squadron, who downed eight V1s, is quoted by Cull:

We patrolled a thousand or two feet higher than the expected altitude of the Divers and were well informed by ground control of their imminent arrival. We would be vectored to the position at which the Diver would cross the coast and given a countdown to its arrival. This was absolutely accurate … As it passed through the flak we pursued it in a long gentle diving turn at maximum revs and boost. They varied in speed and to a lesser extent altitude. We could be doing maybe 450 mph at this stage and we had maybe two and a half minutes to catch it before it entered the balloon barrage.

Most Spitfires were generally too slow to catch V1s and it was the much faster Tempests which bore the brunt of the fighter attacks on the divers — with a valuable and effective contribution from night-fighter Mosquitoes over France, the Channel and England. 486 Squadron and 3 Squadron, the first to be equipped with Tempests followed by 56 Squadron, formed 150 Wing, or the Newchurch Wing. The wing took up the prime role in the battle against the V1s from RAF Newchurch, a steel-mesh field near Folkestone, where the pilots lived in tents. The wing was aided by other Tempest squadrons as they entered service, the later faster Spitfire marks, Mustangs IIIs and by the Meteors of 616 Squadron — the first RAF jet aircraft and the first British jets to go into action, albeit against a passive enemy.

The top V1 killer was Squadron Leader Joe Berry, who had led a flight of Tempests within the Fighter Interception Unit (FIU), a special RAF fighter group.

Cull says that in early August New Zealander Garry Barnett, CO of 501 Squadron (Tempest) at Manston, and twenty of his pilots, were posted to 274 Squadron, also at Manston, which was converting to Tempests. Barnett was designated to take command when the current

CO completed his tour. Meanwhile Berry, accompanied by five other experienced Tempest pilots from the FIU, arrived to take over 501 Squadron. His instructions came from the prime minister himself, directing 501 Squadron to fly at night in any weather, even when other squadrons were grounded. It was felt that the V1s were such a threat that people on the ground must at least 'hear' fighters whenever there was a V1 warning. The squadron was to get airborne even if it was impossible to make an interception, and was to consider itself expendable.

Berry is credited with no fewer than sixty-one V1s, two of them shared, the majority destroyed while he was flying night sorties with the FIU on Tempests, including an astonishing record of seven one night in July. He was killed in October 1944, shot down by ground fire over Holland, too low to bale out. His brave last words: 'I've had it, chaps. You carry on.' He died with a DFC and two bars.

In the V1-kills stakes Berry was well clear of Belgian Remi van Lierde of 3 Squadron who tallied forty-seven, including three shared. A close third was Francis 'Togs' Mellersh, of 96 Squadron on Mosquitoes with forty-three, assisted in thirty-seven of them by his navigator Mike Stanley. Also high on the table was Newchurch Wing boss, Wing Commander 'Bee' Beamont, who usually flew with 3 Squadron. He scored thirty-two V1s, six of them shared.

Behind these leaders were twelve pilots who tallied twenty or more, among them 486 Squadron New Zealanders Owen 'Ginger' Eagleson with twenty-three (three shared) followed by Ray Cammock, twenty-one (two), and Jim McCaw, grandfather of All Black Richie McCaw, twenty (one). Jim Cullen shot down fifteen, Ray Danzey eleven and Harvey Sweetman ten. Best New Zealand one-patrol scores were McCaw's and William 'Wacky' Kalka's four each.

However, the first New Zealander credited with the destruction of a V1 was Spike Umbers, who had flown with 486 Squadron earlier and was to die commanding it in 1944–45. Now with 3 Squadron as a flight lieutenant, Umbers made his mark in New Zealand air war history mid-morning 16 June, while on patrol from Newchurch. His squadron got twelve that day, establishing an early lead against 486 Squadron it never lost, tallying 288 to become the highest-scoring squadron, to 486 Squadron's 241, which was the second highest score.

Less than three hours after Umbers' success, 486 Squadron's Brian O'Connor and Kevin McCarthy were the first to score, O'Connor getting in for the initial kill. Just short of forty years later, O'Connor wrote:

> My only claim to fame … It came in over Dungeness at 9500 feet, the highest ever recorded, at 380 mph. [He shot it down, the bomb landing] … between the officers' mess and the sergeants' mess at RAF West Malling. No casualties. For which I received one bottle of Scotch. My call sign was Fairway, Pink One! The RAF put on a big reception at Eastbourne for the presentation — we all got rotten.

Amazingly, O'Connor also shot down 486 Squadron's last V1 at 7.18 p.m. on 31 August, in the Maidstone area. O'Connor flew 190 ops with the squadron, claimed nine flying bombs, a lot of locomotives and mechanised transports, one and a half FW 190s and 'numerous SS troops'. He also earned a DFC.

McCarthy suffered engine failure returning from a Diver patrol in early August and smashed down into a forest at night, suffering severe injuries. Jim Sheddan wrote: 'Though he survived the crash, his flying days were over. When next I saw him he was in [Archie] McIndoe's hospital in East Grinstead having his face straightened out.' McCarthy was in hospital for almost a year.

However, 486 Squadron paid dearly for its success against the V1s. Three pilots died, another ten were injured and seventeen aircraft destroyed or damaged beyond repair, according to Cull. Some of the aircraft casualties occurred when Tempests were caught in the flames and debris of exploding V1s, but most occurred in forced and crash-landings.

Joe Wright, 24 (Auckland), was killed late on 28 June; a number of sources say he was shot down by American gunners, plunging into the sea. However, the reliable *For Your Tomorrow* says the Tempest dived into the ground three or four miles inland from the coast close to where the V1 he had been attacking, hit the ground and exploded. It was considered unlikely the AA fire was to blame; Wright probably followed his target down, leaving no room for manoeuvre when he was either thrown about or blinded by the blast when the V1 exploded.

On the last day of July, squadron newcomer Alex Wilson, 24, who came from the Helensville area, died when his Tempest collided with a 1 Squadron Spitfire after coming out of cloud at 2000 feet near Bexhill, Sussex. The other pilot was also killed. An inquiry decided the Spitfire had intruded into the Tempest's patrol area. The third, another newcomer, Jim Waddell, 23 (Invercargill), died on 17 August shortly after takeoff on a V1 interception patrol, crashing and exploding.

Gordon 'Sandy' Bonham, 23 (Christchurch), one of the New Zealanders on 501 Squadron, claimed a total of five V1s, four of them on 25 August in two hours on a dawn patrol. It's said he shot one down and then, out of ammunition, flipped the others over with his wing tip, sending them to earth. Countless stories have been written about RAF pilots nudging flying bombs into a downward dive by flying their planes alongside the V1s then putting their wing tips under one of the enemy missile's wings. Such action disrupted the air flow and destabilised the V1, causing it to roll over and plunge down. But there's plenty of controversy and doubt about this issue. Some experienced pilots are doubtful that wing-tipping occurred, among them Harvey Sweetman, who says he never saw it happen and doesn't think it ever did — though some photographs do seem to show otherwise. However, Sweetman flew through the entire anti-diver campaign and his opinion must be respected.

Bonham had won a DFC as far back as 1942, honoured for his flying in Singapore where he operated on Buffaloes with 243 Squadron and suffered severe wounds in combat with the Japanese. He reached England in late 1943 then flew Spitfires (fifty-three ops) and Tempests (forty-one ops) with 501 Squadron. He was killed on 25 September, while returning from an anti-diver patrol. Trying to land in poor weather, he flew into the ground near Harwich, Norfolk.

Sometimes so many fighters attacked an individual V1 that pilots more or less lined up for a go, or were thwarted by other aircraft barging in on 'their' target. On 24 August 274 New Zealander Lyndon Griffith closed on a diver at 3000 feet over the Channel. Cull quotes him:

I attacked from 400 yards astern and saw no strikes. A Spitfire next attacked but no strikes seen and he pulled away. The Diver continued on the same course and speed. I then made another attack from astern and saw strikes. The Diver went down and exploded in the sea.

A few days later Barnett, now commanding 274 Squadron, watched a gang attack on the diver he'd been stalking. A Mustang dived steeply and opened fire at 400 yards, too far away. Then another Tempest closed to 100 yards but his fire missed. When it was all over the diver continued serenely on. Left alone with his prey, Barnett attacked again and this time saw strikes. The diver turned over, went down and exploded in the sea.

In the early stages of diver attacks, Johnny Checketts got one in a Spitfire, despite his plane's relative slowness. But he missed one. Checketts had just taken over command of a wing at Horne, near Biggin Hill, and directed twin machine guns be set up in front of the intelligence officer's hut so that when he wasn't flying he could take pot shots at any that flew over the airfield. The inevitable. Checketts wasn't home when a V1 did roar over Horne and the intelligence officer shot it down.

American units participated in the V1 shoot with some success but were not really welcomed by the RAF. Cull quotes one American pilot:

> When we were flying we were told to keep the hell out of the way of the RAF Spitfires and Tempests which were much lighter and more manoeuvrable than our lumbering Jugs [P-47 Thunderbolts]. But the temptation was great because it seemed the vast majority of the beastly things came directly over our tents [on the south coast]. We did chase a few while airborne but the RAF fighters let us know they didn't like our intrusion and we knew for a certainty that the ack-ack boys would gleefully shoot at anything that moved so we did not press the issue.

Even Bomber Command got into the act. In the right place at the right time, gunners on two Lancasters homeward bound from Germany destroyed V1s and an American Fortress crew got another.

The attacks declined rapidly in the first days of August and by the middle of the month some Tempest squadrons were able to resume flights over France. It was all over soon after. The fighter boys had destroyed 1902 V1s (for the loss of seventy-three pilots), the gunners 1657 and the barrage balloons 264. On 7 September the government announced that 'Except possibly for a few last shots, the Battle of London is over.' The next day the first V2 slammed into London.

Chapter 15

INVASION AND VICTORY

The cross-Channel invasion of Hitler's 'Fortress Europe' by Allied land forces proved impossible in 1943, as the Russians had urged, but during that year Britain and the United States began detailed planning for Operation Overlord, the code name for this enormous undertaking. The invasion was first targeted for May 1944 but planners eventually settled on June, and the build-up of huge numbers of American forces, ground troops and airmen began. On D-Day, 6 June 1944, more than 1.4 million Americans were in Britain.

The first bomber units of the 8th US Army Air Force had arrived in England in early 1942 but it was well into 1943 before the 8th could commit serious numbers of the aircraft for strikes in Europe and they didn't begin deep-penetration raids until the second half of the year. Meanwhile, the RAF began its own changes in organisation for its role in Overlord. In mid-year 1943 its Army Co-operation Command was disbanded and replaced by the creation, on 1 June, of a new Tactical Air Force (TAF) provisionally under Fighter Command with Bomber Command's 2 Group day bombers transferred to it. Five months later Fighter Command was split in two, TAF becoming a stand-alone renamed command, the Second Tactical Air Force (2TAF); its role was to provide support for the invasion. Fighter Command was renamed Air Defence Great Britain (ADGB), an unwieldy title changed back to Fighter Command eleven months later.

In January 1944 the first commander of 2TAF was replaced by a New Zealander, Air Marshal Sir Arthur 'Mary' Coningham. It was just reward for a man who more than anyone had developed and honed the air-support and ground-attack role of the Desert Air Force in North Africa into a key instrument of the victory there. He applied many of the lessons he learned in North Africa and later in Sicily and Italy to 2TAF's campaign in Europe. Coningham served with great distinction in the air over the Western Front in World War I and was a good choice as 2TAF's leader. An added plus was his ability to work closely with the Americans, whom he liked and admired. The Americans, who formed their own 9th Tactical Air Force to support their ground troops, admired Coningham in return.

2TAF had two key strike groups — 83 to support Britain's Second Army, and 84 to support the Canadian First Army. New Zealanders had important roles leading big wings in each group. Group Captain Jamie Jameson was given command of 122 Wing, holding the post from July 1944 to the end of the war. A number of squadrons were attached at various periods but for much of the time the core of the wing were Tempests — 3, 56, 80, 486 and 274 Squadrons. The Meteors of 616 Squadron were also attached for the week of their combat life in April-May 1945. Des Scott, a wing commander when he was appointed and then promoted to group captain, led 123 Wing of Typhoons — 198, 609, 183 and 164 Squadrons. 35 (Reconnaissance) Wing in 84 Group was commanded by New Zealander Peter Donkin. Other New Zealanders held 'Wing Commander Flying' posts in several wings, notably Bill Crawford-Compton (April 1944 to January 1945) in 145 Wing (Spitfire), 84 Group. Cam Malfroy commanded the wing briefly in April 1944, followed by Al Deere, in charge from May to July in 1944. Deere was followed by the South African Sailor Malan, now a group captain. 485 Squadron was attached to 135 Wing.

2TAF had wings of fighters, fighter-bombers, reconnaissance aircraft and night fighters. The fighter and fighter-bomber wings were highly mobile and self-contained — packing and moving to set up at new strips had been practised assiduously in England before the invasion. Because of their short range the fighter types moved quickly to Normandy after the initial landings so they could be in close contact with their own ground troops and close to the German forces they were attacking. As the fighting moved away from the beachhead areas after D-Day the wings moved on to other airfields further afield in France, Belgium, Holland and eventually Germany, keeping pace with the Allied armies.

The first field built in Normandy was 'B1' (Asnelles-sur-Mer) in countryside a bit inland from Gold Beach. It was a strip designed for emergency landings only. The next step was the building of Advanced Landing Grounds, or ALGs. They were constructed by simply bulldozing areas of flat land and laying steel mesh tracks of various types — 1200 yards long for fighters and 1650 yards for fighter-bombers. ALGs B2 and B3 were first operational on 13 June, just a week after the initial landings, and more were quickly in use. Aircraft operating from these early grounds were able to refuel and rearm, but until the strips could take full wings permanently, squadrons flew home to England at night.

On the eve of D-Day 2TAF had fifty-one squadrons of fighters and fighter-bombers, twelve of light and medium bombers, ten

DAY AFTER DAY

reconnaissance squadrons and twelve squadrons of defensive fighters, according to *2nd Tactical Air Force* by Christopher Shores and Chris Thomas. In addition ADGB had thirty-four squadrons of fighters.

The Allies totally dominated the air space over the beachhead on D-Day and the Luftwaffe, weakened to the point of exhaustion by sustained suppression attacks on their aircraft and airfields far inland from the landing beaches, and by other factors, was unable to mount any effective opposition. Basically the Luftwaffe had been swept from the skies.

Allied pilots providing the umbrella at Normandy were astonished by the D-Day armada of ships streaming back and forth across the Channel, the greatest line-up of vessels in history. They were also astonished by the strength of German ground fire and anti-aircraft fire from the Allied fleet, whose aircraft recognition was poor and whose sailors blazed away at anything that flew — despite the clear painted strips on RAF aircraft that were supposed to signal 'friendly'.

Johnny Checketts, now a wing commander leading the Horne Wing (three squadrons; one British, one Canadian and one Polish) from a new improvised airfield of the same name southwest of Biggin Hill, was briefed about D-Day on 5 June but had to keep the news to himself until he could tell his men at midnight. Vincent Orange's biography of Checketts says the New Zealander remembered the mood when he broke the news. 'Loud cheers rolled round … everyone was laughing, weeping, shouting and dancing about; Canadians, Poles and Britons were all slapping each other on the back and, for a moment, they were indeed a band of brothers.'

Checketts flew four separate sorties on D-Day for a total flying time of seven hours and thirty-five minutes, his Spitfire holed by bullets from friends and enemies alike. 'Seamen and soldiers, whether Allied

336

or German, seemed to be united in regarding all aircraft as fair game,' Orange wrote. 'Johnny's wing was supposed to help troops fighting on the eastern beaches, but their fire — combined with that of the ships lying off shore and the German defenders — drove the Spitfires away.'

'Lots more bloody flak from our own ships,' Checketts wrote in his logbook on 7 June. On D-Day he'd led his wing over Caen before first light, protecting the huge fleet of bombers, and gliders carrying paratroops to drop behind the beachhead.

Two New Zealand aircrew died on D-Day but neither was on single-engined aircraft. One was Edward Atkinson, 22 (New Plymouth), bomb aimer on a Stirling briefed to drop paratroopers of the 6th Airborne Division near Caen. It was brought down over France in the early hours of the morning. Only two of the crew and a number of paratroopers survived. The other was James Chalmers, 21 (Invercargill), navigator on a 2TAF smoke-laying 88 Squadron Boston, shot down by shore flak or E-boats off Le Havre. His body was never found and he is commemorated at Runnymede.

Few RAF pilots saw aerial combat in the invasion area on D-Day. One who did was 485 Squadron's Johnnie Houlton, 21 (Auckland), credited with a Ju 88 bomber, the first enemy aircraft destroyed by a 2TAF pilot that day. Using a new gunsight the squadron was testing, he blasted a three-second burst at the 88's starboard engine. According to his book, *Spitfire Strikes — New Zealand Fighter Pilot's Story*, the engine 'disintegrated, fire broke out, two crew members baled out and the aircraft dived steeply to crash on a roadway, blowing apart on impact'. Three other pilots from his squadron joined with him to down a second. He remembered this aircraft crash-landing at high speed, one propeller breaking free 'to spin and bound far away across the fields

DAY AFTER DAY

and hedges, like a giant Catherine wheel'. Houlton enjoyed a purple patch in those early days of June, downing two Me 109s and damaging a third. On 8 June he attacked a 109 flying starboard of a group of twelve near Caen. His combat report says he opened up astern at 300 yards and watched pieces fly off the enemy fighter and black smoke gush from its engine.

> He porpoised in and out of cloud a few times and as he came out I got in one or two more bursts without effect; on the last occasion, however, I followed him up and hit his slip stream in the cloud. I fired again and the black smoke came past me in the cloud. He broke cloud simultaneously and I saw him go down in a shallow dive to crash in a wood. Just before crashing an object came away but no parachute.

His victim three days later was a 109 fighter-bomber flying at low level. At 200 yards Houlton opened up with a three-second burst. Pieces flew off, the engine burst into flames and the 109 pulled up sharply. 'At a height of about 600 feet the pilot was thrown clear and his parachute opened. The E/A then crashed and blew up.'

Houlton served briefly on 485 Squadron in June 1942 before volunteering for Malta. He damaged two Ju 52 transports over the Mediterranean in November 1942, postwar research showing both may have crashed into the sea. Some sources credit him with nine victories, *Aces High* says five, two shared and four damaged. Houlton rejoined the squadron for a long stint when he returned from the Mediterranean at the start of 1943. He was later posted as a flight commander to 274 Squadron, flying a Tempest in the last stages of the war. His final victory was a Dornier 217, southwest of Kiel, a couple of days before hostilities ended in northwest Europe.

On 6 June 485 Squadron pilots destroyed two fighters, with four more on the 8th and another two on 12 June, one of them Houlton's, the other downed by Bill Newenham, a former two-tour bomber navigator much earlier in the war. He requested and was granted pilot training, earning his wings in Canada before joining the squadron.

One New Zealander who missed the D-Day drama was Bob Caldwell, nicknamed 'Grid' because his surname was the same as New Zealand World War I fighter ace 'Grid' Caldwell; they were not related. Caldwell, a Waikato bank officer, volunteered in January 1940, 'subject to the very real adrenaline surge of youth', enlisted in May 1941 and arrived in Britain in February 1942. After AFU and OTU he served on two squadrons, both posted to the bleak Shetland and Orkney Islands north of Scotland. This was followed by lots of sun and flying in Malta and Italy with 126 Squadron (Spitfire) before its return to Britain in April 1944 and posting to Culm Head, Somerset, in mid-May in preparation for the invasion.

Caldwell wrote in a memoir:

The morning of D-Day dawned to find me on leave in London! A prompt return to my unit allowed me to become airborne over the beachhead on D plus 2, in loads of time to get seriously involved. D plus 3 saw the squadron patrolling in terrible weather in the vicinity of the famous Mulberry Harbour installation which was being thrashed about by an unexpected storm … In spite of a stuttering start in June, I completed fifteen offensive sorties for the month. Some of the trips were longish [using] overload tanks to extend our normal range up to say 2–2½ hours … On an early-days patrol inland … we were astounded to view the bombardment of Caen by battleships and cruisers lined up close to shore. [The town was stoutly defended by the Germans and

DAY AFTER DAY

damaged so badly by RAF bombers that the British advance completely stalled in its rubble] ... A goodly number of shells, some as large as 16-inch, must have passed under or through us as we cruised by. The effect of these huge missiles as they exploded caused tremendous shock waves across the ground in a rippling pattern ... An absolute hell for those on the receiving end. [Caldwell noted the] ... almost complete absence of enemy air response ... [in June and July] ... and indeed August ... [while the navy fought off E-boats and submarines and the soldiers plugged on.] ... We 'Blue Orchids' seemed somehow removed from most of the real nastiness.

Typhoon pilots often joked, sometimes sarcastically, about the patrolling Spitfires, 'swanning about overhead' as their 'Tiffies' prepared for takeoff, and the deadly ground flak as they swooped to drop bombs and fire rockets and cannon at low level in support of the troops battling the Germans. The Typhoons bore the brunt of single-engined aircraft casualties in the three months of the Normandy campaign, with 151 pilots remembered on the Normandy Typhoon pilots' memorial at the entrance to the village of Noyers Bocage near Caen. Six of those are New Zealanders — Warrant Officer Doug Burke, 20 (Matamata), 247 Squadron, killed 15 July 1944; Pilot Officer Peter Price, 20 (Napier), 609 Squadron, killed 27 July; Pilot Officer Robert Hemmings, 21 (Invercargill), 247 Squadron, killed 8 August; Pilot Officer James 'Joe' Stellin, 22 (Wellington), 609 Squadron, killed 19 August; Flying Officer George Trafford, 23 (Gisborne), 164 Squadron, killed 25 August; and Flying Officer Ian Hutcheson, 28 (Hastings), 137 Squadron, killed 27 August.

All except Stellin were victims of the ever-present flak, which took an enormous toll on Typhoons and other fighters. Stellin is remembered as a young man who died trying to avoid a Normandy village. He was on an eight-aircraft patrol in the Orbec-Bernay area on the morning of 19 August — fellow New Zealander Rod Harkness was among the pilots — that attacked tanks and motor vehicles. As the Typhoons headed back to B7 Martragny, Stellin was given the okay to make a lone attack on another vehicle he had just seen. He winged over and went down. Later, apparently lost, he was heard asking for a course home followed by a message saying he was running out of fuel and about to force-land. He never did. As he glided towards the ground out of fuel and deciding to jump, Stellin saw the little village of St-Maclou-la-Brière in his path. He banked sharply to the right to avoid crashing into the village. Once clear of it he baled out but was now too low — his parachute didn't open in time and he died as he hit the ground.

The 400 people of St-Maclou-la-Brière mourned the death of this young man who had come from the other side of the world to fight for their freedom and sacrificed himself to save lives in this tiny speck of a foreign land. They buried him in the village churchyard where he lies today, his name engraved on the village's own war memorial and the area in front of the church named 'Place Stellin'. In 1947 the French Government posthumously bestowed on him the Croix de Guerre avec Palme. In Wellington his parents donated a piece of land on Tinakori Hill ridge in memory of their only son. The site, James Stellin Memorial Park, and its engraved stone cairn, look out over the city, a reminder of the short life of a brave young pilot.

Less than two months after Stellin's death, New Zealander Ivan Cain, 20 (Auckland), another Typhoon pilot, gave his life in similar circumstances over Holland. Cain took off with seven other 175 Squadron planes at 7 a.m. on 6 October, on an armed reconnaissance.

As the aircraft fired rockets at barges on a waterway just inside Germany, Cain's Typhoon was hit by flak. Streaming glycol, he reached friendly territory, but passing over Reichswald Forest he continued to lose height as smoke from the engine rapidly increased. Nearing the southern outskirts of the Dutch city of Nijmegen he fired off his remaining rockets into a wooded area apparently in preparation for a forced landing south of the city. When Cain found the area densely populated, he steered his plane to crash on a small plot surrounded by houses. His body, found thirty metres from the wreckage, was buried locally but later reinterred in Jonkerbos War Cemetery.

Dutch-born Wellingtonian Nick Lambrechtsen, who has researched this incident and plans a memorial on the crash site, quotes a Reuters correspondent on the scene that day in 1944 who called Cain's death 'an heroic act' because he stayed with his plane when he could have baled out.

Between 6 June and war's end fifty-four New Zealand pilots of single-engined day fighters and fighter-bombers lost their lives on ops with 2TAF — twenty in Typhoons, sixteen in Spitfires, thirteen in Tempests and five in Mustangs. Four of the Tempest pilots lost their lives during the anti-diver campaign in England.

Flak was the main killer, the Germans firing millions of rounds from multiple-barrelled 20 mm guns (a rough equivalent to the Allied pom poms), and from 37 mm and 88 mm pieces. They clawed down countless Allied planes by day and by night, the scourge of the Typhoons and other fighters. Every German target had its flak defence and they threw up a hail of shells, many of them radar-directed. The Germans were brilliant at disguising flak sites, with innocent-looking buildings, trains and woods turned into deadly traps. Flying into flak was heart-churning. Pilots jinked from side to side and moved up and down to make themselves more difficult targets. Flying straight was courting disaster.

In early September 1944, John Church, a 74 Squadron Spitfire pilot and lifelong mate of Bob Caldwell (they met during initial training at Levin), arrived with the squadron at Bernay field in France. Postwar he never wrote a word about his service in the final year of the war, but his log reveals dozens of what must have been hair-raising ops. Definitely not one of those Spitfire squadrons swanning around upstairs, 74 Squadron dropped bombs, fired rockets and pummelled ground targets with cannon and machine-gun fire. On almost every op flak hosed up at them. On 28 October after attacking a gun post northeast of Flushing, he summed it all up in four words that would have appealed to thousand of flyers: 'Flak unfair to pilots.'

Pilots of some planes hit by flak were able to nurse their aircraft back to base, others force- or crash-landed or jumped. The lucky ones lived to either evade or be captured on the ground. Some aircraft simply blew up in mid-air in vast explosions, while others disintegrated in fireballs on the ground. Rob Hemmings, killed on 8 August, was lost in an attack on a convoy of six tanks on a road between Caen and Falaise. Caught by a burst of flak while firing rockets, his Typhoon broke away to port, rolled over and exploded on impact.

Typhoons reigned supreme in Normandy, smashing German armour and motor transport and wreaking general havoc among the Nazi forces. They broke up a key German armoured thrust at Mortain and played a huge role in the destruction of armoured forces in the Falaise Gap. German troops feared and hated the Typhoons; British and Canadian soldiers cheered them. Day after day the Typhoon squadrons whirled over the battlefields, plunging down to knock out strongpoints, artillery, tanks and other German units holding up progress on the

DAY AFTER DAY

ground. Cooperation between ground and air was refined to such a point that Typhoons could attack targets just in advance of British and Canadian forces with deadly accuracy and without casualties among the 'friendlies'.

In late May 1944, when Rod Harkness joined 609 Squadron at Thorney Island on the south coast in preparation for D-Day, two other New Zealanders also arrived — Pete Price and Joe Stellin. They both died in Normandy; Harkness had a charmed life. He flew with 609 Squadron right through to war's end while the squadron lost thirty pilots, including five COs, in that time. New Zealanders Tom Annear and Allan Scott arrived as replacement pilots during the year and while both survived, Annear was injured in a nasty crash that ended his flying. On 1 July 609 Squadron, along with 164, 183 and 198 Squadrons of 123 Wing, under Des Scott, arrived in France. A couple of weeks later they were settled in at Martragny.

Harkness wrote about Normandy years later, recalling the stress under which pilots operated.

[The flying was] … very concentrated and the heavy amount of flak took toll of the pilots. On top of that at night our own ack ack guns would open up on enemy aircraft; army artillery was on the go and occasionally warships just off the coast would open up with their big guns so some nights sleep was out of the question. The ingredients were there, and signs of exhaustion became apparent among us.

Most RAF pilots lived in tents at ALGs in France, Belgium and Holland, often just a mile or two from the front lines, and German artillery made life uncomfortable. Pilots dug slit trenches in their tents and rolled into them when shells or bombs were falling. Some slept in their trenches;

even group captains did at times. Jamie Jameson, commanding 122 Wing in the Normandy beachhead, wrote to his wife in England on 27 July 1944 that he had 'a lovely big hole dug in my tent and put my bed in it'.

Harkness also remembered the 609 Squadron Typhoons over the Falaise Gap.

[We] went down through a gap in the clouds and on a vehicle-choked road there they were — MET [Mechanised Enemy Transport], tanks, buses, huge covered troop carriers, tractors pulling guns, everything moveable. They were all over the place between villages and you could see dust rising everywhere ... Our CO said on attack 'a pair of rockets only' and in we went for our first attack ... you only had to fly along the road and let go — you couldn't miss. We made four attacks with a pair of rockets at a time and strafed with cannon fire. We attacked everything. Some vehicles blew up and smoke rose to 4000 feet and it seemed to flatten out at the top like a big cloud. The spirals of smoke rising into the still air marked the area for other squadrons who would be on their way to have a turn at the Germans ... it was a wizard show, and in the excitement I hadn't realised I had been hit by flak.

Pilots visiting Falaise after the battle were astonished and appalled at the carnage they had wreaked. Hundreds of dead Germans still lay where they died, in a terrible mix of wrecked tanks, artillery, vehicles and the poor horses used to haul transport. The smell was indescribable.

Both 609 and 183 Squadrons claimed something rare in the RAF — pilot brothers born in Germany. Ken Adam flew on 609 Squadron,

Denis Adam on 183 Squadron. Their wealthy Jewish family, penniless when they fled Germany in the mid-1930s, settled in England. Ken, known affectionately to his RAF mates as 'Heini', became a noted screen production designer postwar, famous for his sets for a number of the James Bond films and an Oscar winner. He was knighted in 2003.

Denis, called 'Who Dat' on 183 Squadron, immigrated to New Zealand in 1947, arriving with £6 in his pocket. He settled in Wellington, grew rich as an astute businessman, and is well-known and appreciated as an art collector and benefactor.

On 183 Squadron Adam watched pilots die, necks broken when their Typhoons flipped on landing. In a 2009 newspaper interview he said he always lowered his seat as far as it would go when landing. He figured that and his short height (5 feet 6 inches) might preserve his life in a landing accident. Other pilots could only see the top of his head peering out of the canopy and someone drew the age-old cartoon of a face peering over a wall on the back of his flying jacket and the line 'Who Dat'. Hence his nickname.

One of the men he may have seen killed in an accident was New Zealander Des Perrin, who joined 198 Squadron as a flight commander a week before his death. Just after 7 p.m. on 10 September Perrin was on his takeoff run, leading three other Typhoons to rocket a strong point at Le Havre, when a tyre on his aircraft burst.

Byron Lumsden, who flew in to the squadron as a replacement pilot on 13 August after his tour on 3 Squadron and a spell of instructing, wrote in his memoir that Perrin was doing 80–100 mph when the tyre was burst by a stray end of tie wire on the mesh runway.

[The Typhoon] flipped on to its back and as the aircraft hit the ground the cockpit canopy was crushed and the armour-plate behind [Perrin's] head was bent over and broke his neck. This was very saddening and resulted in an instruction to lower your seat completely before takeoff and if you had a tyre burst on takeoff or landing you were instructed to bend forward and grip the bottom of the seat in the hope this would save you from the bending of the head shield.

Adam was proved to be doing exactly the right thing when he huddled down in his cockpit. The sortie led by Perrin was abandoned after his death but the war went on and Lumsden wrote: 'Immediately after that we took off to attack a strongpoint at Mervilliers.'

Lumsden was no stranger to the death of fellow pilots — and friends. Ian Hutcheson, killed in Normandy in August, shared a tour on 3 Squadron with Lumsden. He was best man at Lumsden's marriage to Wren Connie Taylor, in England in July 1943, and godfather to the Lumsdens' first child, a daughter, born when Lumsden was instructing. Hutcheson had been a Hawke's Bay shepherd before enlisting.

Lumsden flew solidly in his three months on 198 but in November, exhausted and suffering health and eye problems, was sent to hospital. Fit for flying again in January 1945 but classified 'tour-expired', he was homeward-bound with his wife and daughter the following month.

He wasn't around in December 1944 when 198 Squadron lost two more New Zealanders, Mate 'Timmy' Milich and Oscar 'Ossie' Oden, but would have known them both. Milich, who was twenty-three, died on 8 December, Oden four days later.

The son of Dalmatian-Maori parents, Milich was educated to Standard Six level at country schools in Northland and was working as a farm hand when he enlisted in August 1942. His limited schooling ruled him out as a pilot and he began training as a WOp/Ag. Someone must have spotted great natural intelligence and flair and he was remustered as a pilot under training two months later. He joined 198 Squadron on 4 June 1944 and had flown 101 ops when he was killed flying from Gilze-Rijen in Holland. The squadron had successfully attacked an enemy headquarters when Milich radioed he was having engine problems. Another Typhoon flying protection as they headed for Allied lines lost sight of the New Zealander in cloud and Milich's aircraft was later found crashed. Milich, awarded a DFC in November 1945 dated to the day before his death, is buried in Woudenberg.

Writing about 198 Squadron in *Wings of Chance,* Denis Sweeting recalled he could not believe he wouldn't see Milich again.

> No more would Timmy joke about my flying boots and we would not sing together again. Oh God, I thought, will it never end. [Sweeting remembered a very heavy party one night with much drinking and singing.] ... My next recollection was that I was outside the mess tent fighting with my friend Timmy, the iron-muscled Maori, which proved I had drunk too much as I would never have considered such a thing sober. I shouted 'what the hell are we doing this for?' and Timmy dropped his hands in equal bewilderment.

At that moment the ack-ack started and planes overhead started dropping bombs. As Sweeting and Milich dashed for cover they sprawled over tent ropes. Danger over, they got up, grinned at each other and went back to drinking.

Oden, just twenty-one and an only son, was well educated in Tauranga, where he worked as a clerk in State Fire and Accident. He joined up in December 1941 and in August 1942 received his wings and commission in Canada. However, he didn't sail for England for almost eighteen months, held back as an instructor or staff pilot in the expanding training scheme, and didn't reach 198 Squadron, his first posting, until September 1944. He was on his 43rd op on 11 December when he was shot down. Returning to Gilze-Rijen from an armed reconnaissance, his Typhoon was hit by heavy flak over Zaltbommel. His aircraft was last seen at 6000 feet in a steep dive, engine on fire. It was learned later he died of injuries in a German field dressing station the following day.

On 28 September 1944 the Tempests of 3, 56 and 486 Squadrons, the new strike force of Jamie Jameson's 122 Wing, roared in to Grimbergen, a grass field just north of Brussels. They replaced Mustang squadrons, which had flown under Jameson's control in the Normandy beachhead since July. Two or three days after the Tempests arrived the wing moved to Volkel, south of Nijmegen in Holland, where it would stay for more than five months before moving into Germany in the final weeks of the war. The wing was strengthened on 7 October when two more Tempest squadrons, 80 and 274, flew into Volkel. Later a Spitfire squadron was attached.

Commanding 3 Squadron was New Zealander Harvey Sweetman, appointed in mid-September following the death of the previous CO in an attack on a V1 site. Sweetman had gone to 3 Squadron as a flight commander after his long spell with 486 Squadron.

Jameson was having a great time commanding a potent wing and resuming ops, even if he was desk-bound much of the time. He flew thirty-three hours on Mustangs over the beachhead and by the time the war ended he'd accumulated 102 operational hours on Tempests. After running wings at Wittering and North Weald, where two Norwegian squadrons had been under his command, he'd been posted to 11 Group Headquarters in mid-May 1943, his first 'rest' since the start of the war and the June 1940 *Glorious* disaster off Norway. His job at 11 Group included the day-to-day running of all fighter operations in south-east England and later detailed planning for D-Day fighter operations, working closely with the Americans.

After the Normandy breakout his wing — self-contained with its own transport, technical and admin sections — moved to Beauvais, forty-five miles from Paris. But as the front line moved quickly towards Brussels Jameson felt the wing was being left behind. He complained to Air Vice-Marshal Harry Broadhurst who told him if he could find an airfield near Brussels he could have it. Broadhurst suggested Grimbergen but warned the Germans might not have left.

Jameson flew to Grimbergen in 'my little communications aircraft, an Auster with my initials painted on the side'. He ran short of fuel on the way and landed in a field after spotting his advance party, carrying gasoline, on the road. The field was deserted but almost instantly he was surrounded by shouting, cheering Belgians who hugged and kissed him and filled the Auster with flowers, fruit and vegetables. His aircraft refuelled from four-gallon jerry cans, Jameson flew on to Grimbergen, where he landed. Nervous of mines, he left the engine running, hand on revolver, in case Germans were still in possession. He learned from Belgian resistance people who came running across the field that the enemy had gone that morning.

Jameson didn't enjoy Volkel nearly as much as Grimbergen. He told his wife Hilda (they married in England in August 1941 after she wangled a ticket on a ship from New Zealand, and he wrote to her almost every second day) that he thought Volkel was a 'bleak, desolate spot after our lovely place near Brussels. The people in the district are quite friendly but not so exuberant as the French and Belgians. They are more reticent, like the English.' But there were compensations. 'I have a new car which belonged to the Huns. It's a snappy Pontiac drop-head coupe with long and slinky lines … she's a little beauty.'

Jameson appreciated the worth of New Zealand pilots in his wing and the New Zealanders benefited from Jameson's nationality. He wrote to his wife on 20 December 1944: 'Rosie Mackie is with me now [on 274 Squadron]. He was in 485 at Witters [Wittering] or rather King's Cliffe [Northamptonshire] when we were there … He's still as keen as mustard.' Four days later:

It's been a beautiful day and the boys clobbered a few Huns. Rosie Mackie and a chap called [Keith 'Jimmy'] Thiele clobbered one each. Rosie has got about eighteen and I'm going to give him a squadron soon [he did, naming Mackie as CO of 80 Squadron]. I think he'll do well and will probably get a wing before long.

Right again. Mackie was appointed wing commander flying in mid-April 1945 when the popular Peter Brooker was killed. Jameson also appointed Thiele to command 3 Squadron in January 1945 when Sweetman finished ops and went to Hawkers as a test pilot, his second spell there. Sweetman survived the war and now lives in Devonport, in Auckland.

On 26 January 1945, writing to his wife again, Jameson said: 'Harvey Sweetman has gone on rest now and I've given Jimmy Thiele the squadron. He's a New Zealander and has done two tours on bombers and got the DSO, DFC and bar. Now I have recommended him for a second bar to the DFC. He's a cracker.'

Pulling away after attacking a German train standing at a station north of Dortmund on 10 February, Thiele's Tempest was hit by flak. He baled out, suffering burns, and was saved from a nasty crowd of train passengers — and possible lynching — by the flak gun crew that had shot him down. He escaped from a POW hospital and made it back to Allied lines. And, yes, he did get that second DFC bar recommended by Jameson, the only RNZAF pilot to get the DFC for flying bombers and fighters.

During its seven months on the Continent 486 Squadron lost eight pilots, including COs Spike Umbers in February 1945 and his successor Keith Taylor-Cannon two months later. However, the squadron took an awful toll on the last of the Luftwaffe in the air and on the ground. On 29 April they destroyed no fewer than twelve enemy fighters, Me 109s and FW 190s, new CO Warren Schrader claiming three and one shared.

Schrader put up a remarkable performance in the last weeks of the war with nine and a half victories scored between 10 April and 1 May. Then he was given command of 616 Squadron (Meteor), the first operational jet unit. 'I had shot down an Me 109 in the early morning with 486 and was refuelling and rearming at our base in Fassberg [Germany] when I was told it was essential that a Meteor shoot down a German aircraft, preferably an Me 262 jet fighter, for political reasons,' he said years later. He didn't manage to achieve an air 'kill' with 616 Squadron, also based at Fassberg, but destroyed several of them on the ground. Schrader had no time for a conversion course to learn how to fly the jets. He more or less jumped from his Tempest into the cockpit of a Meteor, went solo and immediately began ops. He flew two sorties on 2 May, three the next and one the day after before combat ceased. Schrader had served earlier in the Mediterranean, where he scored two victories. Postwar he flew with National Airways Corporation (NAC), retiring as chief pilot in 1976.

486 Squadron's big score on 29 April helped it to a total of fifty-five victories in the air on the Continent, beating 56 Squadron's tally by

one, to achieve top rank among the seven Tempest squadrons on the Continent. The leading 486 Squadron pilots were Schrader (nine and one shared), Mackie (five and one shared), Jim Sheddan (four and three shared) and Ralph Evans (four).

Among the 486's victims was the one and only Me 262 destroyed by the squadron in combat. Jack Stafford and Duff Bremner shared the victory on Christmas Day 1944, when Stafford spotted the jet and climbed to engage. Normally 262s could easily outpace the Tempests but the New Zealanders got into position to attack head on. Stafford saw his shells hit the jet's port engine, pieces break off and then flames as the 262 passed over the top of him. As the German's speed fell away the pair came in behind and finished it off. The jet crashed near Aachen in Germany.

Astonishingly 485 Squadron scored no further successes after its June 1944 spree over the Normandy, although there were reasons. By 31 August when the squadron flew from England to B17, at Carpriquet in northwest France, their Spitfire IXs were no longer the elite interceptors, following the introduction of the Mark XIVs. The squadron's role now largely involved dive bombing and armed recces strafing ground targets, often in support of troops below. It never tangled with enemy planes.

Waipawa-born Max Collett flew with the squadron through that final nine months. He never saw a German fighter on any of his 75 ops and so never had an opportunity to fire. Though the squadron didn't add to its aerial 'kills' tally after June 1944, Collett and Terry Kearins each got a midget submarine with cannon on Boxing Day, thought to be the only such craft destroyed by RAF fighters.

Collett and Kearins were on duty at dawn, a 'very, very cold one' Collett wrote in his diary (he was wearing three pullovers and three

DAY AFTER DAY

pairs of socks and was still cold) when they scrambled to attack the submarines reported off Flushing, a harbour city on the edge of the Scheldt Estuary in southwest Holland.

> We patrolled out to sea for a while and then came in and saw two subs close together. One submerged hurriedly but I managed to get the other. It blew up and left a big dark patch of oil and wreckage behind. Terry got another one about half a mile off Flushing and had it lying on its side, destroyed, before I got there and we sank it between us. Great fun and caused quite a panic when we arrived back with two submarines destroyed.

Collett called it his most 'fruitful' day in the air force. However, what he later said was the 'greatest experience' of his life occurred on 13 February 1945, when he had to bale out. He and another pilot had been operating over the Canadian lines in extremely murky weather and decided to fly home.

> Was just passing out of cloud when I felt a terrific bang. Could find no fault with the kite … [but] … suddenly the radiator temperature went off the clock and the engine caught fire so I was over the side like a shot. Never entered my head to force lob. Have seen too many go like that.

Collett landed at Venray, inside Allied lines, and was well looked after by 52 Division (a big stiff gin and lunch with the officers). His parachute was ripped to pieces on the barbed wire fence on which he landed and he cut it up for scarves — one per pilot. His Spitfire was the squadron's last lost on operations.

Like other New Zealand pilots whose fathers had fought on the

354

Western Front in World War I, Collett explored the French countryside as best he could. Carpiquet village had been bombed flat; only a few walls standing. 'Reminds me very much of Dad's photos of No Man's Land,' he wrote. On 23 September he drove to Merville when the squadron moved there — through Abbeville across the Somme to Arras, where he stopped to have a couple of beers, and Bethune where the New Zealanders fought. He also visited a war cemetery. He said he would never forget the drive — 'Wish Dad had been here with me.' Collett, who lives in Napier today, is a stalwart of the now-tiny band of former 485 Squadron members.

The Germans shocked 485 Squadron with a fiery start to 1945. Just after dawn enemy aircraft swept over Maldegem, Belgium, the field to which the squadron had moved on 1 November. Maldegem was one of a number of Allied bases in France, Belgium and Holland hit by the Germans on the first day of the new year. The attack, called 'Bodenplatte' (Baseplate), was aimed at catching and destroying large numbers of aircraft on the ground. By doing so the Luftwaffe hoped to do something to even up the now great disparity between the opposing air forces. The Germans did inflict major damage but many RAF and American units were already in the air at dawn and Allied fighters and intense ground fire cost the Luftwaffe almost 300 planes. Pilot losses that day, many of them irreplaceable, proved disastrous for the Germans. The aircraft losses were not the problem — it was shortage of fuel due to Allied bombing of refineries, and lack of experienced pilots to fly available aircraft that crippled the Luftwaffe. The Allies had no such problems.

The attack cost 485 Squadron eleven Spitfires with several more damaged — a traumatic experience — but they had new fighters the next day. Max Collett looked out a window as the Germans arrived

DAY AFTER DAY

'to see a big black cross zoom past'. When he got down to where the Spitfires were parked he watched the burning fighters sending up huge columns of black oily smoke:

> Eleven funeral pyres. I could have sat down and wept … had a last look at the remains of 'D' [his fighter]. Boy! Did I curse those bloody Huns. Still give credit where credit is due, they made an excellent job of ground strafing … Spent most of the afternoon clearing up and salvaging what we could but believe me there wasn't much to salvage. We [the squadrons on the airfield] were very lucky … there were only six casualties, none fatal.

Collett went on patrol that afternoon as 485 Squadron put up four Spitfires to join fighters from 349 and 453 (RAAF) Squadrons. Volkel, home to 486 Squadron, was one field that escaped attack. The New Zealand Tempests were active and destroyed five German fighters over Holland, Spike Umbers downing two, an Me 109 and an FW 190.

In early 1945, 485 Squadron lost three pilots, their last dead of the war and first fatalities since the previous October. On 6 January veteran Al Stead, 24 (Dunedin), and newcomer Frank Matthews, 20 (Palmerston North), attacked a train in western Holland, both suffering severe damage to their Spitfires from debris when the train exploded. The two men radioed they were okay and said they were going to jump. Stead, however, died when he tried to crash-land in Allied lines. Matthews was also killed but *For Your Tomorrow* says it's not clear whether he died from injuries caused by baling out too low or while trying to land. Stead was on his 198th op, Matthews on his 20th.

Five weeks later on 8 February, Don Taylor, 21 (Cambridge), went so low attacking a train in a Dutch station his wing struck a lamppost in the station yard. The wing tore off, the Spitfire hit the ground, bounced and smashed into a house killing Taylor and two Germans inside.

An unfortunate young man from Wellington became New Zealand's last Fighter Command casualty in the European theatre on 4 May 1945, the day Field Marshal Montgomery accepted the surrender of German forces in Holland, northwest Germany and Denmark.

Basil Natta, 22, was flying a 19 Squadron Mustang as one of a two-squadron group escorting Mosquitoes on an anti-shipping strike over the Kattegat, the long narrow strait between Denmark and Sweden. Natta's aircraft and another Mustang collided after an attack on an E-boat and both plunged into the sea, neither pilot surviving. Natta's body was not recovered and his name is on the panels at Runnymede.

On the same day, Hugh Morrison, 27 (Masterton), an FAA Wildcat pilot flying as part of an escort to Avenger bombers attacking a U-boat base at Norway's Lofoten Islands, was shot down by flak and killed. His body was recovered and he is buried at Narvik.

Natta and Morrison were the last New Zealand aircrew to lose their lives on operations against Germany.

Bibliography

Ashworth, Vincent A with Dhollande, Fabrice; *For Our Tomorrow He Gave His Today — A Fighter Pilot's Story*, Vincent A Ashworth, Morrinsville, 2009

Bartley, Anthony (Tony); *Smoke Trails in the Sky*, William Kimber, London, 1984

Beamont, Roland; *My Part of the Sky*, Patrick Stephens Ltd, Northamptonshire, 1989

Braithwaite, Errol; *Pilot on the Run — The Epic Escape Story of Flight Sergeant L. S. M. White*, Century Hutchinson, London, 1986

Brennan, Paul, Hesselyn, Ray and Bateson, Henry; *Spitfires Over Malta*, Jarrolds, London, 1943

Brickhill, Paul; *Reach for the Sky — The Story of Douglas Bader, Legless Ace of the Battle of Britain*, Buccaneer Books, New York, 1954

Bungay, Stephen; *The Most Dangerous Enemy — A History of the Battle of Britain*, Aurum Press, London, 2000 (p/b edition 2009)

Burns, Michael; *Cobber Kain*, Random Century, Auckland, 1992

Clouston, Arthur; *The Dangerous Skies*, Cassell and Co., London, 1954

Collier, Basil; *The Battle of the V-Weapons 1944–45*, The Emfield Press, Yorkshire, 1964

Cornwell, Peter D; *The Battle of France — Then and Now*, Battle of Britain International Ltd, Old Harlow, Essex, 2007

Cull, Brian with Lander, Bruce; *Diver! Diver! Diver!*, Grub Street, London, 2008

Cull, Brian with Lander, Bruce and Weiss, Heinrich; *Twelve Days in May*, Grub Street, London, 1995 (p/b edition 1999)

Deere, Alan C; *Nine Lives*, Hodder & Stoughton, London, 1959 (Crecy Publishing p/b edition 2009)

Ford, Colin; *Adjidaumo — Tail in Air — The History of No. 268 Squadron Royal Air Force 1940 to 1946*, two volumes, self-published, Canberra, 2004

Foreman, John; *RAF Fighter Command Victory Claims*, Red Kite, Surrey, 2005

Franks, Norman; *Air Battle for Dunkirk — 26 May–3 June 1940*, Grub Street, London, 1983 (2006 p/b edition)

Franks, Norman; *The Greatest Air Battle — Dieppe, 19th August 1942*, Grub Street, London, 1992 (p/b edition 1997)

Gleed, Ian; *Arise to Conquer*, Victor Gollancz, London, 1942 (Severn House edition 1982)

Gray, Colin; *Spitfire Patrol*, Hutchinson, London, 1990

Hanson, Colin; *By Such Deeds — Honours and Awards in the RNZAF 1923–1999*, Volplane Press, Christchurch, 2001

Hill, Larry R; *An Aviation Bibliography for New Zealand*, Larry R Hill, Auckland, 2009

Hillary, Richard; *The Last Enemy*, Burford Books, UK, 1942

Houlton, Johnnie; *Spitfire Strikes — A New Zealand Fighter Pilot's Story*, John Murray, London, 1985

Jackson, Robert; *Air War Over France*, Ian Allan Publishing, Hersham, Surrey, 1974

Jefford, Wing Commander C G; *RAF Squadrons*, Airlife Publishing, Shrewsbury, 1988

Johnson, J E 'Johnnie'; *Wing Leader*, Chatto and Windus, London, 1956 (Reprint Society edition 1958)

Kingcome, Brian; *A Willingness to Die*, Tempus Publishing, Stroud, Gloucestershire, 1999

Martyn, Errol; *For Your Tomorrow — A Record of New Zealanders Who Have Died While Serving with the RNZAF and Allied Air Services Since 1915*, Volumes 1–3, Volplane Press, Christchurch, 1998–2008

Mitchell, Alan; *New Zealanders in the Air War*, George Harrap and Co., London, 1945

National Archives, The (UK) Pilot combat reports quoted herein

Orange, Vincent; *The Road to Biggin Hill — A Life of Wing Commander Johnny Checketts*, Mallinson Rendel, Wellington, 1987

Palmer, Derek; *Fighter Squadron*, The Self Publishing Association, Upton-upon-Severn, Worcestershire, 1990

Price, Alfred; *The Hardest Day — The Battle of Britain, 18 August 1940*, Jane's Publishing Co., London, 1979

Rae, Jack; *Kiwi Spitfire Ace*, Grub Street, London, 2001

Ramset, Winston G, editor; *The Battle of Britain — Then and Now*, After the Battle, Old Harlow, Essex, 1980

Richards, Denis; *The Royal Air Force 1939–45*, Volumes 1–3 (Vols 2 and 3 with Hilary St George Saunders), HM Stationery Office, London, 1953–54 (Vol. 1: *The Fight at Odds*)

Richey, Paul; *Fighter Pilot*, Jane's Publishing Co Ltd, London, 1941 (1980 reprint)

Ross, David; *'The Greatest Squadron of Them All' — The Definitive History of 603 (City of Edinburgh) Squadron, RAuxAF*, Volume 1, Grub Street, London, 2003

Sanders, James; *Venturer Courageous — Group Captain Leonard Trent V.C., D.F.C.*, Hutchinson, Auckland, 1983

Scott, Desmond; *One More Hour*, Hutchinson, London, 1989

Scott, Desmond; *Typhoon Pilot*, Leo Cooper, London, 1982

Sheddan, C J with Franks, Norman; *Tempest Pilot*, Grub Street, 1993 (p/b edition 2003)

Shores, Christopher and Thomas, Chris; *2nd Tactical Air Force*, Volumes 1–3, Ian Allan Publishing, Hersham, Surrey, 2004–06

Shores, Christopher and Williams, Clive; *Aces High*, Grub Street, London, 1994

Sortehaug, Paul; *The Wild Winds — The History of Number 486 RNZAF Fighter Squadron with the RAF*, Paul Sortehaug, Dunedin, 1998

Sortehaug, Paul and Listemann, Philippe; *No. 485 (N.Z.) Squadron 1941–1945*, self-published, France, 2006

Spurdle, Bob; *The Blue Arena*, William Kimber, London, 1986

Sweeting, Denis; *Wings of Chance*, Asian Business Press, Singapore, 1990

Terraine, John; *The Right of the Line*, Hodder & Stoughton, London, 1985

Thompson, H L; *New Zealanders with the Royal Air Force, Volumes 1–3*, War History Branch, Dept of Internal Affairs, Wellington, 1953–59

Thompson, Julian; *Dunkirk — Retreat to Victory*, Sidgwick & Jackson, London, 2008 (Pan p/b edition 2009)

Walford, Eddie; *War Over the West*, Amigo Books, Cornwall, 1989

Walpole, Nigel; *Dragon Rampant — The Story of 234 Fighter Squadron*, Merlin Massara Publishing, London, 2007

Wellum, Geoffrey; *First Light*, Viking/Penguin, London, 2002

Willis, John; *Churchill's Few — The Battle of Britain Remembered*, Michael Joseph, London, 1985

Winton, John; *Carrier Glorious — The Life and Death of an Aircraft Carrier*, Cassell Military Paperbacks, London, 1999

Wynn, Kenneth; *A Clasp for 'The Few' — New Zealanders with the Battle of Britain Clasp*, self-published, Auckland, 1981

Index

Index of New Zealand Aircrew

Ranks listed here are those held at the end of World War II. So too are decorations, but they do include awards announced in the first year or two of peace for events during the war. All those listed are members of the Royal New Zealand Air Force (RNZAF) unless otherwise specified.

† denotes those who lost their lives

♦ denotes brothers

* denotes bar to decoration

Abbreviations

Air Force Ranks

ACM	Air Chief Marshal
AM	Air Marshal
AVM	Air Vice-Marshal
Air Cdre	Air Commodore
Gp Capt	Group Captain
Wg Cdr	Wing Commander
Sqn Ldr	Squadron Leader
Flt Lt	Flight Lieutenant
Flg Off	Flying Officer
Plt Off	Pilot Officer
Wt Off	Warrant Officer
Flt Sgt	Flight Sergeant
Sgt	Sergeant
LAC	Leading Aircraftman
ACW1	Aircraftwoman 1st Class

Others

(A)	Air
Brig	Brigadier
FAA	Fleet Air Arm
Lt	Lieutenant
RAF	Royal Air Force
RAAF	Royal Australian Air Force
RCAF	Royal Canadian Air Force
RNZAF	Royal New Zealand Air Force
WAAF	Women's Auxiliary Air Force

Awards and Honours

VC	Victoria Cross
GCB	Knight Grand Cross, Order of the Bath
KBE	Knight, Order of the British Empire
CBE	Commander, Order of the British Empire
OBE	Officer, Order of the British Empire
MBE	Member, Order of the British Empire
DSO	Distinguished Service Order
DFC	Distinguished Flying Cross
AFC	Air Force Cross
DFM	Distinguished Flying Medal
GM	George Medal
mid	Mention in Dispatches
(bbc)	Battle of Britain Clasp
(pff)	Pathfinder Force Badge

DAY AFTER DAY

A

Adam, Wt Off D, RAF 346

Aitken, Wg Cdr RF, RAF — OBE, mid (3) 245–46

† Allen, Flg Off JHL, RAF — (bbc) 47–48, 50, 225

Annear, Sgt TF 344

♦ Ashworth, Sqn Ldr A, RNZAF/RAF — DSO, DFC, mid, (pff) 318

†♦ Ashworth, Flg Off CP 318–19

† Atkinson, Flt Sgt EHF 337

B

† Bailey, Plt Off GM, RAF 68

Baird, Flt Lt GM, RAF — (bbc) 123

† Baker, Wg Cdr RW — DFC, mid 292

Barnett, Sqn Ldr MG — DFC 292–96, 327–28, 331

† Barrett, Flt Lt R 317–18

† Barton, Plt Off, JE 270, 280–81

† Bary, Wg Cdr RE, RAF — DSO, DFC, mid, (bbc) 101, 192, 319

† Bassett, Flg Off TG, RAF 62–64, 67

Baxter, Flt Lt AC — DFC* 272

† Berry, Sqn Ldr AE, RAF — DFC 270, 280–81, 283

† Bickerdike, Plt Off JL, RAF — (bbc) 165–66, 225

Blake, Wg Cdr MV, RAF — DSO, DFC 186–91, 270, 284

† Bonham, Flt Lt GL — DFC 330–31

Boxer, Sqn Ldr AHC, RAF — DSO, DFC 195

Breckon, Sqn Ldr AAN, RAF/RNZAF — DFC 172

Bremner, Flg Off RD — DFC 353

Brinsden, Sqn Ldr FN, RAF/ RNZAF 101, 109–10, 144–46, 260

Brown, Flt Lt BW, RAF 218, 220–23

Browne, Sqn Ldr SF — DFC* 260, 292, 295–96

† Bullen, Sgt RJ 266

† Burke, Wt Off DL 340

Burton, Wt Off DL — (bbc) 123

† Button, ACW1 EL, WAAF 152

C

† Cain, Wt Off IW 341–42

Caldwell Flt Lt RA 339–40, 343

Cammock, Flg Off RJ — DFC 328

Carbury, Flg Off BJG, RAF — DFC*, (bbc) 126–27, 132, 153–64

Carlson, Wg Cdr D — DFC 274–75

Carswell, Sqn Ldr MK, RAF/RNZAF — (bbc) 101, 111–12

Caulton, Flt Lt JJ 320–22

† Chalmers, Plt Off JC 337

† Chamberlain, Plt Off CJE, RAF 68

Chapman, Flt Lt OR — DFC 309–10

Checketts, Wg Cdr JM — DSO, DFC, US Silver Star, Polish Cross of Valour 155, 248–49, 260, 297, 332, 336–37

† Christensen, Flt Lt AG — mid (murdered by Gestapo, Great Escape, 1944) 270, 284–85

Chrystall, Flt Lt C, RAF/RNZAF — DFC, mid, (bbc) 276–77

Church, Flt Lt J 343

† Churches, Plt Off EWG — (bbc) 128–31

† Clark, Flt Sgt DB, 264

† Clark, Plt Off FD 289

♦ Clouston, Gr Capt AE, RAF — DSO, DFC, AFC*, mid, (bbc) 107–9, 112

Clouston, Flt Lt DT — mid 306

†♦ Clouston, Flt Lt FN, RAF 101, 106–8

†♦ Clouston, Sqn Ldr JG 147–48, 262

♦ Clouston, Sqn Ldr WG, RAF — DFC 91–94, 101, 106, 108–10, 142–48, 262

(Brothers AE and FN Clouston unrelated to brothers JG and WG Clouston. DT Clouston unrelated to the others)

† Cobden, Plt Off DG, RAF — (bbc) 226

† Coleman, Plt Off JH, RAF 60

Collett, Flg Off MA — mid 353–56

† Collins, Flt Lt JN, RAF/RNZAF 60

364

† Collyns, Flt Lt BG — DFC, (bbc) 261, 317–18

Coningham, AM Sir Arthur, RAF — KCB, KBE, DSO, MC, AFC, mid (4) and decorations from France, Belgium, Netherlands, US and Greece 334

† Cooney, Flt Sgt PJD 238

Copland, Flt Lt HG 230, 235–41, 277–80

† Courtis, Sgt JB — (bbc) 254

Cowan, Sqn Ldr NLR — DFC 128

Crawford-Compton, Wg Cdr WV, RAF — DSO*, DFC*, US Silver Star, French Legion of Honour, French Croix de Guerre 155, 248, 260–61, 306, 335

Cullen, Sqn Ldr JR — DFC* 328

† Cunningham, Plt Off VA, RAF 68–70

D

Danzey, Flg Off RJ — DFC 328

Deere, Wg Cdr AC, RAF — DSO, OBE, DFC*, (bbc), US DFC, French Croix de Guerre 98–104, 106, 120, 126–27, 131–32, 150, 155, 160–61, 335

† Dini, Plt Off AS, RAF 54–59

Donkin, Wg Cdr PL, RAF — DSO 251–53, 286, 334

† Downer, Plt Off IW 302–3

†♦ Dromgoole, Plt Off I, RAF 60

†♦ Dromgoole, Flt Sgt SH 60

E

Eagleson, Flg Off OD — DFC 328

† Edwards, Flt Sgt AJ 237–38

† Edwards, Flg Off JE, RAF 68

Evans, Flt Lt AR — DFC 353

F

Fittall, Flt Lt VC — DFC 298–300, 305

Fitzgerald, Wg Cdr TB, RAF/RNZAF — DFC, (bbc) 69–71, 148–50

Fleming, Wg Cdr J, RAF — MBE, (bbc) 183–86

Frame, Wg Cdr A, RAF/RNZAF — DFC 55

Francis, Sqn Ldr GH — DFC 306

† Frankish, Plt Off CR, RAF 55, 62–64, 67

G

Gard'ner, Sqn Ldr JR, RAF — mid, (bbc) 191–92, 194–98, 223

Gawith, Wg Cdr AA, RAF/RNZAF — DFC, (bbc), US Bronze Star 223

Gellatly, Sqn Ldr WR — mid (2) 273

Gibson, Sqn Ldr JAA, RAF/RNZAF — DSO, DFC, (bbc) 52–54, 132–33

Gill, Wg Cdr TF, RAF/RNZAF — DSO, mid (3), (bbc) 76, 218–20

Gillies, Flt Lt JA, RAF — MBE 201–3, 288–89

Goodlet, Wt Off TC 246

Goodwin, Wt Off CSV 287

†♦ Grant, Flg Off IAC — (bbc) 307–8

†♦ Grant, Wg Cdr RJC — DFC*, DFM 260, 306–8

♦ Grant, Flg Off WE, RAF (died 1932) 307

♦ Gray, Wg Cdr CF, RAF — DSO, DFC**, (bbc) 101–6, 120, 126–27, 131–32, 155, 160, 192–94

†♦ Gray, Flg Off KN, RAF — DFC, Czech War Cross 102

† Grieves, Mr BW — pilot under training in RAF 55

Griffith, Flt Lt LP — DFC 331

H

† Harden, Plt Off RC 322

Harkness, Flg Off RD — DFC 341, 344–45

† Hawkins, Flt Lt WT — DFC 309–10

Hayter, Sqn Ldr JCF, RAF/RNZAF — DFC*, mid (2), (bbc) 69–70, 148, 150

† Hemmings, Plt Off RB — mid 340, 343

†♦ Herrick, Flg Off BH, RAF — (bbc) 124

†♦ Herrick, Plt Off DT — GM 124

†♦ Herrick, Sqn Ldr MJ, RAF — DFC*, (bbc), US Air Medal 124

Hesselyn, Flt Lt RB — MBE, DFC, DFM* 312–14

Hickton, Flt Sgt HT 295

DAY AFTER DAY

† Hight, Plt Off CH, RAF — (bbc) 175–79, 182–83, 226

†◆ Hill, Plt Off HP, RAF — (bbc) 200–1, 207–9, 227

†◆ Hill, Flt Sgt PJ 208–9

† Hodgson, Plt Off WH, RAF — DFC, (bbc) 165–74

† Holder, Sgt R — (bbc) 128, 228

† Horton, Flg Off PW, RAF — (bbc) 177–78, 257

Houlton, Sqn Ldr JA — DFC 261, 337–39

† Howarth, Plt Off EE, RAF 60

Hume, Sqn Ldr MRD — DFC 260

Humphreys, Sqn Ldr JS, RAF — (bbc) 57

† Hutcheson, Flg Off IC 340, 347

I

† Irvine, Plt Off IH — DFM 304–5

J

† Jacobsen, Plt Off LR, RAF — DFC 21–22, 27

Jameson, Flt Lt GE — DSO, DFC 237

Jameson, Gr Capt PG, RAF — DSO, DFC*, mid (5), Norwegian War Cross with Swords, Cdr, Netherlands Order of Orange Nassau with Swords, US Silver Star 17–30, 38, 153, 263, 276–77, 317–18, 334, 345, 349–51

† Jones, Sgt JS 264

† Joyce, Sqn Ldr EL — DFM 266–67

K

Kain, Wg Cdr D, RAF/RNZAF 33–35, 37

† Kain, Flg Off EJ, RAF — DFC, mid 19, 32–33, 36–39, 41–46, 68, 76, 318

† Kalka, Flg Off WA 328

Kearins, Flt Lt TSF — French Croix de Guerre 297, 353–54

† Keedwell, Plt Off OH, RAF 66

† Kelly, Sgt AC 244

† Kemp, Plt Off JR, RAF — (bbc) 192–94, 196, 225

† Kidson, Plt Off R, RAF — (bbc) 192, 194, 196, 225

Kilian, Sqn Ldr JRC — French Croix de Guerre 274–75

Kinder, Sqn Ldr MC — AFC, (bbc) 200, 209–12

† Kirkcaldie, Plt Off K, RAF 60

Knight, Gr Capt MWB, RAF — DFC, US Legion of Honour 259–60

L

† Langlands, Sgt NM 305

Lawrence, Sqn Ldr KA, RAF/RNZAF — DFC, (bbc) 177–78, 223

† Liken, Flt Sgt JR 246–47

† Lovell-Gregg, Sqn Ldr TG, RAF — (bbc) 175, 179–82, 226

Lumsden, Flt Lt BC 230, 281–83, 346–47

M

† McArthur, Flt Lt DH RAF — DFC 172

McCarthy, Plt Off K 329

McCaw, Flt Lt JH — DFC 328

Macdonald, Sqn Ldr KJ — DFC 260

McGregor, Air Cdre HD, RAF — CBE, DSO mid (5), (bbc), US Legion of Merit 101, 113–14, 179

Mackenzie, Sqn Ldr JN, RAF/RNZAF — DFC, (bbc) 101, 136–42, 159, 172–73

Mackie, Wg Cdr ED — DSO, DFC*, US Silver Star 237, 248, 261, 351, 353

Magill, Wg Cdr GR, RAF — OBE, DFC*, mid 272–74

Malfroy, Wg Cdr C, RAF — DFC, US DFC 52–54, 335

Mart, Flt Lt WG — DFC 303

† Martin Flt Lt JC, RAF — (bbc) 260

Maskill, Sqn Ldr IPJ — DFC 237–38

† Matthews, Plt Off FC 356

† Miles, Brig R, 2NZEF (Artillery) — CBE, DSO*, MC, mid (2), Cross of Valour (Greece) 21

† Miles, Lt (A) RJ, FAA 21, 27

† Milich, Flg Off MA — DFC 347–48

† Miller, Flt Lt CW, RAF — DFC 165

366

INDEX

†♦ Mitchell, Plt Off JS, RAF 39–41

†♦ Mitchell, Plt Off SS 40

† Morrison, Lt (A) H, FAA — mid (2) 357

Mortimer, Flt Lt JE — DFC 297

† Morton, Plt Off EE, RAF 66–67

Mowat, Wg Cdr NJ, RAF — DSO, mid, (bbc) — † postwar 101, 112–13

♦ Murphy, Sqn Ldr F — DFC 300–1

♦ Murphy, Wt Off SOJ 265

N

† Natta, Plt Off BMC 357

Newenham, Sqn Ldr WA — DFC 339

Newman, Sqn Ldr HD, RAF 174

† Newton, Flg Off KE, RAF 57, 94, 101, 115

† North, Flt Lt HL, RAF — DFC, (bbc) 101

† Nuttall, LAC RRH, RAF 61

O

O'Connor, Flg Off BJ — DFC 329

† Oden, Flt Lt OH 347–49

† Ollerenshaw, Plt Off AC, RAF 60

† Orgias, Plt Off E, RAF — (bbc) 165, 227

P

Park, ACM Sir Keith R, RAF — GCB, KBE, MC*, DFC, mid, French Croix de Guerre, US Legion of Merit 100, 122–23, 143–44, 153, 209–10, 245

† Paterson, Flt Lt JA, RAF — MBE, (bbc) 79–90, 198, 200, 203–8, 227

Pattison, Sqn Ldr JG — DSO, DFC, (bbc) 128, 200, 212–16, 246–48, 260

† Perrin, Flt Lt DP — DFC 302, 346–47

Peryman, Flt Lt BW, RAF 76–77

† Pheloung, Sqn Ldr THV 314–15

Porteous, Sqn Ldr JK — DFC 261

† Price, Plt Off PM 340, 344

† Priestley, Plt Off JS — (bbc) 127, 226

R

† Rabone, Sqn Ldr PW, RAF — DFC, (bbc) 75–76

Rae, Flt Lt JD — DFC* 261, 287, 289–91, 306, 308, 312

Ralph, Flt Lt LM — DFC 246–47

† Rasmussen, Sgt LAW — (bbc) 124

† Rawson, Flg Off GE 315–16

† Rea, Flg Off KN, RAF 68, 77–78

† Robinson, Sqn Ldr PB, RAF — DFC 165

Robson, Flt Lt AR — DFM 308

Ross, Asst Section Off R, WAAF 171–73

† Roy, Sgt JC 238

† Russell, Wt Off DM 248

† Russell, Plt Off WH 287–88

Rutherford, Flt Lt RS — DFC 271–72, 274

S

Sames, Flt Lt AN — DFC 299

† Saunders, Plt Off GC, RAF 47

Saxelby, Sqn Ldr CK, RAF — DFC 174–75

Schrader, Wg Cdr WE — DFC* 262, 352–53

Scott, Sgt AD 344

Scott, Gr Capt DJ — OBE, DSO, DFC*, French Croix de Guerre, Belgian Croix de Guerre, Netherlands Orange Nassau 114, 249–51, 262, 265–68, 282, 301–3, 334, 344

Shand, Flt Lt MM — DFC (bbc) 128, 131–32, 216

Sheddan, Sqn Ldr CJ — DFC 249–51, 262, 329, 353

Shorthouse, Wg Cdr JS — DFC, mid 71–75, 77

† Simpson, Flg Off GM, RAF — (bbc) 58, 101, 106–7, 228

Sise, Wg Cdr GD — DSO*, DFC* 128

Smith, Sqn Ldr AH — DFC*, mid 230, 262, 298–301, 303–4

Smith, Wg Cdr IS, RAF — DFC*, (bbc) 133–36, 263

367

DAY AFTER DAY

† Spence, Flg Off DJ, RAF — (bbc) 101, 112–13

Spurdle, Sqn Ldr RL, RAF/RNZAF — DFC*, mid, (bbc) 128–31, 213, 233–34

Stafford, Flt Lt JH — DFC 326–27, 353

† Stanley, Sgt DO — (bbc) 128, 228

Stark, Flt Lt RG — MBE, US Bronze Star 203

† Stead, Flt Lt AB — DFC 356

† Steed, Sgt RJ 308

† Stellin, Plt Off JK — French Croix de Guerre 340–41, 344

† Stenborg, Flt Lt G — DFC 261, 310–12

† Stewart, Plt Off C, RAF — (bbc) 128, 131–32

† Stone, Plt Off IS 306–7

† Strang, Flt Lt RH, RAFVR — (bbc) 219

Stratton, Sqn Ldr WH, RAF/RNZAF — DFC*, mid 33

Sutherland, Flt Lt MG 287, 289

Sutton, Sqn Ldr KR, RAF — DFC, mid (2), (bbc) 77–78, 272

Sweetman, Sqn Ldr HN — DFC 260–63, 328, 331, 349, 351

T

† Tait, Flt Lt KW, RAF — DFC, mid, (bbc) 47–49, 182

† Taylor, Flg Off DGL 356–57

† Taylor-Cannon, Sqn Ldr KG — DFC* 262, 352

Thiele, Sqn Ldr KF — DSO, DFC** 351–52

† Thomas, Flg Off GG 299

† Trafford, Flg Off GR 340

† Trenchard, Plt Off HA, RAF 41

Trent, Sqn Ldr, LH, RAF — VC, DFC 64–65

Trousdale, Wg Cdr RM, RAF/RNZAF — DFC*, (bbc) — † postwar 101, 177

U

† Umbers, Sqn Ldr AE — DFC* 262, 329, 352, 356

V

Verity, Sqn Ldr VBS, RAF/RNZAF — DFC, (bbc) 59, 101, 106, 150–51, 177

† Vernon, Flg Off JE, RAF — DFC 68–69

† Vessey, Sgt RW 305

† Vickery, Plt Off HE, RAF 21, 23, 27

W

† Waddell, Plt Off JW 330

Waddy, Sqn Ldr ID — DFC 262

† Walker, Sgt DM 265

† Wallace, Sgt JT 266

† Ward, Sqn Ldr DH, RAF — DFC*, (bbc) 47–48, 50–52, 94–97, 180–82, 266

† Waters, Plt Off LJB 270, 273

Wells, Wg Cdr EP — DSO, DFC*, (bbc) 128, 140–42, 155, 260–61, 292

† Wendel, Plt Off KV, RAF — (bbc) 55, 226

Westenra, Sqn Ldr DF, RAF/RNZAF — DFC*, mid 257, 316–18

Wetere, Flt/Lt JH — DFC 284

† Wheeler, Wg Cdr AB, RCAF — DFC 273–74

White, Flt Lt LSMcQ — DFC 289, 291–92

Whitley, Gr Capt EW, RAF — DSO, DFC 101, 112–13, 124

† Wickham, Plt Off AE, RAF 68–69

† Wilkie, Plt Off JL, RAF 21–22, 177

† Williams, Plt Off WS, RAF — mid, (bbc) 227

† Wilson, Plt Off AA 330

Wilson, Flt Lt DS, RAF — mid, (bbc) 196

† Wipiti, Wt Off BS — DFM 297

† Wright, Plt Off RJ 330

† Wylie, Plt Off CR, RAF 68

Y

Yule, Wg Cdr RD, RAF — DSO, DFC*, (bbc) — † postwar 48–49, 101, 111, 151–52, 274